FATAL FEMALES

Women Who Kill

MICKI PISTORIUS

PENGUIN BOOKS

PENGUIN BOOKS

Published by the Penguin Group
80 Strand, London WC2R 0RL, England
Penguin Putnam Inc, 375 Hudson Street, New York, New York 10014, USA
Penguin Books Australia Ltd, 250 Camberwell Road, Camberwell,
Victoria 3124, Australia
Penguin Books Canada Ltd, 10 Alcorn Avenue, Toronto, Ontario,
Canada M4V 3B2
Penguin Group (NZ), Cnr Airborne and Rosedale Roads, Albany,
Auckland 1310, New Zealand
Penguin Books India (P) Ltd, Community Centre, Panchsheel Park,
New Delhi – 110 017, India
Penguin Books (South Africa) (Pty) Ltd, 24 Sturdee Avenue, Rosebank,
Johannesburg 2196, South Africa

Penguin Books (South Africa) (Pty) Ltd, Registered Offices:
24 Sturdee Avenue, Rosebank, Johannesburg 2196, South Africa

First published by Penguin Books (South Africa) (Pty) Ltd 2004
Reprinted 2005

ISBN 0 143 02440 X

Typeset by DCW Design in10/13pt Bookman
Cover design by Mouse Design
Printed and bound by Interpak, Pietermaritzburg

*This book is dedicated to my father
Calie Pistorius,
my inspiration in life*

Contents

Acknowledgements

The research required for a book of this nature is a major task and I would like to express my sincere appreciation to the following: the South African Police Service Museum; journalists Zelda Venter, Elsabe Brits and Helene Cilliers; Karen Oosthuizen from the SABC library, Laurette Visser from the University of Pretoria, Hester van den Berg from the University of the Free State, Lisa Vetten from the Centre for the Study of Violence and Reconciliation, Dalene Clark from the SA Law Commission, the many detectives I talked to, Danie Lötter, the people of Cradock, and my father Calie Pistorius.

Thank you, too, to Alison, Pam, Claire and everybody else at Penguin Books.

And special thanks to Mondi award nominee, researcher and journalist, Petro Roosendaal, for all her help.

Introduction

In the year 2000 a woman in Zeerust in the North West province of South Africa poisoned her common-law husband, hid his body in a deep freeze for a few days, then burnt it on an open fire, decapitated the charred head, burnt it a little longer, scattered the ashes in the veld and dumped the rest of his remains in a cattle dip.

Hardly anyone opening a newspaper today would be able to ignore the above report, especially since this atrocious crime was committed by a woman. People are inevitably shocked when women commit violent crimes. But despite the fact that it may make them uncomfortable, many people are fascinated by the subject, probably because it is difficult to comprehend that women, bearers of life, are capable of ruthlessly taking it.

Throughout history the opinion seems to have prevailed that women are not inclined to commit violent crimes. But there is no real basis for this opinion. After all, within the Judaeo-Christian framework at least, the first person to commit an act of deception was Eve. If women are capable of deception, they are certainly capable of other nefarious deeds.

Not much research was conducted on the subject of female criminality before the nineteenth century. Current thinking that it is against a woman's nature

1

to commit an act of violence, especially murder, is a remnant from the Victorian era when women were considered paragons of virtue, born to serve and to inspire men.

In her book *Women, Crime and Custody in Victorian England*, Zedner (1991) explains: 'Within Evangelical morality women were regarded as being naturally different from men. Said to be more fragile and morally impressionable, their superior moral standards had to be continually reinforced. Moreover, although women gained considerable power within the limited sphere of their influence, in order to protect their own purity, they were admonished to leave the home as little as possible.'

Women were therefore kept indoors purportedly to protect them from immoral influences. At the same time, being 'kept indoors' also prevented women from being exposed to situations which could awaken the temptation to commit crime. This notion supposes that criminal tendencies are attributable to external influences, and any internal inclination towards such tendencies is negated.

Victorian society imposed strict expectations on the conduct and demeanour of respectable women and any attempt to oppose these resulted in ostracism from that society: '... since women were already in a far weaker position than men, there was less need to employ the coercive agents of police and prison to secure their conformity. So persuasive was this ideal of the "angel in the house", the little wife and caring mother, that only the very lowest stratum of society remained completely immune from its influence' (Zedner, 1991).

Women were regarded as innately non-criminal,

virtuous upholders of morality, and from this pedestal they were supposed to inspire men to greater virtue. 'Simply by being a model of chastity, altruism and morality, she was supposed to induce men to raise themselves to her level of virtue ... The fact that women were more religiously inclined than men was also thought to act as a restraint against crime' (Zedner, 1991).

More realistic Victorian writers recognised that there might be other reasons why women were less inclined to commit violent crime than just fear of moral ostracism. Confined to their homes, deprived of exercise and restrained by their restrictive clothing, they lacked the mobility and physical strength to commit physical crimes.

Appearance and attire played an important role in Victorian society. Women were supposed to look feminine and to act accordingly. They had to reflect cleanliness, which was next to godliness, and this applied not only to their own appearance, but also to their households. If these aspects were neglected, they would forfeit their reputations. 'Deviance from femininity alone, then, was grounds for suspicion and condemnation' (Zedner, 1991).

By and large, Victorians exhibited two reactions when confronted with women who committed violent crimes. They either condemned them more harshly than their male counterparts for betraying the feminine qualities expected of them, and punished them more severely, or they were over-lenient in the punishment meted out, because of the fact that the offender was of the 'gentler sex'.

Both these Victorian attitudes merit further exploration. Let us look first at the harsh attitude. A remark made by the directors of convict prisons in

Millbank, England, in 1859 illustrates this attitude: 'The gentler sex, as a whole, are superior in virtue to the sterner sex; but when woman falls, she seems to possess a capacity almost beyond man, for running into all that is evil ...' (Zedner, 1991).

It may seem from this comment that the directors were disposed to attribute a woman's fall from grace to an internal motivation, but reading between the lines one gains the distinct impression that words such as 'gentler sex' and 'superior in virtue' indicate that they could not forgive the woman for betraying her 'true nature' – a nature that would exclude the capacity for violent crime.

The Victorians linked female criminality to sexual perversion. Both were regarded as influences over which the 'poor creature' had no control, or 'did not know better of'. Again, no internal capacity to commit violent crime was acknowledged. 'The criminal woman, on the other hand, offended against her very social role ... As the ideal woman was compassionate, self-sacrificing, and deferential, so the criminal woman was seen as hardened, self-seeking, and bold. Above all, when the revered innocence of the ideal woman was discarded by her criminal counterpart, it was thought ... to be replaced by sexual degradation' (Zedner, 1991).

The inclination to link criminality to sexuality dates back much further than Victorian times and might even be seen as a remnant of the biblical Delilah who betrayed Samson. In much the same way as a woman's virtue was supposed to inspire a man, so her suppressed sexuality was supposed to temper his desires. 'Maintaining a woman's supposed innocence demanded man's restraint before marriage, and woman's supposed lack of sexual appetite demanded the suppression of his own desire thereafter' (Zedner, 1991).

The link between criminality and sexuality was attributed to the lower classes, who 'did not know better' and it was supposedly up to the refined ladies of the upper and middle classes to rectify this situation with their pious charity work. 'In general, little distinction was made in early criminological literature on women between criminality and unchastity – the female thief and prostitute tended to be grouped together as one' (Zedner, 1991).

While it is no longer considered a crime for a woman to explore and express her sexuality, some women use their sexuality to induce men into becoming their accomplices in crime.

The other side of the coin, the more lenient Victorian approach to female criminality, also deserves exploration. Zedner reflects upon the Victorian stance of being over-sympathetic: 'As today, there was an implicit assumption, common to much nineteenth-century criminological literature, that women were kept out of prison as much by men's chivalry as by their own virtue. This suggested that women were less vigorously pursued than men, that judgements made upon those who were prosecuted were less severe, and that punishments meted out were less harsh' (Zedner, 1991).

The class system certainly played a role in this sympathetic attitude. Should a well-bred woman fall from grace, society would more likely attribute her actions to madness, not believing that in her right mind the offender could be capable of committing such a crime. Such a woman would be confined to a secluded institution and her offspring would be closely monitored for signs of 'inherited madness'. Should a woman of the lower classes offend, it was likely that her actions would be attributed to her depraved circumstances. She would be sent to prison, to become a convenient vehicle for the philanthropic work of upper-class ladies. In neither case – either upper or lower class – was it recognised that some women are innately capable of committing violent crimes, much the same as their male criminal counterparts.

'For the most part women criminals were viewed not so much as economically damaging, physically dangerous, or destructive to property but as a moral menace' (Zedner, 1991). The notion of a woman's fall from grace was considered much more socially scandalous than the crime itself, and punishment reflected this, especially in the upper levels of society. Society preferred not to know the details of the crimes for it threatened the delicate threads that wove their moral safety net. Families were expected to confine the 'unfortunate offender' to the family home or to dispose of her in a secluded institution. Should the case go to trial, the 'unfortunate offender' would often win the sympathy of the court, which would more than likely attribute the crime to mental instability – a delicacy of the nerves. In this way the holy grail of feminine virtue was upheld.

Zedner explains that the majority of 'feeble-minded' convicts were women. 'These confirmed recidivists were consequently redefined as helpless defectives rather than deliberate sinners ... It re-diagnosed them as blighted by a mental incapacity for making correct moral judgements and, therefore, as incurable inadequates. In turn, this diagnosis removed those thus labelled from the sphere of criminality by redefining them as "irresponsible" ' (Zedner, 1991). The benchmark for feeble-mindedness was a woman's degree of self-control and her moral conduct. Feeble-mindedness therefore became a convenient excuse for criminality (and overt sexuality) enabling the Victorians to protect their moral view of women as elevated creatures.

Caesare Lombroso and his son-in-law William Ferrero (Bowker, 1979) were nineteenth-century criminologists who attempted to break away from contemporary stereotyping in researching female criminality. In their *Female Offender*, published in 1894, Lombroso applied to female offenders his atavistic degenerative physical characteristics theory, which he had developed in *The Criminal Man*. By measuring cranial capacities, facial anomalies, facial angles and brain weights, Lombroso and Ferrero came to the conclusion that certain women, who possessed certain 'primitive' physical characteristics, were biologically predisposed to crime.

Bowker (1979) in *Women, Crime and the Criminal Justice System* states that Lombroso had established that 'criminal women were found to possess many male characteristics, both physical and mental ... (However) women were, on the whole, less inclined to criminality because of constitutional and psychological factors. They were organically conservative. Atavistic qualities had been bred out by sexual selection, and feminine qualities such as piety and maternal affection further worked against criminal tendencies. When criminality overcame these factors and "reared its ugly head", it was much worse than criminality as it appeared in the male.' It is quite clear that no matter how much Lombroso attempted to raise a scientific stance towards the study of female criminality, he was still very much caught up in Victorian stereotyping. Lombroso was sincere in his scientific venture, but he was sincerely wrong and has been criticised for his unscientific research methods, as well as for the dubious nature of his atavistic theory.

Bowker also refers to contemporaries of Lombroso who sought to give a more psychological explanation for female criminality. Factors such as sexual repression, envy, jealousy, vengeance and feminine rage were presented as motives for violent crimes committed by women, distinguishing them from violent crimes committed by men. 'Hans Gross, for instance, looked at qualitative aspects of female crime. He postulated that deceitfulness was a trait common to all women and came naturally from a history of concealment (of menstruation and socially disapproved aggression)' (Bowker, 1979). These arguments are ludicrous for they imply that men are *not* motivated to kill for reasons of jealousy, envy, revenge or rage.

Even in the 1930s researchers were unable to rid themselves of stereotyping. Bowker cites Eugenia Lekkerkerker, a Dutch lawyer, who observed that 'women offenders were regarded as "erring and misguided" and in need of protection and help. Shame was an important tool in rehabilitation attempts with females.' In the same manner, Sheldon and Eugenia Glueck found that a good marriage 'was a strong factor in preventing further delinquency. What a woman needed, in other words, was the iron hand of a man' (Bowker, 1979).

The 1940s and 1950s fared no better. Otto Pollak agreed that women were more deceitful than men. 'The relative weakness of the female made deceit necessary as a defence, subversion was found to be a common tactic of all oppressed classes: the biology of the female enabled her to deceive (she could fake orgasm while men could not), and her socialisation

8

taught her to conceal many things (menstruation, aggression and marital frustration)' (Bowker, 1979). To present biology or genes – implicit in the reference to hormonal changes – as an explanation for female inclination to crime, is also ludicrous. By the same reasoning, the effects of testosterone could be offered as an explanation for male criminality.

Pollak acknowledged that female criminals were treated differently from men. 'Men hate to accuse women and thus, indirectly, to send them to their punishment, police officers dislike to arrest them, district attorneys to prosecute them, judges and juries to find them guilty and so on' (Bowker, 1979).

Both Victorian attitudes towards the punishment of women offenders – that is, either treating them more harshly because they were 'sinning' against their nature, or being over-lenient – has prevailed throughout the eras, as did the tendency to link criminality to sexuality. 'In general, an overview of police interactions with women reveals that, contrary to the chivalry hypothesis, police officers routinely violate the civil rights of women they suspect of prostitution ... harassment is a highly significant reminder to women that paternalism accrues only to women who conform to a sex role which requires obedience to men, their passivity and their acceptance of their status as the sexual property of only one man' (Bowker, 1979). Women were even arrested as suspected prostitutes if they were found in areas frequented by prostitutes at night. In effect, they were being punished for not being at home, where society expected them to be.

As Bowker so rightly says: 'The theories on female criminality were generally contaminated by popular stereotypes and myths regarding women.'

It is surprising that despite the industrial revolution,

the world wars, the liberating nineteen sixties and the advent of feminism, both the Victorian attitudes continue to prevail today. Surely it is time that society moved away from excusing women's crimes on account of their 'feeble-mindedness' (without, of course, negating cases where crimes were committed as a result of the serious mental illness of the offender), or because of poverty and circumstances beyond their control. It is time that we recognise that some women are quite capable of committing violent crimes simply because they want to. In some of the cases examined in this book it most certainly was a deliberate decision, a cognitive choice.

Contemporary literature still struggles with the concept of women's supposed innate goodness. Are female criminals really worse than the men, or do we simply perceive them as worse because we believe they should be good?

Eileen MacDonald studied female terrorists and presented her work in a book entitled *Shoot the women first* (1991). The title refers to an instruction allegedly given to West Germany's anti-terrorist squad. Herr Christian Lochtre, director of the German intelligence gathering network, considered this good advice as he found female terrorists to 'have much stronger characters, more power and more energy' than the males. Anti-terrorist agencies all over the world concur with this view. MacDonald found that the premise of female terrorists being more dangerous than their male counterparts still stemmed from the stereotyical question: 'How could a woman do this?' People tended to rationalise the behaviour of female terrorists by branding them as lesbians or feminists gone mad, the implication being that lesbians and feminists are not 'proper women'.

MacDonald draws attention to justifications that the women were either so unattractive that they became killers in an attempt to attract men's attentions, or that they were so pretty that they succumbed easily to the seductions of charismatic terrorists like Carlos (Illich Ramirez Sanchez). The concept of using physical appearance as a yardstick to measure propensity for crime is perhaps a misguided throwback to Lombroso's studies reported in *Female Offender*.

Female terrorists are painted with the same 'romanticised brush' as male terrorists. Depicted in camouflage clothing, cradling heavy, 'virile' machine guns, they are considered sexy and alluring, challenging the male animal instinct to conquer. (Freud would have had a field day analysing the phallic significance of those weapons!) Yet, at the same time, they are condemned for being overtly sexually aggressive. Again, judgement of these women's motives was based upon their sexuality and not upon their political views. If their political views were to be considered they would be ascribed to 'passion', seen as a female emotional weakness, and not a cognitive conviction.

Today, society tends to justify aggression in a woman when she fights off a rapist, defends herself against an abusive husband or defends her children, and then as MacDonald aptly describes it, she is condescendingly branded 'a brave little woman'. Even premenstrual or postnatal depression may be accepted as legitimate reasons for violence, since this distinguishes the woman's behaviour from that of men; it is something 'that cannot be helped' and is beyond her control. When women are forced to join the armed forces in times of war, their ability to kill is accepted, just so long as they return to their more stereotypical roles once peace is declared (MacDonald, 1991).

It seems that Victorian stereotyping has left an inheritance which still regards criminal women as weak, feeble-minded, evil, unable to exert self-control, victims of their own biological make-up, and so on. Society is quick to blame men for upholding and enforcing this attitude which implies that women are victims of male chauvinism. But does society not, in supporting the Victorian view of regarding women as the gentler, nurturing sex, negate these qualities in men? If women are to be regarded as naturally 'good', are men then naturally 'bad'? Is this not discrimination against men? It is clear that neither gender benefits from this attitude. Men can be gentle, sensitive and nurturing. Many men love to care for women and children. This should not be overlooked.

This book is not intended as a platform for feminism, but rather as a mouthpiece for humanism. It is time that society rid itself of stereotypes. While it may be generally agreed that men should treat women with respect and should protect the innocent (a remnant of chivalry, perhaps), by the same token women should respect men and should also learn to take responsibility for all aspects of their own lives.

Once this approach is entrenched in society, it is more likely that men will take a more active role in bringing up their children, especially in teaching their sons to respect women, and in the same way women would realise, when they criticise men for violent behaviour, that they are the mothers of those men. Fathers would realise the harm they cause their daughters when they overindulge them, or rape and reject them. Mothers would realise the devastating effect they have on their daughters when they imprint nagging, castrating role models upon them. Are mothers not also guilty of transferring the image of weak, defenceless, helpless creatures upon their daughters?

In this book I propose equality – not from a feminist viewpoint, but rather from the perspective that all human beings deserve respect. We should all have the opportunity of self-actualisation, incorporating the anima and animus, without shame or condemnation. And if a human being – be it male or female – transgresses by committing interpersonal violence (whether it be verbal abuse, disrespect for property, or murder) that person should be brought to book on an equal basis, regardless of gender. Just as one should not be surprised that there are men who single-handedly raise their children in a nurturing environment, one should not be surprised that there are women who are capable of committing violent crimes.

If women do not commit violent crimes because they are feeble-minded, or because they are victims of their depraved circumstances, or because they do not know any better, why then do they do it? What motivates them?

This book is divided into chapters assigned to different categories of South African female killers. Each chapter will, as far as possible, begin with an introduction to the historical perspective and psychological motivation that induced these women to commit their crimes. This is followed in each instance by a number of case studies which have been selected to illustrate these motives. It was of course impossible to include all documented cases of female killers. Some of the psychological motivations may differ from those of men, but this does not make them better or worse and it may well be that the difference lies precisely in outdated societal norms. Some women acted purely out of motives of greed, some as a result of depression or other mental disturbance, others because of deprivation, and yet others out of self-defence. Whatever their motivation, the question has to be asked: should society condone their actions just because they are women, and if society *does* condone them, what criteria are being applied, and should not the same criteria be applied to men as well?

1

Battered Women

When does a battered woman reach breaking point? And is she justified in killing her abuser, or should she have extricated herself from her situation before she reached the point where she had to defend her life or that of her children? Can all cases of battered women who kill their abusers be attributed to self-defence, or are there cases where the women killed as a result of years of resentment? These are the troublesome questions that come to mind when the motives of women who kill their abusers are examined.

For centuries men had the right to abuse and beat their wives. In *When Battered Women Kill* Browne (1987) states: 'The first known "law of marriage" was formalised by Romulus [in ancient Roman times] and required married women "as having no other refuge, to conform themselves entirely to the temper of their husbands and the husbands to rule their wives as necessary and inseparable possessions".'

Browne also refers to Friar Cherubino who, in the late 1400s, compiled his Rules of Marriage and recommended that husbands should first try bullying and terrifying their wives before beating them. Beatings should be carried out not in anger but in a spirit of charity and out of concern for the woman's soul. At much the same time in England the view was held that since a man was held accountable for his wife's misbehaviour, he had the right to chastise her. Husbands were also pardoned for killing their wives, but for the wife to kill her husband was an act comparable to treason, since he was her lord and master and she was subservient in the way a subject would be to his king (Browne, 1987).

In 1871, Alabama became the first state in the USA to abolish a husband's right to assault his wife. 'The privilege, ancient though it may be, to beat her with a stick, to pull her hair, choke her, spit in her face or kick her about the floor, or to inflict upon her like indignities, is not now acknowledged by our law ...' (Browne 1987).

South Africa implemented the Domestic Violence Act in 1999. This act offers spouses, partners involved in live-in as well as dating relationships, parents, the elderly and children, protection against physical, verbal, sexual, emotional, psychological and financial abuse, as well as against intimidation, harassment, damage to property and stalking. Anyone who has been abused, including children, may obtain a protection order or interdict. Any person who has an interest in the victim's life, including counsellors, health workers, policemen, social workers and teachers, may also obtain protection orders against the abuser.

Protection orders may be obtained from the magistrate's court closest to the victim's place of residence or employment, or the abuser's place of residence or employment, or where the abuse has taken place, at any time of the day or night.

The protection order is enforceable throughout the country. If a victim needs immediate protection, an interim protection order may be issued.

Notice of the impending protection order is handed to the abuser by a sheriff, a policeman or a clerk of the court and the abuser is informed of a court date. If the abuser does not attend the court date, the protection order will be granted immediately. If the abuser appears in court, evidence will be heard from both parties and witnesses may be called. The presiding magistrate will then decide whether or not the protection order will be granted. The victim, as well as the police station closest to the victim, will be provided with copies of the protection order and a suspended warrant of arrest. Police officers have the right to arrest an abuser immediately at the scene of the violation, or to arrest the abuser on the basis of an allegation that the protection order has been violated.

If the abuser violates the protection order, the victim may approach any police officer with the suspended warrant of arrest. The victim may lay a criminal charge against the abuser and the abuser will be arrested and given a court date. Once this arrest warrant has been used, the victim should immediately obtain another in case the abuser violates the order again.

Protection orders prohibit the abuser from continuing acts of domestic violence, or entering the family home or the victim's place of employment. The abuser may also be warned not to make contact with any children involved. In addition, the police may be entitled to remove the abuser's firearms. The police may be ordered to accompany the victim home to remove personal effects and to instruct the abuser to provide money for the victim for lodgings and food and other necessary expenses.

It is imperative for victims to realise that many male abusers experience protection orders as challenges, and are infuriated by them. Within the first month of implementation of the South African Domestic Violence Act, fifteen women were killed by their abusing partners shortly after protection orders were served. It is therefore crucial that abused women and their children move to safe houses and remain there before or on the day the protection order is served. Addresses of safe houses may be obtained from police stations or crisis centres, such as LifeLine.

There is no guarantee that an abuser will be kept in custody after an arrest. Depending on the circumstances, he may be released on bail the same day. This effectively places the victim in immediate danger and she should make arrangements at once to move to a shelter or safe house and to remain there until more permanent accommodation can be arranged. Protection orders should be viewed as a temporary measure to escape immediate danger. Although the maximum sentence for transgressing a protection order is five years' imprisonment and/or a fine of a hundred thousand rand, many men regard protection orders as a direct insult to their egos and will oppose them, the threat of punishment notwithstanding.

It is imperative that victims receive counselling, and this is provided in shelters and safe houses. The victims themselves may not have the strength or courage to leave the abuser, but should be urged to seek help from those who have the appropriate training to assist them. There are literally hundreds of state and private organisations all over the country who are geared to help victims of abuse.

The application of the Domestic Violence Act has been identified as one of the South African Police Service's major priorities. Police officers, especially those at the Child and Family Violence Units, are trained to deal with domestic abuse. Should the victim not be satisfied with the conduct of any police officer, the commander of the police station or unit may be contacted, or complaints directed to the provincial level of command. The Independent Complaints Directorate is the 'watchdog' of the police service and any complaints regarding police conduct may also be directed to them. Although the police services and the judicial processes in South Africa are still riddled with problems – mainly due to lack of manpower and other resources – victims of domestic violence now have legal routes to follow, as opposed to resorting to violence themselves. There is no legal defence for killing an abusive partner, unless it is in self-defence and this can be proved.

Although laws and organisations are in place, battered women often continue to stay with their abusers. The question has to be asked: 'Why?' The first, somewhat simplistic, answer could be that these women grew up in a similar environment and know no better. Childhood patterns may be repeated in adulthood, perhaps in a misguided attempt to resolve them. Yet Browne cites Mildred Pagelow, who found that women who had been abused as children were more likely to leave abusing partners sooner than women who were not abused as children: 'Women who had no exposure to violence in the past often viewed the incidents as isolated occurrences, attributing them to particular circumstances or stresses in daily life, rather than suspecting that this may be a characteristic way of relating for their partner, and attempted to change their own behaviour or the couple's interactions in order to avoid a resurgence of aggression' (Browne, 1987).

As discussed in the Introduction, reasons why women stay with abusive partners may be traced to remnants of the Victorian 'ideal woman' perspective. Women are supposed to be unselfish, self-sacrificing, putting others' needs before their own, and so on, so it is not surprising that they should try to make peace, change their own behaviour or make excuses for their abusers' behaviour, rather than terminating the relationship. Too many women still hope that *their* good conduct will rectify their partners' unacceptable behaviour. They still feel the need to inspire 'goodness' in bad men by their own virtue. These women need to realise that there is nothing 'noble' about allowing themselves to be abused. It is not proof of love for the man. It is an atrocity.

A more realistic, albeit not always practical, reason why a woman does not leave an abusive home, is because she questions why *she* should be the one to leave. After all, she is not the offender and nor is she breaking the law. But when one's life is in danger, it is obviously best to leave the home until the abuser is removed, preferably for long-term imprisonment.

Another reason why women do not leave abusive partners is fear of reprisal. There is no guarantee that leaving him will end the abuse. Lisa Vetten, of the Centre for the Study of Violence and Reconciliation in Johannesburg, profiles abusive men as ordinary individuals who harbour 'traditional' expectations of their partners. Most of their friends and acquaintances would not identify them as wife-beaters. These men deal with stress through violence. Any deviation by

20

their partner from the traditional 'ideal woman' notion will be punished with violence and humiliation. They are also possessive and obsessively jealous, often accusing the woman, without any justification, of being unfaithful. Even looking at or speaking to another man is inexcusable. This kind of jealousy should not be regarded as a sign of his love for the woman. It is pathological behaviour and a way of exerting control over the woman.

An abusive man does not recognise that he has a problem and will not readily agree to therapy. He believes that he is entitled to abuse his partner and will pass the blame on to her, arguing that if she had 'behaved' herself, according to his rules, he would not have had to punish her. The burden of trying to make the relationship work is left entirely to the woman. She is expected to interpret his moods and needs and to adjust her behaviour and the daily running of the home accordingly. She is not permitted to ask him if anything is wrong, for abusive men refuse to discuss their emotions. They view emotions as female attributes; expressing emotions is manifesting weakness. They are uncompromisingly indifferent to the woman's own needs.

Abusive men tend to attach their own self-esteem to their victims. Although they regard their victims as worthless human beings deserving of punishment, they subconsciously believe they cannot live without them. (See the chapter on *Love Triangles*, and the discussion on obsessions and inferiority complexes.) For the woman to exercise her basic human rights and decide to leave an abusive relationship is seen as a rejection of the man's concept of himself. His fragile ego is not equal to facing the fact that the one he regards as 'a degraded creature' had the gall to leave him. As far as he is concerned, she belongs to him and, by leaving, she is challenging his conviction that women are objects or possessions, and not human beings who have rights. Should she achieve this, his whole belief system will come crashing down and he will no longer be in a position to regard himself as lord and master. Such a humiliating prospect is too much for his frail ego and he will risk his life – or take hers – to protect it.

Studies have proved that the longer an abusive relationship continues, the more difficult it is for the woman to leave. Warning signs that a relationship is doomed to develop into an abusive one, which may very well end in tragedy, include the following:

- behaviour aimed at controlling the woman;
- rewarding or punishing her depending on how acceptable her behaviour is to him;
- refusing to take responsibility for his actions and blaming the woman for anything that may go wrong;
- placing all responsibility for maintaining the relationship on the woman and expecting her to 'save' him from bad behaviour.

If any of these signs are detected, it is imperative that the relationship be ended immediately, no matter how much the potential abuser may protest. The woman will be making a grave mistake if she thinks she is the 'chosen one' who will change him either by complying or, worse, through 'love'. Love plays no role at all in these relationships. The emotions and behavioural patterns involved are control, fear, manipulation, lies, violence and terror. There is nothing noble or loving about any of these.

Despite these admonitions, some women find themselves caught in the trap of an abusive relationship.

It should be realised that the abuse is seldom present at the beginning of a relationship. Initial romantic wooing gradually deteriorates into an abusive pattern. Those who do not recognise the early stages risk being brainwashed into accepting abuse as normal. Browne refers to Sheriff and Hovland's model of social judgement, which incorporates a continuum on which incoming stimuli are ordered. 'The "latitude of acceptance" is that range of possibilities an individual is willing to agree with or adapt to; stimuli that fall outside that range are either in the latitude of rejection or the latitude of non-commitment' (Browne, 1987). 'Past experiences may determine what is acceptable and what not. Through continued abuse, the victim begins to assimilate the abuse as acceptable. If a certain stimulus is far beyond the others, it forms a contrast. This is usually the turning point, which causes the woman to leave or to kill. Such a stimulus may be a sudden threat towards the children, which was not previously imminent. The final hope has been crushed, they can not believe that they will survive the situation' (Browne, 1987).

It is difficult to comprehend why battered women do not leave their partners if one has not experienced their situation oneself. It seems, though, that many women find the cycle of romantic seduction, violence, reprisal, promises, and recidivism difficult to resist because it poses a challenge to their virtuous perseverance.

The issue of why some battered women resort to killing their abusers, while others do not, warrants exploration. Might the answer be provided by investigating their childhoods? 'Intergenerational transmission of violence' refers to the concept that children exposed to certain behavioural patterns of their parents will learn this to be the norm and will practise similar behaviour in adulthood.

Yet, in a comparative study between battered women who did not resort to violence and battered women who killed their husbands, Browne (1987) found that witnessing violence as children occurred in the history of both groups. It cannot therefore be considered a justifiable reason for battered women to kill their abusers. Although both groups viewed violence as an acceptable or deserving punishment for bad behaviour, the majority of battered women in this study did not kill their abusers.

Browne (1987) identified seven indicators that distinguished the homicidal group in her comparative study. They are:
- frequency of assault;
- severity of the victim's injuries;
- frequency of forced sexual intercourse;
- frequency of the man's intoxication;
- threats to kill by the man;
- alcohol and drug abuse;
- the victim's being reduced to threatening suicide.

Any one, or any combination, of these may be the trigger for murder.

Battered women who kill their partners have several plea options, the strongest of which is self-defence. Yet self-defence is only justifiable when one reasonably believes one is in immediate danger of unlawful bodily harm and that violence or force was necessary to avoid that harm. Any element of premeditation will rule out a plea of self-defence. A history of abuse alone is not justification for killing the abuser. In court cases the focus often shifts to the question of why the woman did not leave the relationship, instead of focusing on her legitimate right to defend her life.

In cases where self-defence can be proved, it is entirely reasonable for women to be acquitted; would it not, however, have been preferable for these women to have terminated the relationship at the first signs of controlling behaviour or violence, either verbal or physical? They should leave before they find themselves in a situation where they are forced to resort to killing.

Women need to be aware of the characteristics of abusers and not get involved in the first place. There is no acceptable reason for violence towards others, unless it is directed towards the protection of one's own life or the lives of others. If a woman provokes a man to the point where he considers retaliating with violence, he should think twice about the kind of woman he associates with, and walk away with dignity. The same rule applies to a woman who encounters a violent man.

Mens rea (Latin: guilty mind) is a legal term that refers to the state of mind of the offender at the time when the crime was committed. It is that element of the crime that examines the intention or knowledge of wrongdoing (as opposed to the action or conduct) of the offender. Women who kill their abusers sometimes resort to a plea of diminished mental capacity, which is surely a harking back to the Victorian plea of 'feeble-mindedness'. On this issue, Browne refers to Elizabeth Schneider who expresses concern that: 'Judicial willingness to find women's perspective acceptable may relate to the fact that the perspective courts are hearing and to which they are responding is that of damaged women not of women who perceive themselves to be, and may in fact be, acting competently, assertively and rationally in light of the alternatives' (Browne, 1987). The question remains, why did the woman not assert herself at an earlier stage by leaving the relationship?

All the women in Browne's study experienced severe depression after the killings. This is often exacerbated by the inevitable social stigma attached to these women, even if they are acquitted. In some cases this ostracism is extended to children who may have been removed from their mothers while they are in detention, awaiting trial.

There is also another view, a harsh one, but valid none the less. Every adult human being has to take responsibility for his or her own life. Adulthood, almost by definition, implies taking responsibility for decisions that affect one's life. Women who allow themselves to be continuously beaten or abused in any other way, must take responsibility for their situation. They cannot attribute the entire blame to their parents or their partners. This statement does not suggest that the behaviour of the abuser should be condoned – not at all. But the abused woman, as an adult, is ultimately responsible for herself. Many abused women will argue they have nowhere else to go, and will endure the abuse in order to have a roof over their heads. They offer other excuses – they have no skills, do not earn enough money, cannot provide for their children, etc. But millions of other women are able to divorce their husbands and support themselves and their children. Husbands are required by law to pay maintenance, even before the divorce has been finalised. In terms of the South African Domestic Violence Act, they can even be required to offer financial assistance while the woman and her children are accommodated in a safe house. Millions of domestic workers in South Africa are unskilled women who support extended families on meagre wages. If they can manage, there is no reason why other women cannot do the same. Where there is a will, there is a way.

Women who are not prepared to fend for themselves (and would rather tolerate abuse), even if it means lowering their living standards, are denying themselves human dignity. Were they brought up with the notion that it is the man's responsibility to take care of the woman, that it would reflect badly upon them if they earned their own salary, and that being married means enduring whatever the husband chooses to inflict on them? This is a very outdated notion: women today need to empower themselves. Allowing one's body to be abused for the sake of one's keep is a form of prostitution. The choice is the woman's: she can either remain in the relationship, or get out and take charge of her life. There are many government and non-governmental organisations which are equipped to help them get back on track, but it is up to them to take the first step.

In the twenty-first century it no longer seems fair to expect men to be the sole providers for their families. But if they choose to be sole providers – for they do have a choice in the matter – it does not give them the right to treat their families as chattels.

*

Case study: Maria Aletta Krebbs, 1987
On the night of 21 October 1987, Playmates Escort Agency in Johannesburg received a call from a Mrs Krebbs, who requested the services of a girl

at Mantua Terrace, Morninghill, Bedfordview. The receptionist enquired what the girl's services would be needed for and Mrs Krebbs allegedly replied that the girl would be a present for her husband's birthday.

At about ten o'clock that night, twenty-two-year-old Gertruide Magdalene du Preez, alias Patricia, was dropped off at the address by her manager. According to the statement which she made later, Patricia knocked on the door and it was opened by attractive, thirty-four-year-old Maria Krebbs. Forty-two-year-old Ralph Krebbs paid the manager's taxi fare. Maria, who was wearing a pink nightgown, led Patricia towards the main bedroom. Ralph followed. Maria poured Patricia a glass of wine, while Ralph looked in Maria's handbag for cash to pay Patricia. Finding that they had no cash, Maria offered Patricia a cheque for one hundred and twenty rand, which she accepted.

With the formalities over, Patricia slipped into the bathroom and returned wearing only her top, panties and shoes. Ralph and Maria had already undressed. Patricia began caressing Maria, but Maria asked her to divert her attentions to Ralph, which she did. However Ralph was apparently not very interested and Maria shouted at him before walking out of the room. When she returned Ralph wanted to caress her but she told him to leave her alone. She hit him on the head with the bottle of wine and threw a vase at him.

Ralph got dressed and left the room whereupon Maria locked the door. She took a revolver from a cupboard and pointed it at Patricia and pulled the trigger three times. It was not loaded. Maria then walked to her husband's bedside table and took out three bullets. She loaded one into the firearm and left two on the bed. While pointing the gun at her, she told

28

Patricia that her husband had abused her during the eight years of their marriage.

Maria offered Patricia another glass of wine and allegedly said: 'I am going to kill the bastard.' She left the room. Patricia frantically phoned her manager, asking him to come and fetch her before she was killed.

Maria re-entered the room and went to the bathroom, whereupon Patricia grabbed her belongings and fled to the neighbours, where she phoned the police and her manager. She met her manager in the street and they left hurriedly.

The neighbours, Mrs and Mrs Chudleigh, were shocked by Patricia's story. About ten minutes after Patricia's departure, they heard a shot and a short while later there was a banging on their door. They found a naked Maria Krebbs huddling on the porch. Maria said that she had shot Ralph; she had not meant to kill him, but had acted out of anger. She also told them that this was not the first time Ralph had hired a sex-worker. Mrs Chudleigh covered the naked woman with a gown. Maria then remembered her two toddlers and ran back to her house, with the neighbours following. They found Ralph in the passage. He was still breathing and Mr Chudleigh called the emergency services. Maria called a friend who arrived shortly after the police and persuaded Maria to hand the firearm over to a member of the emergency services. It was then that they informed Maria that Ralph had died.

At about half past one that morning, Dr Ernest Sonnenfield arrived and confirmed that Ralph was dead. Maria told Dr Sonnenfield that she and her husband had been making love when he insisted that a sex-worker should join them. She had been humiliated by this incident. In his statement Dr Sonnenfield said that the couple had previously consulted him on a medical matter.

Maria was arrested, but was granted bail.

Mr Justice D O Vermooten presided over the trial, which began in March 1989. Jan Liebenberg, a paramedic who had attended the scene, testified that while the paramedics were attempting to save Ralph's life Maria told him she wished her husband would die. But when he informed her that Ralph was dead, she said she had never meant to shoot him.

Maria Krebbs denied Patricia's version of events. She said Ralph had dialled the number and forced her to speak to the Escort Agency. She said she thought it was a joke, but the doorbell rang soon afterwards and Ralph went to answer the door. She was lying in bed, naked. She was shocked when he entered the room with Patricia in tow. She was repulsed by the thought of Patricia touching her, pushed her away and begged Ralph to stop. Ralph responded by pushing her legs open and attempting to have intercourse with her. She told him to go to Patricia. When Ralph turned towards Patricia, Maria snapped and threw the vase and wine bottle at him. Ralph had intercourse with Patricia and then he grabbed Maria by the arm. She broke free, ran to the bathroom and hid in the shower. Ralph tried to break down the glass door with a hammer but did not succeed. He left the room, threatening to kill her. Maria testified that when she came out of the bathroom, she saw Ralph's firearm and picked it up. Patricia was gone and she never saw her again. Ralph walked into the room, Maria immediately fled and when he pursued her she shot him. Then she ran to the neighbours. She said she loved her husband and had not meant to kill him.

On 13 March 1989, Mr Justice Vermooten acquitted Maria Krebbs on the charge of murder but found her guilty of culpable homicide. She was sentenced to a fine of two thousand rand or one year's imprisonment and three years' imprisonment suspended for five years. She was also declared unfit to own a firearm. Maria paid the two thousand rand fine and walked out of court.

Comment

The judge found that the damage to the shower door proved that Ralph Krebbs had used excessive violence, which corroborated Maria's testimony that he had abused her. The fact that she ran naked to the neighbours' house indicated that she was in a state of shock. He said she was negligent when she fired a shot at Ralph instead of trying to get away from him, and that this negligence had resulted in the death of Ralph Krebbs.

Ralph Krebbs was Maria's second husband. Her first marriage lasted three years and she had one child from that marriage. She remained single for seven years before she met Ralph in Johannesburg. At that stage he was estranged from his wife. Maria was already eight months pregnant with Ralph's child when she married him and she later had another son with him. They were wealthy and Ralph spoiled her, buying her a Porsche 928S, among other things. They went overseas twice a year. After he lost his job and his own business venture failed, he was earning only five thousand rand a month.

In May 1989, two months after Maria walked out of court, she phoned the police to ask them to arrest a boyfriend who had allegedly been living with her in her luxury home for a year. She maintained that he had assaulted her, but he told a newspaper that she had assaulted him as well. Maria allegedly complained that this boyfriend was 'just after her money', as Ralph had been. He did not even own a car when they met and had only two suitcases when he moved in. Another, younger, man reportedly said that he started dating Maria three days after Ralph's death, but Maria denied this, saying she would not date younger men. It is not difficult to see why men were attracted to her. She was a petite and vivacious redhead who shopped at boutiques and who did embroidery with perfectly manicured hands.

Maria Krebbs objected to her husband's perverse sexual games, especially when he wanted a 'threesome' with a sex-worker. This upset her to such an extent that she broke down and shot him. Maria had one previous conviction at the time she was charged with murder – she had been found guilty of possessing pornography in 1986. She said she took the rap for her husband.

Case study: Ann Cantrill, 1992

Ross and Ann Cantrill emigrated from England to South Africa in 1982. Ross, a skilled artisan, found employment at the Stilfontein gold mine west of Johannesburg and Ann worked in a bank. Both had been married before and Ann had three children from her previous marriage. Nine years after they arrived in South Africa Ann left Ross, alleging that he abused her, particularly when he was drunk. Besides assaulting her, Ann alleged that Ross had sodomised her and continually called her names.

Ross moved in with a girlfriend, Alexandra Wilson Dougan. Ann started divorce proceedings but when Ross found out about this, he returned home, allegedly fastened a dog collar around her neck, tied her to the bed and abused her. She dropped the divorce proceedings, but Ross remained with his girlfriend. Ann attempted suicide.

Ann testified that in October 1992 Ross had complained to her that his girlfriend was not a good cook and said that he wanted to move back home. She took him back. On Christmas morning 1992, Ross attempted to have intercourse with his wife, but was unable to. He blamed her for his impotence. By the time Ann's daughter and her boyfriend arrived for Christmas lunch, the atmosphere was very tense. The couple had an argument after lunch and a hysterical Ann rushed into the house and returned with a firearm in her hand. She shot at Ross point-blank range.

During the trial, she testified that she had taken medication for depression, as well as painkillers and alcohol, and could not remember shooting him. She pleaded criminal incapacity.

There are two sides to every story. Alexandra Dougan testified that during October 1992 Ann had arrived on her doorstep at two o'clock one morning and demanded money from Ross. She accused him of being a worthless husband who was unable to father children or make love properly. Ann had allegedly said that she had heard of a woman who was fined two thousand rand for killing her husband (Maria Krebbs?) and that killing Ross would be worth that. Ann's response to this testimony was that she had gone to Alexandra's home to return Ross' laundry.

A colleague testified that Ross was a gentle person who did not smoke or consume large quantities of alcohol. He also told the court that two days before the murder, Ann had arrived at Ross' place of work and threatened him with a firearm. She had allegedly told him she would 'fix him up like a dog'.

Ann Cantrill was sentenced to three years' imprisonment.

Comment

It is incomprehensible why a woman would want to commit suicide if her abusive husband refused to leave his girlfriend and return to her. When Ross moved in with his girlfriend, Ann was finally rid of his abuse. Why would she take her philandering husband's laundry to his girlfriend's home at two o'clock in the morning? Why do his laundry at all? Why on earth did she take him back? Why did she not add an assault charge to the divorce action after he had tied her up like a dog? Ann claimed that she wanted her marriage to Ross to work because her first marriage had failed. Was Ann Cantrill a woman who believed her value as a human being depended on making her marriage work, regardless of how much abuse she endured in the process? In the end, it made her a killer.

Case study: Maria Magdalene Scholtz, 1996

Maria married Frans Scholtz when she was thirty-one years old. Together with her three children from a previous marriage, the family moved to Kirkwood in the Eastern Cape. Within three months Maria realised that she had made a terrible mistake. She alleged that Frans refused to buy food for the family. During the day, when he was not at home, they were allowed only bread and water or coffee. Maria, a nurse, was forbidden to work and was isolated from her friends and family. Frans also had a drinking problem.

Maria sought help from a social worker at the Christian Social Council, but to no avail. Although

Frans used to beat her son, his abuse of Maria was not physical. It was emotional and manipulative. At that stage there was no law in South Africa that protected Maria against this kind of psychological abuse. She left Frans and returned to her parents and began divorce proceedings. Her family, however, advised her to return to her husband.

During the trial it emerged that three events precipitated Maria's decision to kill Frans. Her older son ran away from school, her younger son told her he no longer wanted to live at home, and one night Frans exposed himself to Maria's seventeen-year-old daughter, Charmaine Bruwer.

Maria decided that she would poison her husband and bought *muti* for this purpose. (*Muti* is medicine prepared by traditional healers called sangomas, using plant and animal products.) However the sangoma did not send her *muti* with lethal properties, but *muti* that would reputedly save the marriage. Maria returned the *muti* and demanded her money back. She then asked her domestic worker Mieta Hartney for help. Mieta asked her friends, thirty-year-old Ernest Helmie and eighteen-year-old Samuel Rolls, to pay Maria a visit. Maria asked her older son and her daughter Charmaine to help her kill Frans. The son refused, but Charmaine agreed.

The five of them planned the murder in detail. On the night of 26 January 1996, the older son and Charmaine's boyfriend were away on a fishing trip. Maria made supper for the family and managed to slip sleeping pills into Frans' drink. When they went to bed, Maria had sex with her husband, which she said filled her with loathing. At about midnight, when Frans was asleep, Maria and Charmaine went outside and tied up the dogs. Ernest and Samuel entered the house and Maria and her daughter locked themselves in the bathroom. The two assailants stabbed Frans to death and then ransacked the house and stole firearms in order to stage a burglary.

Shortly after midnight Maria phoned the police and told them that she and her daughter had been in the bathroom when they heard strange voices in the house. When the intruders had gone they found that Frans had been murdered. A thorough police investigation soon turned the tables on Maria.

While Maria and Charmaine were awaiting trial prisoners, their home caught fire and her older son and a friend were burnt to death. Her younger son was placed in a children's home. Charmaine was held at the Enkuselweni Place of Safety for children, as she had not yet turned eighteen.

During the trial Maria testified that Frans had often raped her, and Charmaine testified that her stepfather had sexually assaulted her. In passing sentence on Maria, the judge said he would have sentenced Maria to life imprisonment, but he found the mental, sexual and financial abuse she had suffered to be mitigating circumstances and passed a twenty-year sentence instead. He sentenced Charmaine to two years' correctional supervision. The two killers were given life sentences.

For the first three year she was in prison, Maria lost contact with her children. Her first son was dead, her second son had been placed in foster care and she had no idea what had happened to Charmaine. But before Christmas 1999 Charmaine had been traced and she visited Maria in prison.

Comment

Maria Scholtz is one of five women whose case has

been taken up by the Justice for Women Campaign being conducted by the Centre for the Study of Violence and Reconciliation in Johannesburg. The other women are: Sharla Sebejan (who was sentenced to twenty-five years for having her abusive husband beaten to death in 1995); Meisie Kgomo (sentenced to twenty years in 1994 for asking her brother to kill her husband with a knife); Elsie Morare (sentenced to twenty-one years for the murder of her policeman husband); and Harriet Chidi (sentenced to fifteen years for having her abusive policeman husband strangled). All these women were severely abused by their husbands. On one occasion Meisie's husband stabbed her and beat her to within an inch of her life. He evidently thought she was dead, for when she regained consciousness she found him scrubbing the bed with antiseptic to get rid of evidence.

According to Lisa Vetten of the Centre, at the time when these women were sentenced, men were receiving sentences ranging from six to ten years for killing their wives, while women's sentences for killing their husbands ranged from twenty years to life. Vetten recalled a case where a man had lost control and killed his wife because she berated him for walking over her clean floors. He was found guilty of culpable homicide and received a suspended sentence, because the murder was not premeditated. The fact that the man was capable of murder when he lost his temper was regarded as mitigating, not aggravating, circumstances.

Case study: Maureen Muller, 1998
Like so many women before her, Maureen Muller finally reached breaking point with her abusive husband, Edmund Harold Muller. She conspired

with her sister Faiza Allie, and her sister's boyfriend Marshall February, to hire a hitman by the name of Richard Ortell to kill Edmund. In June 1998, Ortell and February went to the Mullers' house in Jan van Riebeeck Street, Paarl East in the Western Cape province on the pretext of buying Edmund's car. Ortell shot him and the assailants fled.

All four of the conspirators were found guilty of murder and given life sentences.

Comment

This case does not differ much from other cases where battered women have conspired to kill their abusive husbands, but there was one compelling difference. Maureen Muller wrote an emotional letter, which she read out in court: 'I owe you an apology for contributing to the death of your son, son-in-law, brother, father and friend. Your heartache, grief and anger will remain as a reminder of the wrongful choices I have made. It will forever remind me that I did not have the right to pursue the avenues that I did. It will always remind me that you were the last people who deserved that kind of punishment. My regret is that I could not trust you enough to share my unhappiness with you, and I live with the guilt of what I have forced you into ... I understand that society does not truly favour women and their issues, this did not give me the right to take the law into my own hands. I am prepared to face the wheels of justice for my contribution in this matter, however my warning to other abused women is that I hope my case serves as a reminder to rather seek other options.'

One cannot help but respect Maureen Muller. In the end, she realised that she had other choices and it is sad that her insight came too late. Hopefully, her letter will be heeded by other women in similar situations.

Case study: Zelda Theunissen, 1998

On the night of 23 March 1998, Zelda Theunissen a thirty-four-year-old mother of four, a widow and a school teacher who lived in Mafikeng in the North West province, shot her lover, professional golfer Johannes Andries le Grange. Zelda had earlier found Andries in bed with another woman. On the night of the murder, Zelda had gone out to dinner with Andries and friends. When they returned to his home, she confronted him about his other relationship. Andries said he would not give the other woman up and would not have sex with Zelda. She went into the bathroom, planning to shoot herself. She wrote a suicide note and cocked the firearm – and then she changed her mind. She decided she would shoot herself in front of Andries. An argument ensued and the firearm went off, fatally wounding Andries in the heart. When the police arrived, she was kneeling over his body and she asked the police officer: 'How could you do this to one you love?'

During the trial, psychologist Dr Rudolph Horn testified that Andries was playing emotional games with Zelda. Although they had shopped for wedding rings, he never proposed to her. Zelda had had an unhappy childhood during which her father often assaulted her mother. She was sensitive, naïve and could not handle emotional turmoil. Time and again Andries dangled the promise of emotional security in front of her, only to snatch it away again.

Evidence was also led that Zelda had apparently told the other woman, Cheynne Angelique le Roux, that if she, Zelda, could not have Andries, no one else would.

Zelda was found guilty of murder. Mr Justice

Bob Nugent said that although the murder was not premeditated, Zelda should have foreseen that Andries could die when she pointed the firearm at him and pulled the trigger. He gave her a three-year prison sentence, suspended for five years, and she was also sentenced to correctional supervision and community service at a hospital.

Comment

Zelda contended that Andries had subjected her to emotional abuse. The fact that he played with her feelings was unbearable. Of course a person may have several relationships at the same time, but it is in the interest of both parties to be open about the arrangement. It is then up to all parties to decide whether they want to continue the relationship, knowing there are other liaisons involved. Making and breaking promises and conducting a number of clandestine relationships at the same time is a very dangerous game. Setting up hope of marriage, while having no intention of fulfilling that promise, is extremely callous behaviour. In the case of Zelda Theunissen, it had tragic consequences.

It is ironic that the Domestic Violence Act, which makes provision for psychological abuse, was promulgated in 1999, the year that Zelda was sentenced.

Zelda Theunissen's case is similar to that of Sharon van Coller, discussed at the end of this chapter.

Case study: Margaretha Jacoba 'Maggie' Gouws, 1999

'The magnitude of the "torture" Gouws had to endure for years at the hands of her husband was severe, and one could hardly think of a worse abuse within a marriage.' These were the words of Mr Justice Bert Bam when he sentenced Maggie Gouws to seven years' imprisonment, suspended for three years, for culpable homicide.

For twenty-five years Maggie endured the verbal and physical abuse of her husband Cherel Edouard. A police clerk in Nylstroom, every month Maggie had to hand her meagre salary over to her husband, who gambled it away. The family often had to rely on the church to provide them with food. Cherel referred to himself as Jesus Christ and tolerated no disobedience from Maggie. Maggie had left Cherel several times, but as is typical of battered wives, returned every time. When she threatened to divorce him, he threatened to burn the house down. He forced himself on her when he was drunk and threatened to find sex elsewhere if she did not comply. On those nights when Cherel was at his worst, Maggie would escape and wander the streets until he had calmed down or gone to bed.

On the evening of 27 November 1999 Cherel picked a fight with Maggie. In desperation she called their minister. He arrived, read from the Bible and then left. According to Cherel's son from a previous marriage, he was furious about the minister's involvement and the humiliation he had suffered as a result. Maggie ran to their bedroom to gather a few items of clothing, planning to spend the night elsewhere. She claimed that the next thing she could remember was blood pouring from her husband's ears.

According to Cherel's son, who had gone with his stepmother to play pool and have a few drinks earlier in the day, Maggie had returned from the room with a firearm in her hand. She said: 'Bokkie, stop it,' and fired a shot into Cherel's head. The son took the firearm from her and she screamed, 'What have I done', while trying to resuscitate Cherel. A policeman who arrived on the scene testified that Maggie was hysterical and incoherent. Cherel died on the way to the hospital.

During the trial, the minister testified that Maggie had pleaded with him to come to their house, saying that if he did not she would kill her husband. Maggie alleged she had fetched the firearm only to scare her husband and had no intention of killing him.

'I did not want to divorce him, because I wanted to keep my family together. I loved him and could in any event not cope on my own, financially,' she said.

State advocate Wilma Schutte argued that Maggie was suffering from a major depression at the time of the murder and recommended that she be sent to a state psychiatric hospital for clinical observation. Maggie's defence lawyer, advocate Johan Engelbrecht, contended she was not suffering from any mental illness. Her actions had not been premeditated and her mental ability had been only temporarily impaired. Mr Justice Bam ruled that Maggie not be sent for clinical observation.

Maggie enlisted the services of well-known South African forensic psychologist, Dr Louise Olivier. During the trial, Dr Olivier testified that Maggie had disassociated herself from reality and was not accountable for her actions during the murder, but the judge rejected this finding, saying that she should have foreseen and prevented the death of her husband. He also rejected the finding that Maggie had temporary amnesia and only came to when she heard the shot being fired, but he did concur that Maggie had the profile of a battered wife and not that of a violent offender.

In passing sentence, Mr Justice Bam referred to

two opposing views regarding sentencing of battered wives who kill their husbands. One view is that battered women should not even be charged, and the other advocates imprisonment for *anyone* who takes a life. He found her to be negligent and guilty of culpable homicide and gave her a suspended three-year sentence.

Comment

What is interesting in this particular case is that Maggie Gouws had left her husband several times. Also, as an employee of the South African Police Services, she would have known her rights and could have obtained interdicts or had her husband arrested, yet she chose to return to him. On the one hand, she said that she had wanted to divorce him, but backed down when he threatened to burn down the house. On the other hand, she said she could not divorce him for she would not have been able to make it on her own financially. By this statement, was Maggie Gouws conceding that she was willing to tolerate her husband's abuse in exchange for a roof over her head? Her husband had squandered all their money on his gambling habit. Would she not have been better off divorcing him and keeping her salary for herself and her children? One has to question whether Maggie Gouws had options other than killing her abusive husband.

Case study: Nurse Maria Zwelibanzi, 1999

Nurse could forgive her husband Solomon for beating her, for selling everything in their house, and even for stabbing her when she was pregnant, but the day he attempted to rape her daughter, she had had enough.

She discussed her problem with her cousin, twenty-eight-year-old Nxolisi Khumalo. When Nxolisi heard she was prepared to pay ten thousand rand to get rid of Solomon, he contacted a friend, twenty-year-old Michael Msina. The fact that Michael owned a firearm apparently qualified him as a prospective hitman.

On the night of 20 June 1999, Nurse, Solomon and the two appointed assassins went drinking at a shebeen at Pholo, near Ogies in the province of Mpumalanga. When they left they decided to take a short cut home through the cemetery. When Solomon, who suffered from epilepsy, had a seizure, Michael tripped him. Nurse, realising that the murder was about to take place, immediately ran home. Later that night Michael informed her that 'the job had been done'. It was not until the next morning that Nurse plucked up the courage to return to the cemetery. She was appalled, she later said, to find that the assailants had decapitated her husband. She had expected that he would simply be shot.

Both men denied killing Solomon. Nxolisi said he was at home, watching television, and Michael said he was answering a call of nature when Nxolisi attacked Solomon in the cemetery.

Nurse was sentenced to eighteen years' imprisonment for conspiring to kill her husband.

Comment

Nurse Zwelibanzi's case study illustrates the blatant callousness with which some women are able to keep their composure. She was indignant that her husband had been decapitated rather than shot – which would have been a much 'cleaner' death. The fact that she had hired someone to murder him apparently did not bother her much. It was the manner of his death that appalled her.

Case study: Anieta Natasha Fereirra, 2000

Cyril Parkman was twenty years older than his common-law wife Anieta. The two of them lived together for eleven years on a smallholding near Rustenburg in North West province. Anieta, who as a child had been abused by her mother, also suffered abuse at the hands of Cyril. During the trial she testified that apart from physical abuse, Cyril would sometimes lock her up for two weeks without food. A farm labourer smuggled food to her. Cyril once tried to stab her with a knife and on another occasion he throttled her so viciously that she had to undergo reconstructive surgery. He alienated her from her friends and family and cut the telephone lines so that she could not contact them.

Anieta also claimed that Cyril demanded sex up to fifteen times a night and would humiliate her by undressing her in front of his friends and showing off her private parts. He also threatened to hire men to rape her.

Anieta asked her domestic worker to find someone to kill Cyril. Boston Thys Chilambo and his brother George Koesyn were prepared to help. Anieta testified that she offered them ten thousand rand, but they claimed she promised them ninety thousand rand. On the night of 4 February 2000 the men entered the house and found Cyril in a drunken stupor. They strangled him with a shoelace. Anieta paid them five thousand, seven hundred rand and said they could also have Cyril's car. She helped them load Cyril's body into the car and the men drove off to dump the body. However, they accidentally drove the car into a tree and abandoned both car and body.

All three were convicted of murder by Mr Justice

Bill Prinsloo.

Comment

Anieta claimed that when she realised she would never be able to get away from Cyril, she decided to have him killed. This was in spite of the fact that she had at one stage managed to leave him, and had even found accommodation and employment in another town, but she returned to him of her own free will. She was not even married to Cyril. Was Anieta Fereirra one of those women who chose to endure abuse for the sake of a roof over her head? One has to ask why she did not use the money she gave the killers rather to move out and start a new life.

By the time Anieta stood trial she had allegedly already found another boyfriend. In April 2004, in a landmark judgment, the Supreme Court of Appeal found that Anieta should never have gone to prison. The president of the Appeal Court, Mr Justice Craig Howie, ordered that her life sentence be replaced by six years' imprisonment and that the part of the sentence she had not served be suspended for three years. Anieta left prison within a week.

For the first time the judicial system had acknowledged that abused women may develop the mindset that killing their abuser is the only way out of their situation. Anieta's socio-economic circumstances were also taken into consideration. The Appeal Court judges, however, issued a warning that their ruling did not mean that it was 'open season' for battered women to kill their abusers. The Honourable Mr Justice Robin Marais opposed the ruling, emphasising that 'murder is still murder' and the fact that Anieta had hired two killers is, 'in the eyes of most reasonable people, an abomination which is corrosive of the very foundations of justice'.

No mercy was shown to the two killers hired by Anieta.

In a similar case, Anne-Marie Thiearney shot her abusive ex-husband on 18 March 1999. Anne-Marie first claimed that he had been killed by an unknown man but later retracted her story. After she had been found guilty of murder, her son stormed towards her in the dock and demanded that she tell the truth, or else he would. A tearful Anne-Marie then told the court that her ex-husband had abused both her and her children severely. On the night of the murder, he had threatened to kill both her and himself. They struggled for the firearm and she shot him three times. Mr Justice Johan Els found it unacceptable that Anne-Marie had to kill to resolve her problems. 'You were already divorced. There was no reason why you could not have taken your children and left,' he said when he sentenced her to ten years' imprisonment.

Not guilty
The following women were found not guilty of killing their abusive husbands or partners.

Case study: Maria Bekker, 2000
In 1964 Maria was raped by Jurie Jan Bekker and became pregnant as a result. Then she married him. For thirty-six years Maria regretted this decision. Jurie abused her relentlessly, often calling her a slut. Maria did everything in her power to save the marriage but Jurie resisted admonitions by the police and the minister to work at his marriage.

During the trial a psychologist testified that by the time Maria actually shot her husband, on 3 August 2000 on their smallholding near Ogies in Mpumalanga province, she was so terrified of him that even the smallest incident could have broken her completely. The confrontation that finally caused her to snap was Jurie's throwing a packet of condoms at her and telling her she could 'whore with anyone she wanted to'.

Maria managed to slip sedatives into Jurie's tea, hoping to calm him. He was lying down when Maria took his firearm, walked over to him and fired seven shots. She fled to her brother's home and later claimed that she had absolutely no recollection of those few moments in which she killed Jurie.

During the trial her daughter, Leeza Spies, and her sister-in-law testified that Maria had shown them exactly where she was standing when she shot Jurie. Maria denied this. Lammie Treurnicht testified that a few days before the murder Jurie had expressed the wish to change his will in favour of his daughter Leeza. Maria denied any knowledge of this. It was put to her that her husband had two life insurance policies. She acknowledged that she knew about these.

On 14 November 2001, Mr Justice Malan acquitted Maria. A bewildered, tearful, but grateful Maria walked out of court a free woman. None of her family, not even her daughter, had supported her. They were shocked at the outcome of the trial. 'She killed my father and now she is free,' said Leeza.

'I don't know what is going to happen,' said Maria. 'I have to pick up the pieces of my shattered life and make a new beginning. I don't know where or how.'

Comment

Maria Bekker was given a second chance. It is tragic that, at the age of fifty-six, she had no idea what to do with it. Jurie Bekker had raped a woman and then married her. In his mind, because she was raped, she was a whore, no matter that he was the rapist. Yet he still married the woman he considered to be a whore. Jurie punished Maria for thirty-six years for what he had done to her. Despite her efforts to forgive him and to build a marriage with him, he continuously accused her of sleeping with other men. Jurie manifested a classical case of projection, a psychological defence mechanism in which a person projects his own failures, mistakes or prejudices on to someone else, because he cannot face them himself. Had Jurie gone to prison for the rape, Maria's life would have been so different.

Case study: Sharon van Coller, 2001

In early 2000 Sharon van Coller had been separated from her second husband for two years. She was living in her own house with her two daughters and had found employment at a financial institution in Johannesburg. Sharon claimed that it soon became obvious to her that at least two of her female colleagues had a serious crush on the company's external legal representative, advocate Chris Lamprecht, himself twice divorced.

One day in September 2000 Sharon heard that Chris was in the building and she made a point of finding out who he was, this man whom her colleagues found so attractive. Sharon was briefly introduced to Chris but, on first impression, could not understand the attraction.

Sharon declined the invitation to the company's Christmas party in November 2000, as she did not know anyone to invite. But one of her colleagues persuaded her to accompany a male contact of the company.

That night Sharon and her date shared a table with Chris, who had been invited by one of her female colleagues. Sharon alleged that her date behaved badly and she asked him to leave, which he did. When Chris asked Sharon to dance, she accepted out of politeness. He danced with her all night and completely ignored his own date.

Chris told Sharon he had arrived with her date, who happened to be a friend of his, and since this man had left, he had no way of getting home. She offered him a lift. That night they sat in the car for two hours, talking, and Sharon was surprised how much they had in common. She dropped Chris off at his home. When he asked her if he could contact her again she declined, not wanting to upset her colleague. She also noticed that a woman was waiting for Chris at his home.

Sharon maintained that despite several requests from Chris, she refused to see him; eventually, however, she agreed to meet him on 1 December at his home. She arrived in the afternoon and he opened a bottle of champagne. They went out for dinner and returned late to his home. Sharon spent the night, but they did not make love.

Sharon said that, in retrospect, she realised that whenever Chris discussed his previous girlfriends, he was very disparaging. 'Do unto them before they do unto you,' was his philosophy regarding women. He told Sharon that he had met women who were 'begging to be broken'. Another of his alleged infamous quotes was that women began a relationship with him 'with a roar and left with a whimper'. However, he regarded Sharon as his soul mate; she would be the one to save him from his 'sickness', as they called it.

Sharon said that her relationship with Chris

flourished that December, despite many phone calls and messages from other women who threatened to commit suicide if Chris broke up with them. Chris made Sharon listen to these messages to prove to her that they were pursuing him, and not the other way around. He was of the opinion that they made themselves very cheap. He could not bear 'cheap women'.

In mid-December Chris went away on a business trip. When he returned Sharon found evidence that a woman had been staying in his house in his absence. Chris told her that he had not given this woman permission to stay in his house, but that she still had a set of his house keys. This was the first time he showed aggression towards her. He grabbed her by the arm: 'I say I love you and you accuse me!' he said.

Sharon and Chris made love for the first time in January 2001. The following day he admitted to having had sex with another 'cheap woman' the night before. 'If you had told me you loved me before, I would not have slept with her,' was his excuse. Sharon left, intending never to return, but she forgave Chris when he later apologised.

Sharon alleged that she later found out that Chris was conducting affairs with about twenty-two other women at the same time as he was seeing her. All of these women were led to believe that they were the most special person in his life. When Sharon complained to Chris that she had lost thirteen kilograms because the other women in his life were causing her stress, he replied that losing weight because she was concerned about competition was a sign of her love for him.

One night at Chris' house Sharon innocently massaged the neck of one of his male friends. Chris called her outside and threw her on to the ground.

'You behave like dirt, therefore you are dirt,' he said, kicking her. Sharon felt a terrible pain in her back and could not get up. He pulled her to her knees by her hair and forced her to apologise for embarrassing him. Then he bashed her face against the garden wall. Sharon managed to get away.

The next day she went to work, but her employers sent her to a clinic and someone called the police to take a statement. Sharon told the female investigating officer that it was no use trying to lay a charge against Chris because he was an advocate and had warned her that no magistrate would ever find him guilty, because they were all his friends. Eventually, however, Sharon made a statement. Chris was barred by the hospital from visiting Sharon and she refused all calls from him.

But eventually she took his call. Chris apologised, saying it was probably the alcohol and dagga (cannabis) he had taken that night that had made him lose control. Also, he could not stand her touching another man because he loved her so much. Sharon discharged herself. Chris ordered her a taxi to take her to his home.

When she arrived she noticed that there was a security guard on his property. Chris admitted that he had hired the security guard in case Sharon pursued her case against him. He had told friends that she was a danger to him and that he needed protection. However, since they were now reconciled, he dismissed the guard.

Sharon maintained that Chris forced her to inform her colleagues that she had lied about him assaulting her. She complied. He also persuaded her to sell her house and to move in with him. She did this too. He thought it would be a good idea for her to have his name tattooed on her body. When Sharon wanted a tattoo of Batman, their favourite cartoon character, Chris assaulted her because she had chosen Batman instead of him. Eventually she had his name tattooed on her body.

Sharon said that Chris told her that he was using an army tactic, first breaking her down and then building her up the way he wanted her to be. He drew up a list of rules: for example, she should keep her eyes downcast in public, never smoke at work, never oppose him, etc. Throughout their relationship Sharon had to repeat this list on her knees before she could go to bed at night.

Chris often treated Sharon to holidays, or insisted that she accompany him on business trips. On one such occasion she bought a T-shirt as a present for her eldest daughter, but Chris threw it out of the window. Since he was prepared to sacrifice all the women in his life for her, she had to give up all the people in her life for him. He alienated Sharon from her children. She secretly phoned her daughter on her birthday, but Chris found out and punished her, first by almost drowning her and then making her sit on her knees in a bath of ice cold water for three hours.

Chris checked her cellphone records. If she was not at her desk when he phoned her at work, he would punish her that night. By this time Sharon had been conditioned to try to follow his rules, to avoid punishment. She testified he was planning that they should be married at the end of the year.

On the weekend of 13 and 14 October 2001 Chris and Sharon celebrated his birthday at a resort in KwaZulu-Natal. She had arranged this as a surprise and he was very pleased. On Monday, 15 October 2001, Chris and Sharon joined clients of his at the

Vaal Dam. Sharon got into trouble for not averting her eyes when one of the men stripped off his shirt to go swimming. Chris berated her for her sluttish behaviour. That evening when they sat down for dinner, Sharon was ill with sunstroke. On their way home, Chris reprimanded her for embarrassing him. He said she would be punished when they arrived home.

Sharon alleged that when they got home she had to crawl behind Chris on her knees, apologising for her bad behaviour. She was dazed and ill. Chris opened a drawer in the bedroom where he kept his knife collection. He told Sharon he was going to teach her a lesson she would never forget. Sharon, on her knees beside the bed, reached for her pistol which was hidden under the mattress. She held it to her head and threatened to shoot herself. She alleged that Chris said he would help her before she made a mess of it. A shot was fired. Sharon ran out of the room with Chris following. She ran outside, while he collapsed in the kitchen. Sharon called their domestic worker and sent her into the house to see where Chris was. At that stage Sharon had not even realised that the bullet had hit Chris. She collapsed when the domestic worker returned and told her that Chris was lying on the kitchen floor in his own blood. Eventually a neighbour arrived and removed the firearm from her hand. The police arrested her on the spot.

During the trial, Chris' ex-girlfriends made several statements against Sharon in court, which Magistrate Andrews rejected. Sharon later alleged that the Johannesburg legal fraternity had attempted to convince the state prosecutor that the murder was premeditated, because Chris was 'one of their own'. Chris' friends would not believe a word of the abuse.

They said that in fact Chris was scared of Sharon and that he had told them he was going to terminate their relationship directly after his birthday. He had told them about incidents where she had allegedly threatened to emasculate him with a knife and that she had continually threatened suicide if he left her.

On Friday 30 May 2003, Sharon van Coller was acquitted of murder. Furthermore, the magistrate found no proof that she had ever attempted suicide.

Comment

Although relieved at being acquitted, Sharon's nightmare was far from over. She had to pick up the pieces of her life, reconcile with her daughters and try to comprehend why she had allowed herself to become a victim of such an abusive relationship. She had to find employment, enter into litigation with her previous employer and try to recover the profit from the sale of her house from Chris' estate. Although Sharon received threats from some of Chris' ex-lovers, she managed to form a support group with others. It was remarkable how their individual relationships with Chris had all followed the same pattern. All these women needed to understand why Chris had such a hold on them. Sharon is in therapy and has made it her life's task to assist other abused women. Her work is commendable.

Sharon van Coller's case study is based upon her version of events. Chris' friends have a totally different view of the situation, alleging that Sharon assaulted and manipulated Chris. Chris Lamprecht is not alive to defend himself. But the court believed Sharon and acquitted her.

Sharon's version of the abuse she suffered is a typical description of the behaviour of predatory men. They target a vulnerable woman, shower her with gifts, sweet-talk her into believing that they were meant for each other. The more the woman declines his advances at first, the more persistent he becomes. This is not because he truly wants her, but because his ego cannot stand her rejecting his advances. Recognising the woman's vulnerability and low self-esteem, this type of man will initially cast her in the 'heroine' role. Sharon alleged that she felt it was up to her to 'save' Chris from treating women badly. It made her feel good about herself. But if one person in a relationship has to 'save' the other from abusive or other unacceptable behaviour, the relationship is already doomed, for the offender is transferring responsibility to the saviour.

Predatory men will typically isolate women from their friends and family and make them financially dependent on them. According to Sharon, Chris convinced her that she should sell her house and break contact with her daughters. As soon as the woman is in the man's control, he demands complete obedience. At first 'good' behaviour is rewarded and 'bad' behaviour is punished, but later any behaviour is punished, leaving the woman believing that she can do nothing right. Once a relationship has reached this stage it is very difficult for the woman to break away. Her self-esteem has been completely stripped. She does not have the courage or physical energy to leave. Yet even at a late stage, there are professionals and institutions which have the expertise to help.

Why was Sharon van Coller such an easy target? Sharon was adopted at the age of four. She recalls that her biological mother neglected her and sold her for six hundred rand. Sharon's self-esteem never recovered from this childhood neglect and rejection. She adored her adoptive parents, but says her father was very traditional about her upbringing. She always tried to please him by being his 'good little girl'. Sharon alleged Chris knew about this and would often berate her by asking if she thought her father would approve of her behaviour. Of course she would then immediately amend her behaviour to Chris' requirements. Chris had once acknowledged to a female friend that he preferred dating 'desperate' divorcees with low self-esteem who did not have 'drop dead gorgeous looks'. He enjoyed seducing them and then breaking them down. Chris paid with his life for his little game.

Sharon has submitted the following message for this book:

Only a woman who is in this kind of relationship knows how difficult it is to find a way out. Lack of self-esteem is your greatest enemy in an abusive relationship. What is being done to you is not your fault and you cannot fix it. Find someone, anyone, to help you to love yourself enough to leave. It is much easier getting into an abusive relationship than getting out of it. The most important thing to do is to get as much counselling as possible so that you are never again vulnerable to being the victim of an abuser. Yes, I am glad to be free. However coming to terms with being responsible for the death of the man who I loved more than my own life is a punishment I do not wish upon my own worst enemy. To my sisters who are still trapped, be strong, be safe, love yourself enough to leave as soon as possible. My prayers are with you always, Sharon.

Since the year 2000 judges have seemed more inclined to take severe domestic abuse into consideration, provided it can be proved beyond reasonable doubt that the woman's life was in danger when she pulled the trigger, and that the murder was not premeditated. Staging such circumstances is extremely difficult in the light of ballistic evidence and expert psychological testimony. Terminating an abusive relationship with the help of organisations with appropriate skills remains the best option, no matter how impossible it might at first seem.

Notorious teenage killer Marlene Lehnberg's death sentence in 1975 was later commuted to twenty years' imprisonment. (Sunday Times)

Serial killer Daisy de Melker was hanged in 1932 at the age of forty-six. (Sunday Times)

Sonjia Swanepoel was sentenced to fifteen years' imprisonment for the murder of her husband. Her accomplice and lover, Frans Vontsteen, received the death penalty.
(Rapport)

In 1992 Louisa Chatburn was sentenced to fifteen years' imprisonment for murdering her husband with a crossbow.
(Rapport)

In 1947 Maria Lee poisoned her lover with arsenic. She received the death penalty.
(Sunday Times)

Maria Groesbeek used ant poison to kill her husband so that she could marry her young lover. She was executed in 1970.
(Sunday Times)

Margaret Rheeder received the death penalty in 1958 for poisoning her husband.
(Huisgenoot)

Stalker Nina Olivier shot her victim and later hanged herself in her prison cell. (Sunday Times)

Spree killers Peter Grundlingh and Charmaine Phillips. (Sunday Times)

2

Children who Kill

In the Introduction I commented on how shocked people usually are when women commit violent crimes, for it is not 'expected' of them. However when children – and more specifically girls – commit violent crimes, it completely boggles the mind. The most convenient justifications that society can come up with for juvenile killers is that either the children are suffering from psychoses, or they were severely abused by their parents.

In *When Children Kill* Charles Ewing (1990) quotes research findings which indicate that although the *behaviour* of these children may be labelled psychotic, the children themselves are not. Amnesia is often cited by children who commit crimes, and so they are often misdiagnosed as psychotic. What the research *did* reveal were indications that most of the criminal children studied suffered from various personality disorders, which cannot be classified as psychoses. Research has not established that children with a low level of intelligence are more inclined to violent crime. Previous delinquency does not predict homicidal behaviour either, but it has been found that homicidal children often run away from home and play truant.

Ewing found that most studies indicated that children who had killed came from broken, disturbed, neglectful and abusive families where serious marital discord was noted. There is however no evidence that children from single-parent families are necessarily worse off than those from dual-parent families. Those who targeted family members were found either to have been victims of family abuse, or to have witnessed family abuse. Children who killed a parent were often victims of sexual abuse by that parent. Alcoholism and mental illness among parents were definite predictors of violent behaviour in children, and alcohol and drug abuse among the children themselves also played a role.

Ewing comments that enuresis – the involuntary passing of urine after an age at which continence is expected – was an indicator of violent behaviour. Homicidal children reported difficulty in relating to their peers; they never 'fit in'.

Why do children commit violent crimes? The more common reasons found were:
- parents objecting to their children's romantic liaisons, which led to parricide;
- teenage pregnancy, which was a cause of infanticide;
- jealousy which led to the killing of a sibling;
- domestic violence, which could lead to a child killing the violent parent in order to protect the other parent;
- sexual abuse by a parent, leading to parricide; and
- satanism, resulting in senseless killings.

Boys may kill as an initiation rite to become a gang member, but this does not generally apply to girls.

Ewing cites the research findings of Russel, who

carried out a study on two young female killers. In
both cases the girls 'had been neglected, abused and
dominated by their mothers, who demonstrated a
pervasive lack of support and caring'. One of the girls
was exposed to the literal destruction of her family
home, by hurricane and fire. Ewing found that girls
tend to target family members, not strangers. They
often enlist the help of a boyfriend to commit the
murder. In cases where girls were involved in murders
during the course of committing other crimes, such
as robbery, studies have shown that they were more
callous than boys.

In *Killer Kids* Cliff Linedecker (1993) presents the
case studies of ten American children who murdered
their parents.

What is noteworthy in his book is the astonishing
number of firearms that were accessible in the houses
of children who killed their parents. What is less
astonishing is that all these children were severely
abused by domineering parents. Descriptions such
as the following, taken at random from Linedecker's
case studies, paint their own pictures:

- 'He beat his children and wife for such petty
  offences as leaving tub faucets running, chewing
  food with an open mouth, scraping silverware on
  dinner plates, breaking toys or coughing.'
- 'Bob was a strongly opinionated man, who once
  he had taken a stand on issues, was known
  by neighbours and acquaintances for donning
  emotional and mental blinders. He could be
  bullheaded and heavy-handed, and he had no
  time or tolerance for listening to the other side of
  issues he had already made his mind up about.'
- 'Peter Petrovich was an autocratic, domineering

and fastidious man, who ruled Oliver and his mother, Anna, with an iron fist.'

- 'In fact her father beat both his children and his wife, Deborah stated. And she said he had sexually abused her. She described him as a humorless, violent man with an obsession for guns, who was mean to everyone around him ... sometimes he stuck his hand down her pants in front of her mother ...'
- 'The children were expected to be home most of the time. Neither they nor their mother were permitted to hold jobs. (Their father) didn't trust outsiders. He had no personal friends, and didn't want visitors. He avoided attending his children's birthday parties, graduations and award ceremonies, because he didn't like crowds.'
- 'At six feet, two inches tall and a hard-bodied two hundred and fifty pounds, the elder Pierson had close-cropped red hair that matched his temper, and a reputation for being aggressively boisterous. He kept about a dozen guns around the house, including handguns and an Uzi. Neighbours and other acquaintances recalled that he liked to sit on his porch and shoot squirrels and birds.'
- 'He forced her into bed only two days after her mother's funeral. Cheryl claimed they had sex twice a day.'

The following statement was made during the sentencing of a growth-stunted boy, who had all his life been treated by his mother with hormones produced from corpses, and who eventually killed her in a fit of rage: 'On pronouncing sentence, the jurist stated that Miss Cabot's death was precipitated by her own behaviour. "This was a very strange occurrence ... brought on by the bizarre and often irrational behaviour of the victim".'

Given the above, one would tend to take the part of the children who exacted their ultimate revenge. Yet Linedecker warns against losing one's objectivity: 'Juvenile killers know how to take advantage of their innocent appearance, and prosecutors can have trouble convincing a jury of adults that a sobbing or frightened boy or girl willingly committed such a horrible crime as parricide. Dead parents can be accused of physical or sexual abuse, or of dreadful emotional bullying, and there is no way they can be called on to refute the testimony.'

In the 1950s, psychologist Eric Berne developed a theory called Transactional Analysis. It is a process which focuses on three major aspects of ego states, namely Child, Parent and Adult. Each state has positive and negative attributes; for instance, positive aspects of the Child state are spontaneity and creativity, and negative aspects are fear, being over-emotional and feeling excessive guilt. Initially a parent and a child find themselves in the Parent>Child transactional mode, as it should be. But once the child becomes a young adult, both the parent and the child should progress to the Adult>Adult mode.

It is in this transformation process that problems can arise. Some parents find it very difficult to let go and to acknowledge their children's right to autonomy. This is usually because of the parents' need to be needed – a basic inferiority principle that once the child no longer needs the parent, he or she will be redundant. In order to protect the ego from acknowledging this basic fear of redundancy, the parent tries everything in his or her power to control the child and keep the child dependent. The child, in his or her natural maturation process will rebel against the parent trying to keep him or her in the Child ego state.

These difficulties usually arise with over-protective parents and parents who have lived their lives through their children. Once the fledgling leaves the nest, the parent loses his or her reason for living. To preserve their reason for existence, the parent will try to inhibit the child's natural developmental process. The prospect of a child becoming an adult and no longer needing the parent for its survival can become psychologically life-threatening to the parent. The more threatened they feel, the more they exert their iron fists or resort to psychological blackmail and manipulation to control the child. The outcome of this process can only be disastrous for both parties.

In the same way, children who fear growing up, or who do not have the maturity or skills to face adult responsibilities, may stunt their own natural growth processes by attempting to stay within the Child>Parent transactional mode. Through a process of delinquent behaviour, or imaginary illness, they force the parent to keep on taking care of them by generating feelings of guilt in the parent.

Parents give their children the gift of life and have to allow them to live it. Children should appreciate this gift and embrace it. To deny this natural process is to invite emotional disaster. Anyone caught up in this existential crisis should find the courage to seek professional help and not allow 'pride' to stand in the way of their own natural maturation process or that of their children.

*

Case study: Marlene Lehnberg, 1974

South Africa's most notorious teenage killer must surely be Marlene Lehnberg. She grew up in a middle-class Afrikaner family with one older sister and three younger siblings. Initially they lived on a farm, but later moved to Cape Town. She described her father as a hard-working, quick-tempered man who never showed any sign of physical affection towards her. She never dreamt of discussing her problems with her father. She got on well with her mother, though both of them had a tendency not to express their emotions.

Marlene later admitted that while she was in primary school she and a friend stole several items from shops. Her academic achievements were always excellent, but her parents were never interested in attending the many school occasions at which she was usually awarded top honours. Whenever she was awarded a book prize, she would select a book on needlework. She enjoyed making her own clothes.

Marlene was a religious girl who attended church twice on Sundays and was actively involved in extramural church activities. She preferred her mother's religious convictions and joined the Apostolic Faith Mission. Her father was a Seventh Day Adventist.

By the time she had completed grade 10, Marlene decided to follow in her sister's footsteps by leaving school. She promised her parents she would complete her studies on a part-time basis. Her sister found her a job as a receptionist at the Red Cross Orthopaedic Workshop and she started work there in February 1973. She continued to be involved in church activities and attended prayer meetings, youth groups and other gatherings four times a week. She was also a Sunday

School teacher. There was no time for boyfriends.

By September 1973 Marlene had grown tired of her father's complaints about her returning home late at night, even if it was from church activities, and she decided to move out of her parents' home into a boarding house in the suburb of Observatory. One night, shortly after she moved, Marlene Lehnberg took a good look at herself in the mirror. She saw a pious, attractive seventeen-year-old girl, who had never been on a date, never been to the movies nor to a discotheque. It was time for a change, she decided, and that was the end of her life as a devout Christian. Instead of church activities, Marlene began spending her free time posing as a nude model, working as a waitress in a restaurant and studying. All her religious activities came to a halt.

When Marlene was introduced to Christiaan 'Gerald' van der Linde, the senior technician and second in command at the orthopaedic workshop, she immediately felt attracted to him, despite the fact that he was thirty years her senior. She had, however, started dating her colleagues, one young man in particular, whom she dumped when he became too serious.

Gerald van der Linde took Marlene under his wing and promised to train her as the 'perfect receptionist'. She spent a good deal of time in his company, much to the dismay of an older woman with whom he was having an affair at the time.

Some time between March and April 1974, Gerald asked Marlene to stay after work and made his amorous intentions clear. She was over the moon for she had had a crush on him for a long time. He offered to drive her home. She had by then moved into another boarding house called Stowell Lodge in the suburb of Rondebosch.

So began the affair between the married, forty-eight-year-old man and the eighteen-year-old teenager that was to end in murder.

During the following months their affair blossomed and Marlene began making demands that Gerald drop his other mistress. She even had the gall to tell him if he did not want to leave his mistress for her sake, he should at least do so for his wife's sake. The affair began to turn sour when Mrs Susanna van der Linde received anonymous phone calls telling her about the affair. Gerald allegedly promised his wife that he would end the relationship, but he did not. However, to Marlene's dismay, he began to limit the amount of time he spent with her. Their few hours together each day were spent in argument.

Marlene later claimed that Gerald was extremely jealous and often called her a whore. While spending lonely nights in her boarding house room, she befriended another girl and some students, but she maintained she was never unfaithful to Gerald. She spent her weekends at her parents' home, doing needlework with her mother and missing her lover. She once phoned Susanna van der Linde and confessed that she was having a relationship with her husband. Gerald was furious for a day, reminded Marlene that he would never divorce his wife and leave his family, but then continued to see her as before.

By July 1974 Marlene had convinced herself that Susanna van der Linde was the only obstacle in the way of her happiness. Susanna needed to be eliminated, and so she enlisted the help of Marthinus Choegoe, a physically handicapped thirty-three-year-old man who often visited the orthopaedic workshop. She promised Choegoe that he could take anything he wanted from the Van der Lindes' house if he would dispose of Susanna. She did not care what method he used, but warned him to wear gloves so as not to leave fingerprints. She wrote down the address for him: 66 Gladstone Street, Boston. She later wrote Choegoe four incriminating letters, which were eventually used against her.

Choegoe approached the Van der Lindes' house on three separate occasions, but each time his courage failed him. He said later that he had wanted to warn Susanna that Marlene was planning to have her killed, but she refused to speak to him because he was a Coloured man. The third time he went to the house the police picked him up, assaulted him and warned him to stay out of the neighbourhood.

During July Marlene discovered that she was pregnant with Gerald's child, but she did not tell him straight away. She described herself at this stage as a pregnant nineteen-year-old, lonely and miserable, addicted to tranquillisers to relieve insomnia, depressed and confined to her room at night. She lived only for the stolen moments with Gerald. Sleazy sex in the back of a car during lunchtimes and half an hour after work each day before he returned to his wife and family – these were her only consolations.

Eventually Marlene told Gerald she was pregnant. He accused her of trying to trap him. He told his wife about it and she allegedly responded that he should sort out his problems himself. Marlene considered leaving her job and moving to Johannesburg but Gerald begged her to stay.

In the mean time Marlene had stolen a friend's radio and given it to Choegoe.

By this time the affair had become common knowledge, and the lovers decided it would be best if Marlene found employment elsewhere. In October 1974, Gerald found her a job at Vigus Orthopaedic Services in Cape Town. Now that they were no longer working together she saw even less of him. But at least her father had bought her a car.

In desperation, Marlene decided to pay Susanna a visit. Susanna handled the visit with equanimity, telling Marlene that she had been prepared to grant Gerald a divorce, but he had made her promise never to leave him. She was prepared to play second fiddle, if Marlene was willing to do so as well, until Gerald made up his mind who he wanted. She was even sympathetic about the 'mess' that Marlene had got herself into and invited her to visit any time she wanted to.

Marlene told Gerald she had been to see Susanna, which resulted in another row. That night a distraught, confused Marlene returned to the boarding house and slept with a male student. When friends joined them later that evening, the student began showing off his firearm. Marlene asked him to lend it to her to kill Susanna. This was treated as a joke, but when no one was looking, Marlene stole the firearm and hid it in the cubbyhole of her car.

A short while later she had a miscarriage, much to Gerald's relief.

Marlene wrote Gerald a heart-rending letter, which was later read out in court, saying that she had decided to move to Johannesburg. On Friday night, 1 November 1974, she met Gerald at the Rondebosch Common for the last time. Despite his protests she was adamant that she was leaving. They were both in tears when she drove away. What Gerald did not know was that Marlene had a date later that night with a colleague, also a married man, and that she slept with him.

Marlene visited her parents at the weekend and asked her cousin's husband to demonstrate the use of the firearm she had stolen. She told him Gerald had given it to her for her protection. Without her knowledge the cousin removed the bullets before handing it back to her.

On Monday morning, 4 November 1974, Marlene woke before five o'clock. It was raining. Her luggage was already in her car. She slipped out of the quiet boarding house for the last time. She was on her way to Johannesburg to start a new life, without Gerald. She filled the car with petrol at the Rondebosch petrol station and then, for old times' sake, she drove to the Rondebosch Common, where she used to meet Gerald.

She parked her car and sat staring into space for several minutes. She was heartbroken to be leaving Cape Town and her lover behind. She could not get out of her mind the thought that Susanna was the only obstacle to her happiness. She started her car and drove to Choegoe's house in Retreat. When he got into her car, both of them knew what was going to happen. She had taken the firearm out of the cubbyhole.

Marlene drove to Boston and parked the car opposite the Van der Lindes' house. Susanna was the only one at home. Marlene walked up to the front door and rang the bell while Choegoe waited in the garden. When Susanna saw it was Marlene, she invited her inside. Choegoe followed and Susanna, recognising him as the 'undesirable who had been stalking her home recently', immediately phoned the police. But she was assaulted before she could get through.

There are two versions of what happened next. Marlene said she had given the firearm to Choegoe and he had grabbed Susanna by the throat, strangled her and then hit her on the jaw with the gun. Telling him to 'finish her off', Marlene left the house and waited in the car.

Choegoe maintained that Marlene had hit Susanna on the jaw with the firearm and when she fell, he began strangling her. Marlene then handed him a pair of scissors that were lying on a table and told him to stab Susanna in the heart, which he did. Susanna tried to defend herself with a gas pistol. Choegoe took the firearm and the gas pistol with him when they left. They drove off, not knowing that a neighbour had seen them. Marlene dropped Choegoe off at his home and continued her journey to Johannesburg.

Zelda van der Linde, the oldest daughter, was the first to find her mother's body at about lunchtime. Both she and her father had phoned home during the morning, and became anxious when Susanna did not answer. Gerald and the police arrived on the scene soon afterwards.

Gerald was the initial suspect and was taken in for questioning. Then the neighbour reported seeing the white Anglia parked outside the house earlier that morning. She also described Marlene. A woman at the Red Cross Hospital had overheard Marlene and Choegoe discussing their plans, and she informed the police as well.

On 13 November 1974 Choegoe was picked up at his home in Retreat. He confessed to the murder. On the same day, detectives from the Brixton Murder and Robbery Unit picked Marlene up at her uncle's home in Bryanston, Johannesburg. When they questioned her, she did not seem perturbed, but when they mentioned Choegoe's name, she paled.

Mr Justice Marius Diemont presided over the trial.

Choegoe testified that Marlene had promised him a car, a house and sex in return for the murder. The radio, the firearms and the gas pistol were found in his house.

When Gerald took the stand he described his relationship with Marlene as one of 'fatherly friendship'. He reluctantly admitted they had sex, but insisted that he had never told her he was in love with her or that he would marry her. Gerald's other affairs were also revealed in court. Neither the judge nor the public was very impressed with Gerald van der Linde. He later told journalists that Marlene was a very pleasant young woman. If she had been his daughter, he said, he would have supported her during the trial; her parents' absence was notable. Gerald complained about having to spend two thousand rand to transport his wife's body to her family farm in Magaliesburg for the funeral.

About three hundred people attended the trial and the police had to use dogs to prevent riots outside the court. Marlene did not testify. Her lawyer maintained that she had not touched Susanna and did not even know that scissors had been used as the murder weapon. He did not argue that she was not guilty, but pleaded mitigation on the grounds of her youth and the fact that she was obsessed with the older Gerald van der Linde who, he suggested, had planted the seed that Susanna was the only obstacle in their way. Gerald was later to deny this. Her lawyer told the court how Marlene had wanted to end the relationship, but that Gerald had influenced her not to. The prosecutor pointed out that Marlene was not completely under Gerald's influence for she had of her own accord phoned and visited Susanna. He described Marlene as cold and callous.

Finally, on 14 March 1975, Mr Justice Diemont sentenced both Marlene Lehnberg and Marthinus Choegoe to death for a murder he called 'most foul'. When asked if she had anything to say Marlene said only that she was not guilty of the murder. No member of her family was present to support her when the death sentence was passed. There was a public outcry at the sentence passed down to Choegoe, whose common-law wife attended the trial.

Hardly had the judge pronounced the sentence, than journalists descended on Gerald van der Linde's house, where they apparently found him kneeling on the spot where his wife had died. He was praying for Marlene and Choegoe, he said. He also asked them to keep the interview short because he had to take his car for servicing. Gerald van der Linde moved to his wife's family farm in Magaliesburg and died of a cerebral haemorrhage in 1983 while Marlene was still in prison. He never visited her.

Marlene's death sentence was later commuted to twenty years' imprisonment and Choegoe's to fifteen. Marlene completed a BA degree in communications and psychology while she was in prison and she obtained several certificates in business administration. On 15 December 1986 she was released on parole. Choegoe had been released shortly before. He married his common-law wife and became a preacher.

In 1988 Marlene was interviewed by a newspaper. She said she was innocent of the murder, because she had never touched Susanna. She said she did not feel guilty or sorry for what she had done. She regarded the twelve years she had spent in prison as 'unfair', because she was innocent. She had not paid Choegoe to commit the murder, she had only asked him to. Had he not got into her car that fateful morning, the murder would never have happened. Marlene also found it unfair that she had trouble finding employment. She said Van der Linde had caused her to become addicted to tranquillisers and this was why she had acted as she did. She claimed she had never really loved him.

Comment

The case of Marlene Lehnberg is one of cold-blooded murder. Although Marlene had met Susanna and found her amicable, she developed no empathy for the woman. In spite of her religious upbringing and the years she devoted to church activities, Marlene could not view Susanna as a human being. Susanna's forgiving nature and the fact that she had empathy for the nineteen-year-old's predicament meant nothing: Marlene regarded her only as an obstacle to her happiness. Although she spent twelve years in prison and received therapy from the Department of Correctional Services, Marlene Lehnberg never developed any insight into her own behaviour. She could never believe that she was guilty. She blamed Van der Linde for giving her tranquillisers, which she took of her own accord; she blamed Choegoe for getting into her car, yet she drove him to the murder scene. She said she never touched Susanna and therefore she did not murder her. She never apologised for stealing the radio nor her friend's firearm. She never showed any remorse for having an affair with a married man. She blamed society for not wanting to give her a job.

At the age of thirty-three, Marlene Lehnberg still manifested the same narcissistic, selfish attitudes she had possessed as a nineteen-year-old. She was more concerned about her looks and following the latest fashion than repenting taking the life of a mother of three and the damage she had caused Choegoe's wife and children.

Christiaan Abraham Jacobus van der Linde, a married father of three children, who conducted numerous affairs and seduced a teenager younger than his children, was described by the judge as sanctimonious and self-righteous. Many believed Marlene did not testify because she would probably have admitted on the stand that Gerald had influenced her to murder his wife.

Case study: Amanda du Toit, 1994

Shortly before three o'clock on the afternoon of 19 September 1994 Ria du Toit received a telephone call at work from her hysterical sixteen-year-old daughter Amanda. A masked man had stabbed her thirteen-year-old sister Ciska to death in her bedroom at their luxury home in Mount Pleasant, Port Elizabeth, in the Eastern Cape province.

By the time Ria arrived home, the police were already there, but they would not allow her to see Ciska's body. Amanda's head was bandaged. Ria accompanied Amanda to hospital, where her eldest daughter Irene joined them.

A distraught Amanda said that both she and Ciska had been at home that afternoon studying for their exams. Amanda went to the kitchen to find something to eat when she heard Ciska scream. She rushed to her room to find a masked man attacking her sister with a knife. 'I thought only of my sister,' said Amanda, explaining how she had kicked the man away. He fell but when she turned towards her sister, he stabbed her in the head before fleeing. Amanda phoned the police and returned to hold her dying sister in her arms. She then phoned her mother. 'Her white face and the amount of blood will always remain with me,' she sobbed.

The police launched a massive manhunt for the killer. Amanda helped draw up an identikit, although the man had been wearing a balaclava and gloves. She was not sure of his race. A reward of fifty thousand rand was posted for information leading to his arrest.

The community was shocked at the senseless murder. Nothing had been taken from the luxury five-bedroom house, so burglary was ruled out as a possible motive. The police investigated satanic links, although Ria denied that her daughters were involved in satanism. Since her divorce from her husband in 1990, she and her daughters had lived happily in the house she had bought from him. Ria's boyfriend also lived with them.

For weeks the family lived in fear that the attacker might return. Ria could not bring herself to change anything in Ciska's room. A bouquet of roses, saved from Ciska's grave, hung in Amanda's room. Amanda wrote her mother supportive notes in an effort to console her. Newspapers praised her courage in trying to save her sister's life.

Detective Sergeant Derick Norsworthy of the Port Elizabeth Murder and Robbery Unit had a nagging sense of unease about the case. He was puzzled that the attacker should know that the 20-centimetre bread knife used in the attack hung behind the kitchen door. Amanda had minor injuries to her head, while Ciska had been viciously mutilated. Nobody saw anyone fleeing from the house. The police studied photographs taken during the funeral, especially one of Amanda bending over the grave. During Ciska's funeral Norsworthy had noticed Amanda placing a letter on the coffin just before it was lowered into the grave.

About three weeks after the murder, Norsworthy confronted Ria with his suspicion that Amanda might have been involved. Ciska's grave was opened and the letter was retrieved. In it Amanda expressed her deep sorrow at the death of her sister. Norsworthy began interviewing Amanda's friends and the detectives returned to the house to search Amanda's room. Six weeks after the murder, the detectives phoned Ria to advise her that they wanted to interrogate Amanda the following evening. They arrived at about nine o'clock and escorted Ria, her boyfriend and Amanda to the police station. Two of Amanda's friends were already there.

At about midnight, Detective Sergeant Norsworthy informed Ria that Amanda had confessed to killing Ciska. Ria could not believe it. A flood of conflicting emotions overwhelmed her. She just could not face Amanda right then. The following day Amanda was charged with murder.

She entered a plea of culpable homicide before Mr Justice Hennie Liebenberg. At that stage, since she was still a minor, the judge refused to allow her to be named in the press, although many people knew who she was.

Amanda told the court that on the afternoon of the murder she had returned home before Ciska. She went to the kitchen to make herself a sandwich. She had used the bread knife and left it on the kitchen counter. When Ciska arrived home she locked the security gate, but left the front door open, causing a draught. Amanda closed the door, but Ciska opened it again and this led to an argument between the two

77

sisters. They shouted and swore at each other before returning to their own bedrooms. Ciska turned up the volume on the television and when Amanda asked her to turn it down, she turned it up even higher. Another argument ensued. Amanda went to the kitchen to make herself some hot chocolate and Ciska followed, called her names, insulted her and spat in her face. She kicked Amanda on the shin before running out of the kitchen. In a fit of rage Amanda picked up the bread knife and pursued her sister. She stabbed her in the back. Ciska swung around and attempted to hit Amanda. When she saw the knife she began to scream. Amanda panicked and could think only of silencing her sister. She threw her on to the bed, covered her mouth with her hand and tried to strangle her. Ciska put up a fight and managed to seize the knife. She stabbed Amanda in the forehead.

'Suddenly hate and anger overcame me,' Amanda testified. 'I could not focus clearly. I was on top of Ciska; one hand was round her throat and I tried to get the knife with the other hand. Ciska looked cross but not scared.'

Amanda regained the knife and continued stabbing her sister. When she realised what she had done she ran from the room and telephoned the police, concocting the story about the masked intruder. She returned to Ciska's bedroom only to hear her last gasps for breath.

District surgeon Dr Ivor Laing testified that twelve stab wounds had penetrated Ciska's chest and abdomen. Of the six wounds that penetrated her lungs, five could have caused her death. Her lungs collapsed because of the amount of blood flooding them and it would have taken about ten minutes for her to die, after losing consciousness.

A friend of Amanda's, Leonie Reynecke, testified that before the murder Amanda had written her a note saying that she wanted to kill her sister by stabbing her through the heart or giving her rat poison. She also wrote that her sister was her mother's favourite.

Amanda's father, Dennis du Toit, kept his distance from the family during the trial. Amanda would cross the courtroom to greet him before returning to her mother's side. The press found it strange that the whole family seemed to be hiding behind a mask of emotional detachment.

Dr Maurice Magner, a psychiatrist from Lentegeur Psychiatric Hospital who had evaluated Amanda, testified that she suffered from borderline personality disorder. She was emotionally vulnerable and could murder again if provoked.

It turned out that Amanda, whom her mother described as her sensitive, artistic, eccentric child, the one most likely to bring her flowers and write her little love letters, was a disturbed young woman, consumed with hate and obsessive jealousy towards her sister. Amanda had two previous convictions for theft. She admitted to dabbling in satanism earlier in her life. She suffered from an inferiority complex, viewing herself as the 'ugly duckling' of the family.

Psychologists testified that Amanda was a rebellious teenager, and that matters were aggravated by her parents' divorce. She was described as lonely, anxious and confused. Sexual molestation, aggression, violence, alcoholism, favouritism, jealousy and rejection were proposed as reasons leading to the moment when Amanda snapped. Well-known criminologist Dr Irma Labuschagne interviewed Amanda. She told Dr Labuschagne: 'Every knife thrust was not to kill my sister, but I saw my mother's face in front of me. I wanted to hurt her and I knew I did so.'

Mr Justice Liebenberg rejected Amanda's plea of culpable homicide, saying that the evidence of Leonie Reynecke established premeditation. In May the following year, he sentenced Amanda to fifteen years' imprisonment of which five years were suspended. Amanda would have to go to jail for a period of ten years.

After the sentencing Ria struggled to come to terms with the loss of both her daughters. In an interview with a magazine she said that she had brought them up liberally, allowing the older two to start dating at the age of fifteen. Amanda always wanted to join the police, she said, while Ciska was a tomboy who wanted to become a teacher. Ciska had achieved provincial colours in netball. Amanda had been a prefect in primary school and was a favourite of their church minister. Ria denied that she had favourites. Amanda's boyfriend and her older sister Irene, distanced themselves from the family. Ria said the only way she could cope was not to think about her two daughters at the same time. When she missed Ciska, she could not think of Amanda. And when she missed Amanda, she could not bear to think of her as her daughter's killer.

Amanda stuck pictures of Ciska on the wall of her cell. She wanted to be reminded of what she had done, although she still could not believe that she had done it. She turned eighteen in prison and managed to complete grade 12. At eighteen she was transferred to the adult section at the Kroonstad prison for women. She took a course in hair dressing and make-up and worked at the prison hairdressing salon. She also completed a course in commercial art. On National Women's day in 2000 she was crowned

Miss Kroonstad in prison.

Amanda slept with Ciska's small teddy bear every night. She dreamed about her sister and mostly she remembered the fun they had shared. Prison was a time of introspection for her. Her older sister Irene reached out a hand of friendship again, which meant a great deal to Amanda.

On 19 October 2002, after seven years in prison, twenty-four-year-old Amanda du Toit was released on parole. She had cut her long blonde hair and was sporting a neat haircut. She was transported to Port Elizabeth and rejoined her mother in their Mount Pleasant home. Neither Ciska nor Amanda's bedrooms had been changed. Both were still crowded with stuffed toys. Only the blood-stained carpet in Ciska's room had been replaced. Mother and daughter seemed to be emotionally reunited, but when Amanda traced and phoned her father from prison to inform him that she was going home, she alleged that he seemed not to be interested.

Amanda looked forward to clearing her room of its teenage paraphernalia. Psychologically she had changed from an insecure, obsessively jealous teenager to a mature young woman who needed to face her future.

'When Ciska died in my arms, I told her I was sorry and that I loved her,' she had testified in court years before.

Comment

People affected by borderline personality disorder are characterised by the conflicting emotions they feel towards others. They cannot incorporate the fact that one and the same person might have both good and bad traits. They can perceive only good *or* bad. When they love, they love with passion, but when they hate, they hate with a vengeance. On that fateful day when Ciska died, Amanda perceived her as a bad person who deserved to be destroyed. Perhaps Ciska was aware of Amanda's obsessive jealousy and perhaps she baited her on the day of the murder. Thirteen-year-old Ciska's behaviour was fairly typical of a young girl of her age. She certainly would not have expected her sister to kill her.

According to Kaplan and Sadock (1991) borderline personality disorder is defined by psychiatrists as a mental state in which patients are on the border between neurosis and psychosis. They are characterised by extraordinarily unstable affect, mood, behaviour, object relationships, and self-image. They can be argumentative at one moment, depressed the next and then complain of having no feelings at all, all within a matter of minutes. Their behaviour is unpredictable and they manifest repetitive acts of self-destruction. They feel dependent on yet hostile towards others at the same time and can express enormous anger at friends or family members when they are frustrated. One of the diagnostic criteria is that they are impulsive in areas that are potentially self-damaging; these areas may include spending money, sex, substance abuse, shoplifting, reckless driving and binge eating. Personality disorders are not classified as mental illnesses.

If Amanda had been offered therapy after her theft convictions might the therapist have diagnosed borderline personality disorder and treated it appropriately? One can only speculate about whether the tragedy could have been prevented if the adults in Amanda's life had been more sensitive to her needs. Yet Ria du Toit said that Amanda was the child most likely to talk to her about her problems. After her release Amanda said she had made a decision to be more open with her mother, which suggests she had not been completely open with her when she was a teenager. Clearly Ria was under the impression that her daughter shared everything with her, yet she did not know about Amanda's dabbling in satanism. This case study surely demonstrates how parents' perceptions about their children might be seriously mistaken.

Case study: Salomi Deyzel, 2000
What motivated sixteen-year-old Salomi Deyzel to throw a petrol bomb at her sleeping father, forty-five-year-old Solly, and his thirty-nine-year-old girlfriend, Cornelia 'Neeltjie' Reese, at their house in Pretoria West on the night of 16 September 2000?

Solly died at the scene, but Neeltjie made it to Kalafong hospital. She later died of her burn wounds, but not before she had told a priest what happened. The police arrested Salomi, but took down her confession without her guardian or a legal representative being present. In June 2001 the case was dismissed because her confession had been obtained illegally and there was not enough evidence against her.

Yet in January 2003 Salomi, who had turned eighteen in the mean time, was again charged on two counts of murder.

Speaking out for the first time in two years about her unfortunate childhood, Salomi testified that the family had been very poor. Although she and her father had their differences, she had never hated him. And she had a good relationship with her mother. Salomi admitted that she had turned to prostitution to support her father's drinking habit. She was sentenced to ten years for each murder.

Comment

Clearly Salomi was forced into an Adult>Child role reversal with her father. She had to take on adult responsibilities by earning money to pay their bills, as Solly, an alcoholic, never had the money to do this. Salomi, at sixteen, had no skills and worked as a prostitute. It is not surprising that she snapped.

Case study: Tanya Oosthuizen, 2000

Tanya Oosthuizen herself was not a killer, but she was a member of a teenage gang which attempted murder.

Tanya was head girl at her primary school and in 1998 she was elected head girl of the hostel at the highly regarded Pretoria High School for Girls. Tanya was a beautiful, slender young woman who was expected to achieve four distinctions in her final year at school. Although her parents were divorced, she came from a privileged background. No one knew, however, that this attractive, talented school girl worked voluntarily as a sex worker at a strip club in town at night.

Tanya became involved with Andre Venter, a criminal who ruled her with an iron fist. Initially even Tanya's father, Mark Oosthuizen, was impressed with Andre. They had been led to believe that he had a job in Johannesburg.

Andre persuaded Tanya to give up prostitution, seducing her instead into the world of crime. In 1999 when Andre and Tanya were arrested for car theft and armed robbery, they agreed between themselves that Tanya would turn state witness in order to keep her out of jail. So she was given a second chance, but she chose instead to remain loyal to her boyfriend. From jail, Andre continued to rule her life.

Tanya's diary revealed the extent of the power he had over her. Under a 'must do' list she wrote: 'Speak to Baba until he says goodbye, listen to Baba, do what he says; trust in Baba, believe in Baba; try to calm Baba down when he is stressed, help him; get things done properly; ask Baba if I want to do something – when, where, time and with whom; stay at home from 5:00; when Baba says keep quiet, listen.' Under a 'must not' list she had written that she must never put the phone down on Andre or be stubborn towards him; she should not ask too many questions and should not speak to other men.

Tanya wrote everything down in her diary and took it with her when she visited Andre in prison, when he would 'mark' it and cross-examine her on her daily routine. Plans to free Andre from prison were also detailed in the diary. One day, after a visit from Tanya, Andre attacked a police sergeant, stabbing him seventeen times with a knife. The policeman survived the attack.

Tanya organised a gang of teenagers (William Prinsloo, Manuel da Silva, Mark Flascas and Adriaan van Zyl) to assist her in armed robberies to obtain money to pay Andre's legal fees. The boys were pupils at Capital College in Pretoria and Tanya seduced them with sex. She planned the robberies from a flat in Sunnyside, allocating a role to each gang member. They consumed drink and drugs before each spree. In March 2000, the gang stole a car from a woman in Meyerspark, robbed a woman in Lynnwood Manor of her jewellery, and also robbed a video store of equipment worth five thousand rand. A firearm was used in the robberies. The gang was arrested on 2 April 2000, during a robbery in progress.

During the trial, Tanya's lawyers pleaded mitigating circumstances. She had been molested by farm workers' children when she was four years old, had been sexually assaulted by a domestic worker when she was eight and was allegedly raped by a psychologist in his consulting rooms when she was fourteen.

Magistrate Kallie Bosch accepted these facts, but agreed with prosecutor Johan Kok that thousands of children are molested and raped, but they do not all turn to robbery.

Tanya's co-accused all pleaded guilty and were sentenced to terms of imprisonment ranging from six to twenty-four years. Tanya was sentenced to forty-five years, of which she had to complete an effective fifteen years. Her father Mark advised her not to appeal against the sentence as the continuous media attention would be detrimental to her. Tanya, however, then twenty years old, gave her lawyers permission to appeal. Advocate Johan Scheepers said he would waive his legal fees for the appeal.

In August 2001, Mr Justice Johan van der Westhuizen and Mr Justice Ronnie Bosielo reduced her sentence to twenty-four years of which she had to complete an effective twelve years. Tanya had in the mean time come to her senses and broken up with Andre Venter. Mr Justice van der Westhuizen said it was clear that Tanya had been influenced by Andre, finding that he had to a large extent orchestrated the robberies from prison. Although Tanya's childhood history of sexual abuse did not constitute special circumstances, it did explain why Andre was able to exert such a strong influence over her. He took into consideration that she had shown remorse, that she had progressed in therapy and that she was a first offender. Her privileged circumstances and the fact that she was intelligent, and had acted as the leader of the gang, counted against her.

Comment

From this case study it is apparent that not all delinquents come from poor and abusive family backgrounds. Although they had their marital problems, Tanya's parents did everything in their power to secure their bright daughter's future. Even her stepmother adored her. Yet to this teenager, loving parents and a privileged background were not enough. Like many girls of her age, Tanya subscribed to the romantic notion that 'true love conquers all', and all the more so when one believes oneself in love with a criminal or a delinquent. Only an immature personality would attribute romance and adventure to a Bonnie and Clyde lifestyle. (See chapter on *Spree Killers*.)

Somewhere along the line, girls like Tanya develop an emotional deficiency that is only fulfilled by the egotistical tyrants they choose as boyfriends. One cannot say this is a deficiency in love, for what they feel for their boyfriends and what their boyfriends feel for them, is definitely not love.

Perhaps Tanya felt betrayed by the fact that her parents had not protected her against childhood abuse, but parents cannot keep their children under twenty-four hour observation, and naturally they would trust a psychologist not to abuse a patient in his care. Perhaps, subconsciously, Tanya felt her father was not strong enough to protect her, or perhaps he overindulged her. She therefore cherished the strict twenty-four hour surveillance that Andre kept on her.

To her, his control represented love. She may have thought that someone who wanted to know where she was every moment of the day must care about her. What young girls like this do not realise is that controlling men suffer from a major inferiority complex. The girls' 'everlasting adoration' feeds their depleted egos. These are not strong men, they are pathetic losers. Perhaps, too, Tanya subconsciously wanted to punish her parents for not protecting her and turned to crime to achieve this.

The fact that Tanya was sexually molested and raped as a child means that she was robbed of control over her own life. She felt she needed someone to control her. Very often such girls will turn to prostitution, or promiscuity at the least. They have already lost their virginity and in their reasoning it does not matter thereafter if they sleep with other men. At least they are now doing so of their own free will, and they soon learn to use their sexuality as a tool to manipulate. They have not learned that sex is a gift, not a tool. Psychological counselling would help these girls to regain control of their lives. They also need to accept that although others may support them in this process, it is ultimately something only they themselves can accomplish. It is a long and difficult road, but it can be done, as rape victim Alison described in her book, *I Have Life* (1998).

Women need to learn their value as human beings when they are still little girls. They are not the objects of men, they can exert control over their own lives and even if they are abused, they have the internal power to regain that control. Tanya obviously had an internal need to control as well, for she controlled the members of the gang. Her internal ability to regain control was thus present all along, but she was directing it along the wrong route, because she had convinced herself that it would be 'in the name of everlasting love'.

Loving is not just about giving and serving, it is also about receiving respect as an autonomous human being. One needs to love oneself first in order to accomplish this, and to trust one's inherent inner strength to succeed. If a man does not respect a woman's autonomy or her right to individuality, he does not deserve her love. No one has the right to enslave anyone else, and willingness to become the slave of another is a sign of emotional disturbance. Women need to acquire a sense of self-respect that ensures that they do not tolerate abuse from anyone.

Perhaps men should also practise some introspection. What can be said of a man's self-respect if he is willing to commit crime in exchange for sex? Is he not allowing himself to be debased as well? Tanya's co-accused obviously did not realise this.

Case study: Alta Willene Pretorius, 2001

Alta was twelve years old when her father committed suicide. Although he was an alcoholic, she adored him. Because of her father's alcohol problem, she, her mother Santie, and her older half-sister Natasha lived a nomadic life. Alta attended eight different schools in the space of ten years, yet she was an intelligent girl and never failed a year. When her father died her life was shattered and she blamed her mother.

Alta consoled herself by smoking dagga (cannabis). In 1998 the family moved to Pretoria and Alta gave up the drug. Yet in January 2000 she again started taking drugs and not only dagga, but she used heroin, LSD and Ecstasy as well.

She was a grade 9 pupil at the Hercules Secondary

School when she met and became infatuated with Theunis Frederick Jacobus (Jaco) Steijn, who was in grade 11.

Jaco had had a disrupted childhood. He was the second of three children and his parents were divorced when he was three years old. For two years his mother and her children battled financially. Jaco completed grades 1 and 2 at Eendragt Primary School and during his second grade he stole fifty rand. Because he exhibited behavioural problems he was placed in the school hostel. He attended Bysonderheid Primary School for part of grade 3, but then his mother remarried and he returned home. At Bysonderheid he became involved in satanism. He moved to Tuinrand Primary School to complete grades 3 and 4. During his grade 3 year he stole a bicycle and during grade 4 he stole sweets, which he gave to his sister.

Jaco started his high school career at the Pretoria-Tuine Technical School where he began smoking dagga in grade 8. He was expelled in grade 9 as a consequence of his aggressive behaviour. He moved to Tuine Secondary School, but was again expelled. He was then sent to Middelburg Secondary School where he was expelled from the hostel. It was at this time that he began using Ecstasy and LSD. His father took him in, although he did not get on with his father's new wife, and moved him to the D F Malan Secondary School. He was expelled yet again. He was admitted to Birchley Secondary School where he began smoking rocks and using heroin. He finally returned to Pretoria and attended Hercules Secondary School, where he met Alta.

In 2001 both Alta and Jaco ran away from home, but they were apprehended by the police and placed in Tutela Juvenile Institution. Here Alta allegedly attended a satanic ritual, with Jaco as an observer. During April and May 2001 she was referred to Castle Carey for drug rehabilitation and Jaco was referred to Magalies Oord for the same reason. But as soon as they were discharged they both began using drugs again.

Santie Pretorius, who was a nurse at the Moot General Hospital, had scarcely moved into her new flat in Ontario building in Gezina when her teenage daughter Alta invited her boyfriend Jaco to move in with them. Both children had recently been released from drug rehabilitation centres and at that stage neither was attending school.

Later psychological reports revealed that Santie was very dependent on her daughter. She objected to Alta's relationship with Jaco, probably because she was scared of losing her. On Saturday, 7 July 2001 Alta and Jaco had used heroin. That evening mother and daughter had an argument during which Santie told Alta that Jaco was allowed to visit her only on Friday nights. A short while later Alta regretted the argument and called out to her mother that she loved her. But Santie did not respond.

Later that night Santie, Alta and Jaco were sitting on the couch watching television. Alta and Jaco went to the kitchen to have sex, but shortly after they had started making love, Santie called Alta. This irritated the teenagers. They joined Santie and spent the rest of the night watching television until Santie fell asleep on the couch.

At about two o'clock the next morning Alta looked at Jaco and said simply: 'Let's kill her.' She went to the kitchen and fetched a knife, which she handed to Jaco. They both counted to three, whereupon Jaco began stabbing Santie. Santie woke up and pleaded for her life. Alta, who had been watching, ran to the kitchen and fetched another knife and started stabbing her mother as well. When Jaco's knife broke she ran to the kitchen and fetched yet another. Santie was stabbed more than twenty times. Jaco then strangled her with a shoestring, just to make sure. The couple smoked dagga and decided to go for a walk. They smoked more dagga and returned to the flat where they had sex before going to sleep.

That morning (8 July) they fetched a saw and more knives from Jaco's mother's home. Jaco suggested they saw up the body and flush the remains down the toilet, but when they returned to the flat, he felt disinclined to start cutting up the body. Instead the couple moved into one of the bedrooms when the stench of the decomposing body began to disturb them. That same night they heard a noise at the window, hurriedly left the flat and spent the night in Sunnyside, using heroin. They returned to the flat on Tuesday 10 July. Natasha and Santie's sister had telephoned in the mean time and Alta told them her mother had gone off with a man in a red Golf motor car and had not yet returned. Jaco and Alta were worried that her uncle would arrive at the flat, so they covered Santie's body with a duvet and dragged it behind the couch so that it was not visible from the window. They covered the blood-spattered floor with a blanket. When the uncle arrived they did not answer the doorbell and he left.

The next day, 11 July, they visited a friend of Jaco's where he discovered a firearm in a cupboard. He stole it. The couple made plans to hijack a car and to flee to Durban or Kempton Park, where Jaco had friends. They first returned to the flat, but ran away when they saw that the police were there. The caretaker of the building spotted them.

They decided to hitch-hike and eventually a car stopped for them. As they got into the car Jaco immediately pressed the firearm against the driver's head, demanding that he stop. The man begged them not to shoot him, saying that he had a young child, but he did not stop the vehicle. Jaco pulled up the handbrake and the car came to a screeching halt. The man pulled the keys out of the ignition, leapt out of the car and ran to a nearby house where he called the police. Jaco and Alta fled, but the man went after them, while talking to the police on his cellphone. Jaco and Alta were eventually apprehended.

Having had no response from her mother, Natasha asked the police and fire brigade to investigate on the morning of 11 July. They discovered the badly mutilated and decomposing body of Santie Pretorius hidden behind the couch. Apart from blood, there was food all over the beds and floors. The kitchen was full of unwashed crockery. It was clear that someone had been living in the flat with the body for a few days. Then they found a letter.

10 July 2001: 10:59

Right now, we, (me & Jaco) are waiting for my uncle to arrive here at the flats where my mom's body is lying. We just moved her so nobody can see her when they are looking through the window.

Adam: Present: My heart is beating like a drum at all the excitement that's happening around us. My girlfriend's uncle is on the way to the flats of Ontorio. Where moments ago (me & Alta) moved the furniture to hide her old lady so that if her uncle arrives heal only see furniture and me & Eve will be in one room full of sadness and paranoia.

*You see we are not bad people, we really do love each other. I'm not going to give in. I'll stand by my man. This Adrenillin rush is not good for my heart. I know my Baby's also scarred, he just sits there full of stress and mixed emotions. I really didn't want anything bad as this happening, I'm also in my fuckyou in if they catch us today. Ill go on loving my true love and also waiting for him. God I think my uncle is here, please help us.

Alta and Jaco were interrogated by Captain Riette Everton, national section chief of the Occult Related Crimes Unit. Both of them voluntarily and separately made full confessions. They said that they were not seriously involved in satanism at all, save for a few encounters, but that they were both drug addicts.

Alta and Jaco were charged with murder, theft, robbery with aggravating circumstances and being in possession of an unlicensed firearm and ammunition. The case came before acting Mrs Justice Lizette Meyer. They pleaded guilty to all charges. Both children were sent for psychiatric evaluation. At that stage, since both were minors, they were referred to only as Adam and Eve. Both have since turned eighteen. During their initial court appearances Alta and Jaco professed their love for each other and wrote each other love letters. Not one of their family members was prepared to post bail for them so they were kept in custody throughout the trial.

Psychologists found that Alta had narcissistic traits; she was manipulative and impulsive. Her deep emotional insecurity led to aggression. She experienced her mother as abandoning and insensitive to her needs. Unsatisfied needs of an infantile nature were present.

It was obvious that Jaco's behavioural problems put a strain on his relationship with his mother. His father was absent during his childhood years, yet Jaco hero-worshipped him. He got along with his stepfather, but the man was unable to discipline him.

Dr Irma Labuschagne, a well-known criminologist, testified that Alta had received no love from her mother. She alleged that she would be burned with a pan if she refused to eat. Alta grew tired of her mother's incessant demands and of doing her work. 'Since I was a little girl, my mother threatened to give me away, like she gave away my other sisters. I dreaded this every day,' Alta told Dr Labuschagne. Jaco told her how he and his sister were neglected after school because their mother worked shifts in order to make a living. He said that after his father had left the family to live with another woman, no one discussed the situation with the children. Dr Labuschagne said he was a textbook example of someone who manifested antisocial behaviour. Both Dr Labuschagne and Mrs Justice Meyer were of the opinion that the system had failed Jaco earlier in his life.

By the time Mrs Justice Meyer was ready to pass sentence, 'Eve' was no longer in love with her 'Adam'. Alta ignored Jaco in court and refused to speak to him, although he still professed his love for her.

Mrs Justice Meyer sentenced them both to twenty-one years' imprisonment. She stated that Alta had to complete at least fifteen years of her sentence and undergo rehabilitation before she could be considered for parole. She said it was clear from Alta's diaries that in the months before the murder she and Jaco had lived a life in which unrestrained sex, drugs and alcohol featured prominently. They had shown no respect for any form of authority.

The judge said they should be treated equally. Although Jaco was two years older than Alta, and both of them were master manipulators, it was clear that Alta was the intelligent one who manipulated Jaco with sex to do what she wanted.

Comment

This case reveals how the system had failed the young Jaco. Instead of addressing his problems at an early age, he had been passed from one relative to another and placed in hostels when they felt they could no longer cope with him. Jaco claimed that at the tender age of eight he had been exposed to satanism in primary school. (Yet primary schools continue to deny that they have a problem with drugs and satanism.)

Alta, on the other hand, was forced to take on the role of Parent with her mother in the Child role. This is unnatural and should not be expected from a sixteen-year-old girl. Santie Pretorius objected to Alta's relationship with Jaco not because she did not want Alta to grow up, but rather because she feared she would lose Alta and would have to face her adult responsibilities on her own. Santie's family described Alta as a rebellious teenager, while her father's family described her as a peacemaker. Her older sister Natasha forgave her and promised to support her.

The fact that Alta and Jaco, both from troubled backgrounds, met each other was cataclysmic. Yet it is not uncommon for disturbed teenagers to seek each other out. Jaco's teachers commented that it seemed as if he was about to make a positive change in his life when he entered Hercules Secondary School. Even his relationship with his mother improved after he left Magalies Oord. If he had not met Alta, he might have made it. Alta also performed well at school and was described as friendly and cooperative by her teachers and friends. The combination of their personalities and drugs led to a very different outcome for these two teenagers.

Mrs Justice Meyer was correct when she identified Alta as the leader in the relationship. Despite her immature declarations of 'true love' and her promise 'to stand by her man until the end', Alta ditched Jaco when she no longer had any need for him.

The judge was of the opinion that since the two offenders were young, they might have a chance of rehabilitation.

Not guilty

Case study: Sweeny-Pai Thorne, 1996

When Sweeny was still in diapers, her father took pictures of her posing with hand grenades instead of teddy bears. In her pre-puberty years her father took pictures of her and her younger sister Nicole, dressed only in their panties, cradling automatic machine guns to their chests. He used to discipline his little girl, still in pigtails, by making her sit in the veld and firing shots around her. She was not allowed to show fear.

James Thorne had been a member of Koevoet (an unconventional and controversial paramilitary police unit) who fought in the Namibian war. He was a martial arts expert and ran the South African Combat and Survival School on a farm called Killarney near Lady Grey in the Eastern Cape province. James was an adherent of the doctrine of eschatology – that part of theology that is concerned with the final destiny of humankind. He believed that only those who were prepared would survive doomsday and he devoted his life to training his family to be ready.

James met his Asian wife Shirley when she was sixteen years old. They settled in Gaborone, Botswana, where Shirley's sister, Maureen joined them. James and Shirley were married shortly after Sweeny's birth in 1977. He took Maureen as his concubine. In 1979 they all moved to the then Rhodesia and lived on a farm belonging to his brother Richard. Both Shirley and Maureen fell pregnant and James insisted that both of them abort the babies, but the women refused. James forced Shirley to give up her child for adoption and ordered her to be a mother to Maureen's daughter Nicole. Sweeny was two years old at the time.

The family moved to South Africa and settled in what was then known as Bophuthatswana, where James joined the police. He had progressed to the rank of captain when he resigned and the family moved to the then South-West Africa, where he joined the notorious Koevoet unit. When one of his comrades committed suicide, James resigned and the family moved to Mossel Bay. From there they moved to Walvis Bay, but finally settled on the farm Killarney near Lady Grey.

Here James established his Survival School and took in volunteers. He ruled his world with an iron fist. Sweeny was the apple of his eye and she became his second in command. James had One Rule concerning his daughters: anyone who touched them would die. No man was permitted to be alone with them, only conversations about work were allowed and no one was to laugh or smile.

James would often wake his wives and daughters at three o'clock in the morning to recite the Rule to him. The punishment for transgressing the Rule was the 'Dover method'. This entailed the transgressing man digging a ditch and getting into it. A sheet of corrugated iron would be placed over the ditch and a fire would be lit on top of the corrugated iron. This would be done a distance from the house so that no one should be disturbed by the screams of the dying man. In addition, his wives and daughters would be beaten so severely that they would not be able to walk for ten months.

When Sweeny went to primary school in Mafikeng, James made Shirley write a letter to the headmaster giving him permission to beat her daughter as much as he liked if she did not do well in class. When Sweeny and Nicole had an argument one day, James made the little girls dress in their karate suits and beat each other up. Only when their little bodies were bruised and they were exhausted, did he order them to stop. He told their mothers to give them each a Disprin and sent them to bed.

When James suspected Shirley of having an affair he chained her to the car and drove away at escalating speed. This happened in the town for all to witness. When he suspected Maureen of having an affair he beat her with a sjambok and also assaulted Shirley.

It was under circumstances like these that Sweeny grew up. Her favourite book was *Miko* by Eric von Lustbader – the story of a woman who kills her master. As time went by, Sweeny formed a secret friendship with Peet Grobler, one of the survivalists.

In July 1996, nineteen-year-old Sweeny escaped from the farm. She left her father a letter in which she expressed her heartbreak and disappointment. 'I scream without sound in godforsaken valleys,' she wrote, 'it is like a godforsaken valley where storm winds blow with no one near to hear my screams.' Sweeny had been isolated and lonely throughout her teenage years. She excelled in all the combat training her father had subjected her to, but he never appreciated her efforts. She could not turn to him for comfort and understanding. She had had enough.

James was furious. He interrogated everyone on the farm. He vowed he would find Sweeny if it was the last thing he did and decided to go to Pretoria to ask a friend to help him find his daughter. Peet Grobler and Hanco Ferreira (the latter was attracted to Nicole), decided they would search for Sweeny in Potchefstroom in the North West province. Sweeny had once given Peet the phone number of a friend in Potchefstroom. They found her there. She had cut her hair short, showing off her beautiful oriental features.

Peet tried to convince Sweeny to return to the farm, but she refused. She said she feared for her life. Eventually he persuaded her at least to contact James and on 19 July, about a week after she had run away, she was ready to phone her father, but not yet ready to return to the farm. Sweeny phoned home and Shirley gave her her father's number in Pretoria. But he refused to speak to her. It was only after three days that James agreed to talk to her. In a six-hour conversation he threatened, cursed and pleaded with her. He promised her he would disband the survivalist group and the family would resettle somewhere else and start a new life. Sweeny agreed to return to the farm on these conditions.

When Sweeny arrived at the farm, James had not yet returned. He had, however, ordered the group to disband and he threatened to kill Peet and Hanco if he found them on the farm. The two men were concerned about the young women's safety and decided to camp at a safe distance, but still be able to observe the farmhouse through binoculars.

James had ordered Shirley to chain the girls by their necks to their beds at night, which she did. One night Sweeny signalled to Peet with her torch and within minutes he was at her window. She had written a letter to Louwene du Plessis, an ex-survivalist, begging her to send her sleeping pills. She could not sleep because she dreaded her father's homecoming. She asked Peet to take the letter into town to Louwene. But one of the other ex-survivalists, Hendrik Mills, found the letter and told Shirley about it. Hendrik was worried that Sweeny might try to commit suicide with an overdose of sleeping pills. Shirley passed this information on to James and he phoned Sweeny. 'If you want to know what death is about, I will introduce you to death and you will scream for life,' he threatened her.

Sweeny again signalled Peet. When he arrived at her window she told him that her mother had confiscated both her firearms. She asked him to bring her a firearm. Peet borrowed Hanco's pistol and gave it to her. James was now on his way home.

At half past eight on the morning of 2 August 1996, James arrived back at Killarney. He greeted Shirley and his children but did not talk further to Sweeny. She could not bear the suspense. What was her father going to do to her?

Later that night James was sitting in his study warming himself in front of the coal stove. As always, he was armed. Shirley was preparing food in the kitchen when Sweeny entered and asked for a glass of water. Then she went to her father's study, stood behind him and fired six shots into his back and one into the back of his head. The shots to his back were neatly grouped, as he had taught her. She covered his body with a blanket so that her sister Nicole should not see it. Then she drove to the Aliwal North police station and gave herself up. 'He would have killed us all,' she told the officer.

After interviewing Sweeny and her family, Advocate Malherbe Marais, Deputy Attorney General of the Eastern Cape, decided not to prosecute Sweeny because there were mitigating circumstances.

At the inquest hearing, James' brother Richard said he believed Shirley and Maureen had conspired to kill James. He said the women actually controlled James and that James was mostly just bluster. He said only if James had sexually molested his daughter, would Sweeny have had the right to kill him, but James loved her too much to have done that. James had never killed anyone in his life and could not even kill cattle on the farm, said Richard.

When Magistrate Johan Terblanche confronted Sweeny with the fact that her father was actually a failure, she defended him, saying: 'He knew everything. Not even in ten million years would others know everything he knew.' When she was asked why she forbade her family to call for medical help after she had shot her father, she said that if he had survived he would have been confined to a wheelchair for the rest of his life and that he would never have been able to endure such a humiliation. It would have been cruel to him.

Comment

The case of Sweeny-Pai Thorne is one of the saddest in the legal and criminal history of South Africa. From the time she was in diapers, this young girl had been denied a normal life. Her individuation process was completely stunted. She had been turned into a highly effective soldier, trained to defend her own life, which, ironically, she did. Sweeny could not be certain that her life was in danger on the fateful day when she shot her father, but her young soul retaliated in the only way it knew how, against years and years of captivity at the hands of a cruel, disturbed abuser.

James Thorne thought he was doing his best for his family. He wanted to protect them from Armageddon. No one can deny that being a soldier is an honourable vocation. Anyone prepared to risk his or her life to defend others deserves respect. However some people, mostly men, develop an unhealthy obsession with the military. They become rigid in their expectations of others. Everything has to be executed with military precision and discipline. The military interest is no longer a vocation, but spills over into all other areas of their lives. They collect military paraphernalia, read only military books and talk about military matters to the exclusion of all else. (People involved in the military, who are able to function outside military bounds in other aspects of their lives, naturally do not fall into this category.) These men are obsessed and although they may outwardly seem to be strong, macho individuals, inside they are consumed by fear. They fear life, they fear living and they fear loving. Their only defence against this fear is to attempt to control their external environment, for they cannot control their internal fear. They rule by fear, for they are consumed by fear. They wrap their frail egos in camouflage uniforms, arms and ammunition and military precision in order to present a tough image. Many people are intimidated by this facade, but inside these men are scared and emotionally incompetent. It is sad that they become paranoid and distrustful of others, when their worst enemies are their own egos.

They might be described as courageous soldiers by others, but they lack the courage to face their own inner fears, and to allow others to live their own lives freely. James Thorne was a parent who gave life to his daughter, but refused to allow her to live it; he eventually paid with his own life to set her free.

It later became apparent that when James went to Gauteng after Sweeny had run away, he went to see then deputy minister of Tourism, Peter Mokaba. He told the deputy minister that he was afraid of being assassinated. James had joined the African National Congress Party in 1993 and feared retaliation from his previous associates. He was allegedly appearing before the Truth and Reconciliation Commission, giving information about security police atrocities committed against his wives in the 1970s.

When last heard of, Sweeny was managing a photographic shop.

Case study: Jaudine 'Nikki' Marks, 2000

On the night of 29 November 2000, seventeen-year-old Nikki Marks and her friends Quinton Herbst, Jan Michael van Heerden (both seventeen), twenty-three-year-old Godfrey Lucky Vili, and two sixteen-year-old girls went out looking for trouble.

Only a few days before Nikki, a self-proclaimed sex worker, lured two male attorneys into a trap at Burgers Park in Pretoria. She and the other gang members succeeded in tying both men up in their home in Centurion and robbed them of household goods and their car. The men at least escaped with their lives. The group hid out in a squatter camp near Brits where they obtained *muti* to protect them from detection.

They returned to Pretoria with the stolen car. On

29 November 2000, they found business at Burgers Park rather slow and moved to the Austin Roberts Bird Park in Brooklyn. Quinton acted as the bait to pick up a client. Not long after they had parked their car, forty-six-year-old Petrus Johannes Campher got into the car with Quinton. Quinton alleged that the man immediately began fondling his private parts, whereupon he slapped him. Lucky got into the car, held a knife to Petrus' neck, and the gang then forced him into his own car and drove to nearby Magnolia Dell Park. The three males assaulted Petrus, stabbing him with a knife, while the girls looked on. Petrus begged for his life, saying that he lived with his ageing mother and would like to spend Christmas with her. He even offered them money if they would spare his life. The males responded by attempting to strangle Petrus with a tie, forcing broken glass down his throat, cutting his throat with broken glass and piercing his heart with a screwdriver. They then wrapped the body in a duvet and drove out to the Hartbeespoort Dam. They threw the body over the dam wall, but it landed on a cement shelf. The boys climbed down the wall and kicked the body into the river. The remains of Petrus Campher were found four days later and taken to the Brits mortuary as a John Doe.

In the interim, the mother of one of the sixteen-year-old girls had reported her missing. Both girls had run away from home and one of them was the mother of Quinton's five-month-old baby. Inspector David Andries Smith of Hercules Police Station managed to trace the girls. He was astounded when the girls told him about the robbery and the murder of Petrus. He had Petrus' body identified at the mortuary.

Shortly afterwards, the police arrested Quinton, Michael, Nikki and Lucky. Nikki decided to turn state witness along with the two sixteen-year-old girls. They were all part of a teenage subculture that frequented city parks at night, selling sex to sustain their expensive drug habits. They had all run away from home.

During the trial, the boys said they never intended to rob anyone, but they needed money to support the sixteen-year-old girls who had joined their gang shortly after running away from home. At first all the males denied that they were sex-workers. But they soon turned on each other. Lucky claimed that he had been in prison from April to December 2000 and could therefore not have participated in the murder. A convict testified that Quinton had boasted to him in the awaiting trial section that he and Michael were going to frame Lucky for the murder, since Lucky was older and he was a black man and they were still juveniles. He had told Lucky about this. Lucky said Quinton had promised him that his family would pay him one hundred thousand rand if he took the blame for the murder. Throughout the trial Lucky proclaimed his innocence. Michael testified that he had only participated in the assault because Lucky threatened him with a firearm.

The trial took an unexpected turn when Mrs Lorna Vosloo, a house mother at a home for destitute children opposite Burgers Park came forward of her own accord. She testified that she had seen Lucky at Burgers Park at the time of the murder. She also said that Lucky and Nikki were very close.

Criminologist Dr Yvonne du Plooy testified on the background of the youngsters. She said Michael had a low intelligence and was placed in a reformatory at the age of ten because he was uncontrollable. She identified Quinton as the more dominant of the two. Michael admitted to her that he had sold the clothes his mother brought him in prison for drugs. Dr du Plooy was of the opinion that the boys would not quit their drug habit, not even in prison.

Mr Justice Dion Basson rejected Lucky's alibi. He sentenced him to life imprisonment, since he was an adult when the crime was committed and had not pleaded any mitigating circumstances. The judge acknowledged that Quinton and Michael came from dysfunctional families, which had forced them on to the streets. They fell into drug abuse, and then into prostitution in order to sustain the habit. He sentenced both of them to twenty-eight years' imprisonment, of which they will serve an effective eighteen years.

The judge said that although they were both juveniles when the crime was committed, they should nevertheless be thrown 'in a dark hole', and the key 'thrown away'. He urged them to try to take advantage of any rehabilitation programmes offered them.

When the boys were sentenced their mothers broke down in tears with them. Quinton belatedly apologised to the Campher family.

All the girls were indemnified. Nikki said she had turned to prostitution when she ran away from an orphanage and the people who had adopted her. At the time of the crime, as a seventeen-year-old, she lived in a flat in Pretoria Central and was a sex worker in Burgers Park at night.

Comment

One cannot blame the parents of these children for the murder of Petrus Campher. Yet one has to ask whether the support they offered their sons during the trial was years too late. Teenagers who elect to make adult decisions have to take full adult responsibility for those decisions. When children are not taught to take responsibility for their decisions and when they are not taught to consider the consequences of their decisions, they are not equipped with the life skills needed to face adulthood. Many parents fail dismally in this regard, perhaps because they, in turn, were not adequately taught by their parents. The outcome of this cycle is usually catastrophic; someone is killed and youngsters have to face years of imprisonment where they are exposed to hardened criminals. Their chances of learning adult coping skills are virtually non-existent.

Did the teenage girls in this case get away with murder? One can only hope that the three girls will have the strength of purpose to break the cycle.

*

One feels that the lives of all the children in the case studies discussed in this chapter could have turned out differently if more attention had been paid to the problems they were experiencing, if the parents had been more in touch with their children, if the children had received counselling and, most of all, if they had been better equipped with coping skills and self-esteem when they were younger. One cannot apportion all the blame to the parents. Some of these children had everything going for them, yet they made decisions of their own volition and had to take responsibility for them. Having to endure childhood abuse is tragic beyond words, but it gives no one the right to commit crime and to murder. It may be a reason, but it is not, and never will be, an excuse.

3

Female serial killers

The following theory offering an explanation of the psychodynamics underlying the financial profit motivation of female serial killers is the intellectual property of Dr Micki Pistorius.

Male serial killers do not kill for financial gain; they kill to gratify a deep subconscious psychological need. Surprisingly, Dr Eric Hickey, a professor in criminology at the California State University, has found that the majority of female serial killers are motivated by financial gain.

In his book *Serial Murderers and their Victims* (2002), Hickey reports that 74 per cent of female serial murderers were motivated at least partially by money, and that 27 per cent of them killed purely for money. 'Female serial murderers are more likely to kill in response to abuse of various forms, although this motive appears to be less apparent than greed and desire for money.'

Men who commit multiple murders for financial gain are more likely to be classified as assassins or robbers than serial killers. The difference between robbers and assassins on the one hand, and male serial killers on the other, is that assassins and robbers are motivated by greed. They are not urged to kill regardless of financial benefit, as male serial killers are. Is there such a major difference, then, in the motivations of male and female serial killers, since female serial killers *do* kill for money?

As a forensic psychologist who initially specialised in the psychodynamics of serial killers, I was puzzled by this question, for at first it did not fit the theory that I had previously developed that serial killers kill to gratify a deep unconscious psychological need. Surely money does not present itself as an internal need, but rather as an external gratification. 'For some, the needs for economic and psychological wellbeing are virtually the same,' says Hickey. I decided to research the correlation between the economic and psychological needs of women, and I found the answer in the motivational theory of Abraham Maslow.

Maslow postulated that human behaviour is motivated by a hierarchy of basic needs. Once lower needs are gratified, the organism – or human – will move to higher needs. A basic need will dominate behaviour if it is thwarted or when the organism is deprived of it. Once the need is gratified, the need releases its domination of the organism.

Maslow identified physiological needs as the lowest level of the hierarchy. These needs encompass hunger, thirst, sleep and sex. If a person is deprived of one of these needs, his or her behaviour will be directed towards gratifying this need. Depending upon the intensity of the deprivation, such a person may put the gratification of all other higher needs on hold, in order to satisfy the physiological needs.

In *Motivation and Personality* (1970, 2nd edition) Maslow explains that if a need has been continually satisfied in the past, the organism will be able to cope better with future deprivation: '... those individuals in whom a certain need has always been satisfied (who) are best equipped to tolerate deprivation of that need in the future, and that furthermore, those who have been deprived in the past will react differently to current satisfactions than the one who has never been deprived.'

Is it possible to say that those individuals who have been severely deprived of a certain basic need during crucial childhood years, will always yearn for gratification of that need, and that no matter how much gratification occurs later, it might just never be enough to fill the void? It is possible to say that the infant's basic physiological needs are mostly gratified by the mother or primary caregiver. If one follows Freud's postulation that children are polymorph perverse, in other words they are sensually stimulated by other bodily parts than necessarily the genitals, one can also include the mother as the gratifier of the infant's sexual needs. The mother is the one who bathes, strokes and caresses the infant. I have discussed the male serial killer's fixations in early developmental phases leading to specific patterns during the execution of their crimes in my two earlier books, *Catch me a Killer* (2000) and *Strangers on the Street* (2002), both published by Penguin. It is quite clear that early deprivation caused consciously or subconsciously by the mother figure may lead to her son developing into a serial killer.

The second stage in Maslow's hierarchy encompasses the safety needs. These include such concepts as security, stability, dependency, protection, freedom from fear, as well as from anxiety and chaos, need for structure, order, law, limits, strength in the protector, etc (Maslow, 1970). It is also possible to say that traditionally the toddler's security needs are gratified by the father figure, who is recognised as the protector. What I am postulating is that early deprivation by the father figure of a girl's safety needs may lead to her becoming a serial killer.

Maslow explains that should these security needs not be fulfilled 'the organism may equally well be wholly dominated by them. They may serve as the almost exclusive organisers of behaviour, recruiting all the capacities of the organism in their service, and we may then fairly describe the whole organism as a safety-seeking mechanism' (Maslow, 1970).

If one bears in mind that female serial killers are willing to kill for money – which is a form of security – the following observation by Maslow seems very accurate in explaining their behaviour: 'Practically everything looks less important than safety and protection (even sometimes the physiological needs, which, being satisfied, are now underestimated). A man (or woman) in this state, if it is extreme enough and chronic enough, may be characterized as living almost for safety alone' (Maslow, 1970).

If one looks at the history of female serial killers one often finds that they have been sexually abused by a father figure, that there was domestic violence or discord between the parents, and very often the families were nomadic. If a parent treats a child harshly, the child might fear the loss of the parent's love and protection. A girl who has been sexually abused by her father faces a double predicament First, her basic trust in the father as protector has been broken, and secondly, she fears that if she

112

reveals this secret, she will also lose his love and protection. It is understandable that such a child will grow up with a thwarted concept of sexual intimacy and a basic deprivation of her security needs. It is not surprising that many female serial killers who have been sexually abused are promiscuous as well. '(Her) safety needs often find specific expression in a search for a protector, or a stronger person on whom (s)he may depend ... The neurotic individual may be described with great usefulness as a grown-up person who retains his (her) childhood attitudes towards the world' (Maslow, 1970).

Many female serial killers marry affluent men, whom they identify as protectors who have the means to keep them safe and to 'spoil them' as if they were children. Money, therefore, becomes a substitute for security. However, the woman's continual childlike behaviour may frustrate the husband's expectations of a wife, and he might begin to express his irritation. This irritation triggers the woman's childhood fear of rejection by the father figure. She fears that her husband may divorce her and she will lose her security, so she kills him in order to inherit his money – to gratify her need for security. If the woman is promiscuous as well the husband may threaten to leave her, or he may become an obstacle to her sexual pursuits. Such women have learned to exercise control over men through their own sexuality. In this case, the female serial killer would also kill to retain her security. Although she may seem childlike and vulnerable, and therefore very attractive to the kind of man who wants to protect her, she is at the same time an outstandingly manipulative *femme fatale*, who will use her sexuality to lure men into her traps, and she will show no remorse for doing so. No wonder some

113

of them are classified Black Widows.

Maslow calls the third stage in the hierarchy the need for belongingness and love. He explains the effects that deprivation of this need may have on an individual. 'From these we know in a general way the destructive effects on children of moving too often; of disorientation; of the general over-mobility that is forced by industrialization; of being without roots, or of despising one's roots, one's origins, one's group; of being torn from one's home and family, and friends and neighbours, of being transient or a newcomer rather than a native.' All serial killers, male and female, interviewed by my colleagues and by me complained that they have always felt that they would never really 'fit in'. They all felt like outsiders in a group. I explained in my earlier books that male serial killers do not socialise during the latency phase (six to twelve years). They do not acquire empathy for others and because of a lack of identification with the father figure, they never develop a conscience. Since they never feel part of a group, they can easily treat their victims with a callous objectivity that amazes the rest of society.

If a girl was abused by her father, she became his sexual object. Should one then be surprised if she treats her subsequent partners as objects, since this was the role model that her father had imprinted upon her? Victims are merely objects who gratify serial killers' (both male and female) needs. Once victims lose their usefulness, they will be disposed of.

Maslow also points out that an individual who did not receive love would not be in a position to give love. A woman in this situation often confuses love with sex, which is a lower need. When they receive sex from men, they confuse it with love and they are also more inclined to offer sex, believing that they love. A man who then accepts the sex for what it is, will be punished by the woman for not reciprocating her 'love'.

The fourth stage in Maslow's hierarchy comprises the 'esteem needs'. Maslow described these as follows: 'These are, first, the desire for strength, for achievement, for adequacy, for mastery and competence, for confidence in the face of the world, and for independence and freedom. Second, we have what we may call the desire for reputation or prestige (defining it as respect or esteem from other people), status, fame, glory, dominance, recognition, attention, importance, dignity, or appreciation' (Maslow, 1970).

To men, wealth represents the above needs.

The fifth and last stage in Maslow's hierarchy is the need for self-actualisation: 'It refers to man's desire for self-fulfilment, namely to the tendency for him to become actualized in what he is potentially. This tendency might be phrased as the desire to become more and more what one idiosyncratically is, to become everything that one is capable of becoming' (Maslow, 1970). Obviously if an individual is thwarted or deprived in any of the previous stages, he or she would not easily reach this level. However, once an individual has reached this stage, he or she can tolerate deprivation of lower needs more easily. For instance, a person may voluntarily go on a hunger strike for a cause that would serve greater humankind. People like Mother Teresa and Mahatma Gandhi are good examples.

Maslow's theory on the hierarchy of basic needs led me to hypothesise that while wealth represents gratification of one of the higher needs, namely self-esteem, to men, it represents gratification of one of the more basic, more subconscious needs, namely security, to women. Wealth makes men feel important and successful; wealth makes women feel safe. The need for security is a much more primitive, subconscious motivation for behaviour than the need for self-esteem.

My theory on the psychodynamics underlying the financial profit motivation of female serial killers may be stated as follows: Although wealth may seem to be an external gratification to others, female serial killers kill for money to gratify their deep, deprived psychological need for security. In this sense they do not differ from their male counterparts. Both genders kill to gratify a basic, mostly subconscious, deep psychological need. Most male serial killers combine their murderous act with sexual gratification. This is as basic and primitive a need to them as security is to women. Sex and money might be two vastly different concepts, but subconsciously both are manifestations of basic primitive needs, depending upon the gender. Serial killers differ from other human beings in that the urgency to gratify the unfulfilled basic need is so overwhelming that they will kill to preserve it, never grasping that it will always remain out of reach. No matter how many insurance policies the female serial killer inherits, the money will never be enough. The void will never be filled.

Thus my theory on the apparent external difference in the motivations of male and female serial killers (sex versus money) postulates that both genders are none the less intrinsically motivated by the urge to gratify a deep, subconscious, basic psychological need.

There are, however, further differences between male and female serial killers. As Hickey so aptly states:

116

'To say the woman cannot be a "true" serial killer unless she acts like a man, is myopic' (Hickey, 2002).

One of these characteristic differences is that female serial killers are 'quiet' killers. They may go undetected for long periods, probably because no one associates such dark deeds with women. Kelleher and Kelleher (1998) in *Murder most Rare* examined a hundred female serial killers and found that it took an average of eight years to apprehend them, while the average period for apprehending a male serial killer was four years.

Another difference is in their choice of victims. Three quarters of female serial killers do not kill strangers. 'When family members were victims, husbands overwhelmingly became the primary target' (Hickey, 2002).

Poison is the preferred method of killing. Hickey found that 45 per cent of female serial killers used poison, while others used a firearm, bludgeoned their victims to death, suffocated them, stabbed them or drowned their victims.

Female serial killers are also less mobile than their male counterparts. '... female serial killers were classified as predominantly stay-at-home killers who operate carefully and inconspicuously and who may avoid detection for several years' (Hickey, 2002). Keeny and Heide in their article *Gender Differences in Serial Murderers* (1994) are of the opinion that because female serial killers are mostly static, linkage blindness (which refers to the difficulty of tying together murders committed over a large geographic area) should not occur. They ascribe the reason for the slow detection of female serial killers to the failure of law enforcement and other professionals to recognise that a homicide has been committed and to respond appropriately. They add to this the fact that family and friends may be reluctant to confront female killers with their suspicions. They cite the case of Marybeth Trinning, a New York mother who murdered nine of her children, but whose husband did nothing to stop her behaviour, rather suggesting that she seek therapy or take steps to prevent further births.

Keeny and Heide also found that female serial killers tend not to do damage to their victims in the sense that male serial killers may mutilate, dismember and exhibit overkill in their murders. Female serial killers are also less likely to torture their victims. They apparently do not stalk their victims as their male counterparts do, although some of them are aggressive in procuring victims by actively seeking out boarding house tenants, or insure and kill multiple lovers/partners, or solicit prostitution for the purpose of robbery and murder.

Yet it seems that female serial killers *do* possess several personality traits that occur in male serial killers: 'The women tended to be insincere, amoral, impulsive, prone to exercise manipulative charisma and superficial charm, without conscience, and with little insight, because they failed to learn from their mistakes' (Hickey, 2002).

Hickey refers to Freiberger who, in her 1997 study, stated that the current classifications used for male serial killers do not apply to female serial killers.

Kelleher and Kelleher (1998) found that the 'organised' versus 'disorganised' classification developed by Federal Bureau of Investigation (FBI) profilers in the 1980s was inadequate for female serial killers. They devised another system of classification for female serial killers, dividing them into two main groups: those who act alone and those who act in partnership.

Those who act alone were further subdivided into the following categories:
- Black Widows, who systematically kill multiple spouses, partners or other family members;
- Angels of Death, who systematically kill people who are in their care for some form of medical attention;
- Sexual Predators, who systematically kill others in clear acts of sexual homicide;
- Revenge killers, who systematically kill for reasons of hate or jealousy;
- Profit for Crime killers, who systematically kill for profit or in the course of committing another crime.

'Killers of this type are often mature, careful, deliberate, socially adept, and highly organized. They usually attack victims in their homes or places of work. They tend to favor a specific weapon, like poison, lethal injection or suffocations' (Kelleher & Kelleher (1998).

Female serial killers who act in partnership are subdivided into the following categories:
- Team Killer: kills or participates in the killing of others in conjunction with at least one other;
- Question of sanity: kills in an apparently random manner and later judged insane;
- Unexplained: kills for reasons that are totally inexplicable or for unclear motives;
- Unsolved: a pattern of unsolved killings that may be attributed to a woman.

'Killers of this type tend to be younger, aggressive, vicious in their attack, sometimes disorganized, and usually unable to carefully plan. They usually attack victims in diverse locations. They tend to use guns, knives, or torture' (Kelleher & Kelleher, 1998).

I would like to expand on the two most common categories of female serial killer, namely the Black Widow and the Angel of Death.

The Black Widows usually commence their criminal careers at the age of twenty-five years and target spouses, partners, family members, their children and anyone else with whom they might have formed a personal relationship. They may also kill a person who threatens to expose them. Their preferred weapon of choice is usually poison and the main motive is profit from insurance policies and inheritances. Some of them are attractive and some are 'plain Janes', but their sexual prowess far exceeds their physical appearance. They instil trust in their unsuspecting victims. They also have an uncanny ability to adopt a chameleon-like persona to suit the specific characteristics a male victim might be looking for in his 'ideal woman'. The public often regard them as dutiful wives and doting mothers, although some are not able to conceal their promiscuity and those close to them might observe elements of child neglect in their conduct.

Angels of Death generally commence their criminal careers at the age of twenty-one years. They operate in hospitals, clinics or nursing homes, where the murders may be disguised as medical fatalities, and they have the medical knowledge to choose weapons to facilitate this. They also have easy access to life-sustaining equipment. They enjoy the power they have over life and death and might sometimes also benefit from insurance policies they have persuaded their geriatric patients to cede to them.

Although not mentioned in Kelleher and Kelleher's typologies, I would like to explore the phenomenon of

Münchhausen by proxy. This is a psychological term (also called factitious disorder by proxy) to describe a syndrome in which one individual deliberately exaggerates, invents or induces an illness in someone else in order to gain attention. The condition was first recognised in 1977. The majority of individuals afflicted by this syndrome are women.

The general characteristics of persons exhibiting the syndrome are as follows:
- They focus on their victims' symptoms and not on their abilities or personalities;
- They like dressing up as medical personnel;
- They take over the duties of nursing staff and interfere with doctors' diagnoses and prescriptions;
- They try to play off medical personnel against one another;
- They doubt nursing staff and physicians' capabilities and attempt to blame them or the hospital for the victims' illnesses or deaths;
- They read up on the particular illness and are generally very knowledgeable about medical conditions and medication, although they might not have had formal medical training;
- They use appropriate medical terminology;
- They insist on certain medications, remedy or care and become aggressive when medical personnel do not comply with their wishes;
- They might consult several doctors at the same time, or 'hop' from one doctor to another;
- They are excited when visiting a doctor and dress up as if they are going on a date;
- Initially they are subordinate and friendly towards doctors, but become more demanding and aggressive if they meet with resistance;
- They manipulate doctors not to trust their own

instincts;

- They will withhold food, or supplement the victims' diets with harmful food, to keep them ill;
- They take control of every aspect of their victims' lives;
- They are narcissistic and crave attention;
- Although they may appear well-dressed and in control in public, at home they are unstable and often threaten suicide;
- At home they can become verbally and physically abusive towards the patient, although in the hospital they will feign concern;
- They have no insight into their condition and will deny vehemently that they had anything to do with the victims' illnesses or deaths;
- They will unburden their emotions upon their children;
- They prefer to find employment in a medical environment.

The childhood years of persons with this syndrome will indicate probable sexual abuse by the father figure, resulting in their sexual manipulation of men as adults, repressed hostility towards authority and father figures, emotional neglect by parents, and they might have had a parent employed in the medical field.

The FBI's *Crime Classification Manual* (1992) lists them under Hero Homicides:

- The offender does not necessarily plan the murder, but seeks attention by inducing illness in the victim;
- As soon as the victim is removed from the offender's care, the victim recuperates;
- There have been cases where Münchhausen by proxy correlates with Angels of Death profiles.

When they benefit financially from the death of the victims, they may be Black Widows.

Cynthia Lyda of Orlando (USA) was an Angel of Death serial killer who pleaded Münchhausen by proxy, and so was Bobby Sue Terrel of Illinois (USA). It would be very easy for a calculating female serial killer to study the phenomenon and feign Münchhausen by proxy in order to kill her victims and then plead innocence by reason of insanity.

✳

Case study: Daisy Louisa de Melker, 1923, 1927, 1932

Daisy Louisa Hancorn-Smith was born on 1 June 1886 at Seven Fountains, near Grahamstown in the Eastern Cape province. She had ten siblings – six sisters and four brothers. At the age of ten Daisy went to Bulawayo, in what was then Rhodesia, to live with her father and two brothers who had settled there. At the age of thirteen she was sent to boarding school at the Good Hope Seminary in Cape Town. She was a bright pupil with a high level of intelligence.

After school she trained as a nurse at the Berea Nursing Home in Durban. She was educated in medicine, drugs and surgery. On vacation in Rhodesia she met, fell in love with and got engaged to Bert Fuller, but tragedy struck when Bert died of blackwater fever. Daisy returned to South Africa, to live with an aunt in Johannesburg. She inherited two hundred rand from the estate of her deceased fiancé. This may have set her mind working. Death was a form of income, and it did not require any work.

On 3 March 1909 Daisy married William Alfred

Cowle, a plumber who worked for the Johannesburg City Council. William was not a wealthy man, but he was a member of a pension fund. The couple had five children, of which only the son, Rhodes Cecil, born on 21 June 1911, survived. They lived in Tully Street, Turffontein. William was a hard-working man who provided adequately for his family. But Daisy, who had grown up poor, wanted more. She remembered the easy money she had received from Bert.

On the morning of 11 January 1923, William went to the kitchen and drank a glass of Epsom salts. Then he took his lunch box and set off for work. But before he reached the front door, he doubled up with pain. Daisy put her husband to bed and called Dr Fourie, who diagnosed a nerve condition. Later that day, an anxious Daisy called her neighbours, telling them that William was dying. Dr Fourie returned to find William dead. He diagnosed cerebral bleeding. Daisy, a widow of thirty-seven, inherited about three and a half thousand rand as well as the house.

Three years later, on 1 January 1927, she married Robert Sproat, a forty-six-year-old bachelor. Robert was also a plumber at the City Council, but he had an extra income because he had made some clever investments. They lived in Terrace Street, Bertrams, Johannesburg.

One Sunday evening in October 1927, Robert became violently ill after Daisy had given him a glass of beer. Dr Fourie was summoned again and suspected that Robert had a bleeding ulcer, or maybe arteriosclerosis, or maybe he was also suffering from cerebral bleeding. Dr Fourie was not sure of his diagnosis, but he prescribed medication. Robert asked Daisy to call his friend William Johnston to his bedside. He told William to make sure that Daisy inherited everything, since his will was still in favour of his mother in England. This upset Daisy tremendously. She summoned Robert's brother William Sproat from Pretoria, who arrived the following day. She asked him to persuade Robert to draw up a will in her favour. William did not want to discuss the issue of the will with his ailing brother. A short while later Daisy presented Robert with a will that she had drawn up. With a trembling hand, Robert signed the will, with his brother William and a neighbour as witnesses. Remarkably, he recovered.

But he was not well for long. On 5 November 1927, Robert again fell ill. The doctor diagnosed cerebral bleeding. Scarcely had the diagnosis been made than Robert breathed his last. Daisy inherited about nine thousand rand from her husband. Her insatiable greed led her to make a mistake. She wrote to her mother-in-law in England complaining that there was not enough money to cover Robert's funeral expenses, and would Mrs Sproat be so kind as to make a contribution. Mrs Sproat senior referred this letter to her surviving son William, who angrily confronted Daisy and warned her to stay out of their lives. She obliged.

Daisy had other problems. Her son Rhodes was sixteen by this time. After school he completed an apprenticeship as a plumber, but he was a lazy boy who was more interested in partying and riding the motorbike that his mother had bought him on a trip to England. Daisy found him work in Rhodesia, which he quit, and again in Swaziland, where he contracted malaria. He did not know that his mother had taken out an insurance policy on his life when he was eleven years old.

While he was in Swaziland, Rhodes received the news that his mother was to become Mrs Sidney

Clarence de Melker on 21 January 1928. His new stepfather was not only a plumber on a mine, but he was also an ex-Springbok rugby player. The couple moved to Simmer East Cottages in Germiston.

Although Daisy was not a particularly attractive woman, she had a magnetic personality. Most people who met her could not resist her vivacity. Men fell over their feet to attract her attention and her husbands considered themselves lucky to be chosen by her.

In 1931 Rhodes returned home, ill with malaria. His mother nursed him diligently. He repaid her kindness by assaulting her twice. Daisy had had enough of her son, who spent her 'hard-earned' money without a second thought. Rhodes did not realise how precarious his position was. Assaulting his mother was the last straw.

She none the less found him a job at a garage. On 2 March 1932 he took his lunch box and a flask of coffee and went to work. By three o'clock that afternoon he had a terrible stomach ache. But he decided to go to his usual rugby practice, hoping that the pain would ease. But it woke him again in the middle of the night. He had to get up the following morning since he was charged to appear in court in connection with a traffic violation. He paid the fine and went to work, feeling very ill. At three o'clock his boss sent him home. Daisy put her son to bed. At six o'clock she gave him a glass of ginger beer and wished him a good night. Rhodes never woke up again. The cause of his death was attributed to malaria. Daisy inherited two hundred rand.

When William Sproat, who had quietly been keeping tabs on his former sister-in-law, heard about Rhodes' death he went to the police and informed them about the similarities in the three deaths. The police took note and on 15 April 1932 the three bodies were exhumed at the New Brixton Cemetery. Forensic analyses indicated that both William Cowle and Robert Sproat had been poisoned with strychnine and Rhodes with arsenic. Daisy de Melker was promptly arrested for murder.

But the state had a problem. Despite intensive police investigations, no poison could be found in her home, nor could the police trace where the poison had been bought. Without this, they had no hard evidence that Daisy was responsible for the murders, no matter how suspicious the circumstances may have seemed. At this stage the newspapers were having a field day with the trial of Mrs Daisy de Melker, but no one had a photograph of her. At last *The Star* newspaper obtained one and published it.

Mr Abraham Spilken of Spilken Pharmacy looked at the photograph and recognised the by now notorious Mrs Daisy de Melker as the same Mrs Daisy Sproat who had bought arsenic from his pharmacy. He went to the police. Daisy had visited his shop on 25 February 1932, he said, and bought sixty grams of arsenic. She signed her name as Mrs Sproat from Terrace Road. He knew her as Mrs Cowle, a former customer. Daisy told him she had remarried and she needed the poison for a cat. At that stage he did not know that she was actually Mrs de Melker.

Abraham Spilken was introduced as a surprise witness. The moment he took the stand, Daisy's expression changed from her customary smirk to deep concern and anger. At last the state had its proof.

The trial lasted from 17 October to 25 November 1932. Mr Justice Greenberg finally found that the state could not prove beyond doubt that Daisy de Melker had administered poison to her husbands, but before her smile grew too wide, he found her guilty of the murder of her son and sentenced her to death.

Daisy de Melker, South Africa's first documented female serial killer, was hanged on 30 December 1932 at the age of forty-six.

Comment

The case of Daisy de Melker illustrates my theory of how women will kill for money in order to fulfil a basic security need. She grew up in poverty, one of eleven children who had to vie for their parents' attention. Daisy also experienced dislocation when she had to move to Rhodesia and to boarding school. No matter how many life policies she inherited, they would never have been enough. Despite her appearance, Daisy was known to cast a sexual spell over men. Her last husband supported her throughout the trial.

Case study: Letitia Erasmus, 1988, 1992

For four years, Letitia Erasmus got away with the murder of her first husband, fifty-four-year-old Andre Nel, despite the fact that he was shot under suspicious circumstances. They had been married for thirty-one years and lived in the small town of Cradock in the Eastern Cape province. They had three daughters. Andre, who was employed by the South African Railways, was a jovial person and popular with his friends and neighbours. He was regarded as a perfectionist and was a specialist in firearms who hunted regularly. He also loved roses. Letitia, on the other hand, was reserved with an apparently calm disposition. Friends said that she sometimes appeared to be in a 'trance'. They also commented that Letitia 'wanted a better life', and that she loved spending money.

Some time before his untimely death, Andre became ill. Their doctor, Dr Herman Neethling diagnosed a brain disease with symptoms of amnesia and confusion. Andre's health deteriorated to the point where he had to retire on medical grounds. During Letitia's trial, Dr Neethling testified that he later realised that Andre's symptoms were not unlike the effects of an overdose of Ativan, an antidepressant which he had prescribed for her.

On the night of 18 February 1988, friends of the family received a frantic phone call from Letitia, who said that Andre had shot himself. When Dr Neethling arrived at Andre's deathbed, he noticed that although Andre was right-handed, he had been shot from the left. He conceded that, despite the fact that Andre had been right-handed and had a tremor, it was possible, though unlikely, for him to have shot himself. Given his brain disease, he could understand why Andre had no will to live. When friends arrived at the Nels' home they were puzzled by the fact that Andre's body had already been removed and the bed was stripped down to the mattress. But no one queried anything.

It appeared strange to Letitia and Andre's son-in-law, Etienne Engelbrecht, that Andre, who was an avid hunter, had apparently shot himself with his 7.62 pistol rather than his preferred 9 mm pistol; he had found that the 7.62 was too small for his hands. Yet he had committed suicide using this weapon.

After her husband's death, Letitia, originally a nurse from Port Elizabeth, moved to Pretoria to be closer to her adult children. She arranged for her house in an affluent neighbourhood in Cradock, of which she was the usufructuary, to be sold. She benefited financially from Andre's death.

Letitia eventually returned to Cradock and, much to the surprise of her friends, she decided to marry retired pensioner Petrus Johannes Erasmus. No one could understand why she agreed to marry Petrus, whom they considered to be below her social standing. Letitia, however, told one of her friends that she had married Petrus because he had a lot of money. Petrus, who had retired on medical grounds, suffered from asthma and a heart condition. Letitia moved in with Petrus in his house in Cawood Street before the marriage.

Stephney Nortje, a friend of Petrus, visited the couple in January 1992, shortly before the wedding. She was amazed when, while they were having tea, Letitia told Petrus he had to change his will in her favour. Petrus agreed, but did not get around to it.

Mr Christoffel Michau, a bank official, later testified that the couple visited him a few days before the wedding. Petrus arranged for Letitia to have signing powers on his bank account. Half an hour later, Petrus returned alone and asked him to hold back the authorisation until further notice. The transaction never went through.

On the morning of 29 January 1992, Letitia insisted that before they were married later that day, they should visit the bank again where Petrus had finally to change his will, making her the sole beneficiary. Cradock undertaker Thomas Ferreira testified later that Letitia had updated Petrus' funeral policy twelve days before his death.

When Petrus was rushed to hospital on 23 March 1992, after apparently attempting suicide by shooting himself, the police became suspicious. After all, Petrus and Letitia had been married for scarcely twenty-one days. Petrus died in hospital and the police arrested

Letitia on suspicion of murder shortly afterwards. She was referred to Valkenburg Psychiatric Hospital for assessment, but was found fit to stand trial. While awaiting trial, she stayed with her daughter in Pretoria. Here, Letitia wrote a letter to the investigating officer, Captain Marlize van Zijl, confessing to the murder of Andre.

> When he came out of the hospital, he pleaded with me to kill him since he did not want to be committed to a psychiatric institution. I told him I had wonderful parents and I can not be a murderess. I have learnt to be a Christian of the Ten Commandments. He pleaded and pleaded. I asked him to shoot me first and then himself. His eyes pleaded with me and I had to take four Ativans before I could commit the deed. He was alive for a little longer and said 'Thank you Tiet', his pet name for me.

Until then no one knew that she was the one who had pulled the trigger. Marlize van Zijl arranged for Letitia to make a confession before Magistrate Anna Meyburgh.

At Letitia's trial, Professor Christopher Stones, a psychologist, testified that she had a very low level of intelligence and a history of depression, anxiety neuroses and psychosomatic problems. She experienced men as dangerous, threatening and possessing a potentially destructive force. In a letter to Captain Marlize van Zijl she wrote that her first husband Andre, had destroyed her young life. Her physician, Dr Neethling, testified that he had prescribed Ativan for her. She had become addicted to sedatives. During the trial her lawyers described her as a pathetic figure who constantly consulted doctors and constantly took medication.

Mr Justice Jean Nepgen presided over the trial in Port Elizabeth in August 1993. Letitia, aged fifty-five, alleged that she shot her second husband Petrus, aged sixty, because he tried to rape her. Her testimony was contested by Dr Herman Neethling, the family doctor of both Letitia's husbands, who said that Petrus was impotent. Because he had a heart problem and had been an alcoholic for many years, the doctor had prescribed potency drugs for him. But it would have taken months for them to become effective. There was no way in which he could have raped Letitia.

Letitia continued to deny that she had murdered Andre and was convinced she would be found innocent of both murders, since God had already forgiven her. She wrote this in her letter:

> But there is one God, Almighty Father, whom only I believe in. At this moment I am ready for Him to take me. He does not want to. There are to be more tests. He will have mercy on me, for I love Him dearly. He will set me free without punishment or mitigation. I will walk out free to my children and serve Him, as I have promised all my life. He will free me for He loves me.

But Letitia was wrong. She was found guilty of both murders and on 27 August 1993, her birthday, Mr Justice Nepgen sentenced her to seven years for the murder of Andre and twelve for the murder of Petrus. The sentences were to run concurrently.

Comment

Cradock is a small town and, as in all small towns, people gossip. It became quite clear to the towns-people that Letitia had married Petrus for his money after her inheritance from Andre had run out. He was a reasonably easy target. People also gossiped that Letitia had been fired by her previous employers because of missing funds, but no one could confirm this allegation. Yet all who knew her, knew she loved spending money.

Perhaps the fact that Letitia had a low intelligence made her believe that she could get away with murder twice. To commit two murders using the same modus operandi and to expect the police and the community to fall twice for the same transparent ruse can, however, only be ascribed to stupidity. Letitia was blinded by greed and managed to convince herself of her innocence, hoping that everyone else would believe her too.

What is less amazing to an expert is the fact that people, even the doctor, could have been fooled the first time. No one would believe an elderly, small-town woman of low intelligence capable of committing murder. Although her son-in-law had his doubts about Andre not using his favourite firearm, he preferred to believe that his mother-in-law was not a killer. Yet, as with their male counterparts, female serial killers also hide behind a mask of mundane normality. They buy groceries, they prune roses, they shop for clothing, they bake and they clean their houses. They can be anybody – one's neighbour, one's friend, one's wife, one's daughter or one's mother.

Letitia fits the profile of a Black Widow perfectly. Perhaps, since she had been trained as a nurse, she would have preferred to use some form of medication to kill her husbands, which would have qualified her as an Angel of Death. Perhaps she grew impatient as her money ran out and so resorted to using a firearm. A psychologist testified that Letitia experienced men as dangerous, threatening and destructive. Clearly she would not trust men to fulfil her need for security and so instead she substituted financial wealth for security. However, men still had to provide this substituted form of security for her. She would kill to secure it, rather than attempt to earn it for herself. This is typical Black Widow behaviour. In the end, one is left wondering who exactly was the dangerous, threatening and destructive partner.

4

Infanticide

In a general sense, *infanticide* refers to the practice of deliberately causing the death of an infant within the first year of life. I am, however, extending the term to mean the killing of a child by its mother, regardless of age. In nearly all past societies throughout history certain forms of infanticide were considered acceptable, but most modern societies regard the practice as both immoral and criminal.

I have only researched cases of women who have killed their children in South Africa, that is, within a Western context. There is a huge body of literature on female infanticide (that is, the killing of female infants) but that is beyond my frame of reference.

The practice of 'babyfarming', a term coined by the Victorians, was rife up to the nineteenth century. Women were paid to foster unwanted babies, with the tacit understanding that the baby would either be killed outright or would die from neglect and malnutrition. The mother could therefore claim ignorance of the death of her child, and perhaps soothe her conscience, but in effect she was, by proxy, responsible for the death. Of course the 'babyfarmers' themselves were directly responsible for these murders, but they were protected by an oath of silence on the part of their customers. When this practice was discovered and revealed in the late nineteenth century it caused a moral outcry and thereafter it became increasingly difficult for a mother – or her family – to rid herself of an unwanted child in this manner.

The two opposing Victorian attitudes towards female criminality – either over-lenient or over-harsh – also applied to instances of infanticide, with the exception that society tends to be more forgiving towards mothers who kill their infants as a result of hormonal imbalances affecting their behaviour. (One has to ask whether society would be as lenient towards a father who killed his children as a result of overactive testosterone?)

Society also seems to be more understanding towards single mothers in desperate economic circumstances. Although such women are still punished, there is leniency because of their adverse circumstances.

'... such women were motivated by the feminine quality of shame and the natural desire to save their child from a life of misery and themselves from possible further degradation by the need to turn to prostitution to survive. Less sympathetic participants, on the other hand, ascribed infanticide to a lack of chastity and characterized offenders as callous single mothers concerned only to get rid of an encumbrance' (Zedner, 1991).

Sex workers who killed their children were severely punished in the past, for society regarded them as callous women who rid themselves of their children because they were an encumbrance to their trade. The notion that sex workers might also have been destitute women who had no other way of earning their living, and suffered the same predicament as 'moral' single women, did not cross the minds of the Victorians. While they regarded 'depravity' as a justifiable reason for 'moral women' to kill their infants, sex workers – who may well have shared the same circumstances – were condemned because they were seen as betraying their feminine role. Double standards clearly applied.

In 1922 a law was passed in the United States, which declared infanticide to be manslaughter as opposed to murder. 'This leniency was due to a belief in "puerperal" or "lactational" insanity which could affect women in the months following birth' (Bowker, 1978).

Some mothers may kill their children to 'save them from a life of poverty'; some to inflict suffering or revenge on their spouses or partners; and some because they are an obstacle in the way of a new relationship. Infanticide may also be brought about by a combination of postpartum depression (a condition attributed to hormonal imbalances and of varying degrees of severity) and a psychological unreadiness to raise children.

Should society be harsher, or more lenient, towards a woman who kills her children than to a woman who kills anyone else? Is society not thereby painting motherhood with the brush of 'ultimate virtue and femininity'? Are childless women any less 'virtuous' or feminine than mothers? Should women who commit infanticide be treated any differently from women who kill adults?

Case study: Marie Cornelesen, 1996
Forty-one-year-old Marie Cornelesen and her

husband Hendrik lived in Triomf in Johannesburg, a few blocks away from Hendrik's cousin Sean Cornelesen. Sean and his wife Ria had three children: Jacques and Isabel, who were already adults, and the apple of Ria's eye, eighteen-year-old Andries.

Problems arose when Marie Cornelesen believed herself to be in love with the juvenile Andries. She seduced him, and it must have been an easy matter for her to convince Andries that he felt the same way about her. Both families were aware of the affair and the young man's mother, Ria, objected strenuously. Marie was, after all, old enough to be Andries' mother.

In mid-1996 Andries met a young girl, Anne Gerber, and fell in love with her. This, Ria believed, was the reason why Marie killed her son.

Marie and Andries were in the habit of meeting either at the Emmarentia Dam or the Westdene Dam in Johannesburg or at her home for sex. On 16 June 1996, she asked Andries to meet her at Emmarentia Dam. Andries was probably reluctant, since he was planning to become engaged to Anne, but may have decided to meet Marie to tell her that he was finally ending their relationship.

Marie knew ahead of time what the outcome of that day would be. She went to the dam armed with her husband's firearm, some pills and a suicide note that she had written the previous day. The couple duly met and had sex in the back of a van. When they got out of the vehicle Marie produced the firearm and shot Andries in the stomach. Then she swallowed the pills. A municipal security guard heard the shot and went to investigate. He found the seriously wounded Andries and the suicide note in the car, but of Marie there was no trace. She had simply disappeared.

The guard summoned the police. Andries managed

to tell them that Marie had shot him and that she would probably shoot herself too. He gave them her address before being taken to hospital, where he died eight hours later.

The police called in a helicopter and dogs to assist them in their search for Marie, but there was no sign of her in the area. That night, they arrested her at her home in the presence of her husband and their three teenage children. Marie was sent for psychiatric observation.

Marie had addressed the suicide letter to Sean and Ria. She thanked the couple – who were her own age – for their love, describing them as having been like parents to her. If only they had accepted the love between her and Andries, they would both still be alive. She asked that they be buried in the same grave.

Marie was found fit to stand trial and Mr Justice L Goldblatt presided over the trial in 1998. Marie testified that she had taken her husband's firearm with her on the day she met Andries for the last time, in case her attempt at suicide by overdosing on medication failed. However Marie did not use the gun on herself; she used it on Andries.

Marie's lawyer, Mr Henk Louw, alleged that Marie had been sexually abused by her father when she was a child and that she was an emotionally battered woman. Marie testified that Andries had been the dominant partner in their relationship. She said he had ordered her not to have sex with her husband and to phone him every day. She did everything he asked. The judge objected to the deceased being represented as the guilty party. Marie's abuse as a child was tragic, he said, but no reason for her to commit murder. Nor was he convinced that a suicide pact existed between the couple, accepting instead that Andries had told

Marie about his fiancée and that she could not come to terms with this.

In April 1999, Mr Justice Goldblatt sentenced Marie to twelve years' imprisonment for murder and the illegal possession of a firearm.

Comment

Marie Cornelesen told journalists that she regarded Andries as her own son. In psychological terms her relationship with him can therefore be considered incestuous and she can also be considered as having committed infanticide.

There is a naturally close bond between a mother and her son and many mothers resent having to step back for their sons' girlfriends or wives. To Marie, the presence of Anne in Andries' life presented a double rejection. She would not only lose her 'son', but also her lover. She set out for her last meeting with Andries with premeditated murder in her heart. If she could not have Andries, then no one else would. The emotional suicide letter, which she signed in both their names, was written the day before. Andries did not sign it and there had been no indication that he was contemplating suicide. In fact, he was planning to become engaged to Anne. The so-called suicide pact was a fiction.

It is illegal to have sex with a boy under the age of eighteen. Marie and Andries' relationship began before he turned eighteen. Since she had had sex with a minor, in terms of the law she was also a paedophile. If Marie herself was the victim of childhood sexual abuse, as maintained by her lawyer during the trial, it would add substance to the theory that victims are likely to become abusers themselves. Although she was caught up in this vicious cycle, she had no right to 'abuse' Andries. Of course her abuser had had no right either, but it is unlikely that he had any insight into the cycle of violence that he had set in motion.

Sean and Ria had been opposed to the relationship from the outset, but when they discussed it with Marie's husband Hendrik he said he knew about it, but there was nothing he could do. It is regrettable that he did not suggest his wife seek therapy, or try to persuade her to attend family counselling.

Marie Cornelesen had the audacity to blame Sean and Ria for their son's death. If you had accepted our relationship, she wrote in the 'suicide' note, he would not have died.

Case study: Elizabeth Margret Alberts, 1996

Elizabeth Alberts could never accept her parents' divorce. And when she married her husband Robert, she believed their marriage would last for ever. The couple had three children, of which the middle child, a daughter, was disabled. They lived in an army base in Centurion in Gauteng province.

The marriage ran into trouble and in June 1996, when Robert packed his bags and moved in with his mother, Elizabeth felt her life was crumbling. She blamed her mother-in-law for their problems. Robert was her anchor in life and she could not face trying to carry on without him. Their younger daughter was staying with her uncle on the night that Elizabeth dispensed sedatives to her older daughter and her son. She wrote five suicide letters to her family and then went into her daughter's bedroom and smothered her with a pillow. She could not bring herself to smother her son as well, so she hit him on the head with a pressure cooker, knocking him unconscious. He regained consciousness, however, and managed to phone the emergency services. Because he was concussed he could not remember the address. Elizabeth took the phone from him and told the police where they lived. They arrested her immediately. Her son was treated in hospital and discharged after a few days.

Seven weeks after the murder, Elizabeth and her husband were reunited. He and their children had forgiven her.

Elizabeth was sentenced to three years' correctional supervision.

Comment

Elizabeth Alberts was an adult who had not worked through the problems of her childhood, despite the fact that her husband's position as a Defence Force employee made access to psychological help easy. She could have discussed her parents' divorce as well as her own marital problems with psychologists who were available on a twenty-four hour basis. For some reason, she did not. It was perhaps easier for her to blame the problems of her youth than to take responsibility for her adult choices. Elizabeth had never learned to acknowledge her value as a human being. Whatever self-worth she felt she anchored in her husband. People are fallible, but each one of us is blessed with the capacity to value our own worth as human beings.

Taking one's own life or those of one's children to 'punish' a spouse accomplishes nothing. It is indicative of manipulative cowardice. Many thousands of children survive the divorce of their parents and grow up as well-adjusted adults. Others manage to make a success of their lives, despite disruptive childhoods, but some will fail, mostly because they hold others accountable for their circumstances.

Case study: Aletta Barnado, 1998

Sixteen-year-old Rianette Barnado left Brandwag Secondary School in her grade 8 year because she was pregnant. She got engaged to her twenty-one-year-old boyfriend, Malcolm Blewitt. The couple did not want to know the gender of the child they were expecting but looked forward to being surprised when the baby was born.

Rianette lived with her mother Maryna, her stepfather Dirkie Swanepoel and her brother, twenty-four-year-old Riaan and his nineteen-year-old wife Aletta, in their home in Uitenhage in the Eastern Cape province. Rianette's godmother, Sarie Koekemoer, lived across the street.

On the morning of 12 January 1998, Rianette phoned Malcolm. He was surprised to hear from her, for she hardly ever called him at work. She was evidently missing him. 'I just wanted to hear your voice,' were the last words he would ever hear his fiancée say.

An hour later Rianette was brutally murdered. She was stabbed more than sixty-two times and was also strangled. One of the wounds penetrated the back of her eight-month foetus.

That same morning, the police received a call from a hysterical Riaan, informing them that he had discovered his sister's body on his stepfather's bed. The police arrived on the scene and conducted a house search. When they found bloody clothing hidden under Riaan and Aletta's bed they decided to question both of them. Riaan had scratches on his face, which he was asked to explain. Aletta responded and initially lied to the police about the cause of the scratches, but after further interrogation she confessed that she and Riaan had murdered her pregnant sister-in-law. The police ordered paternity tests to be done to establish whether Riaan could have been the father of the baby. A devastated Malcolm heard from the pathologist who conducted the post-mortem that the dead child was a boy.

The motive for this senseless killing appeared to be totally incomprehensible. But both Riaan and Aletta were charged with murder and appeared before Mr Justice Joseph Ludorf.

During the trial, Sarie Koekemoer testified that she had taken her young goddaughter Rianette under her wing. Some days earlier she and her pregnant daughter Kleintjie heard sounds of an argument at the Barnados' home across the road. They went there immediately and found Riaan pursuing Rianette, armed with a kitchen knife. Aletta cornered Rianette and slapped her face. Kleintjie tried to intervene, but Riaan hit out at her and she fell down the kitchen steps. She was rushed to hospital, but fortunately a miscarriage was averted. When Sarie confronted the couple about the altercation, Aletta allegedly told her that she hated pregnant women because she herself could not fall pregnant.

In her testimony Aletta said that she had been abused by Riaan. He was extremely possessive and used to keep her captive in their room. She stabbed Rianette with the knife because Riaan had told her to. Riaan, however, testified that it was Aletta who had initiated the murder and that he had only strangled his sister afterwards with an electric cord. Aletta refused to sit next to Riaan in court, saying that she was afraid of him.

Mr Justice Ludorf rejected Aletta's plea that she

had committed the murder because she feared her husband. He found that she had been the instigator because of her obsessive jealousy of her sister-in-law's pregnancy. He pointed out that she had lied to the police about the scratches on Riaan's face and had confessed only when she was confronted with the bloody clothing that was found under her bed. He sentenced Aletta to fifteen years' imprisonment and Riaan to twenty years. Aletta burst into tears when sentence was passed as she was convinced she would only be sentenced to correctional supervision. Riaan did not utter a word, nor did he console his wife. Aletta was not granted leave to appeal.

Comment

Much has been said and written about a woman's maternal instincts. Perhaps Aletta Barnado killed her sister-in-law because she suspected her of carrying her husband's child – the child she could never have. Did she, in a jealous rage, try to cut the foetus from Rianette's body, as she had once threatened to do? Procreation is an act of giving life yet, obsessed by her need to give life, Aletta took life.

Many young women who feel rejected either by their parents or by their boyfriends or husbands yearn for a child. This is not a maternal instinct, but rather a manifestation of narcissism. These women expect the baby to fulfil their own need for love. Once the baby is born the young 'mothers' are severely disillusioned, for instead of the baby fulfilling their needs, they find themselves in a situation where they have to attend to the needs of a demanding individual around the clock. This selfless task may prove ungratifying and they often abuse their babies.

Riaan Barnado was known to be an obsessively

jealous young man. He treated his wife as his possession. He possibly blamed her for her inability to conceive. It was never established whether Riaan was the father of Rianette's baby, but it is not unrealistic to speculate that his possessiveness extended to his sister as well. He may well have found it hard to accept that she had found happiness with Malcolm and that they would soon have a family of their own – something that he could not have.

In their jealousy, Riaan and Aletta Barnado destroyed the lives of Rianette and Malcolm and the future of a baby boy.

In his sentencing, Mr Justice Ludorf took both the offenders' youth into account, as well as the fact that they were first offenders. He acknowledged that Aletta was under Riaan's influence, but none the less found them equally responsible for Rianette's death. The question has to be asked: why, then, did he not also sentence Aletta to twenty years?

Not guilty

The following woman was found not guilty of infanticide.

Case study: Maria Fernandes,* 1998

Maria Fernandes was a doctor who had taken the Hippocratic Oath, devoting her life to saving the lives of others. She was sincere when she took this oath and fulfilled her promise in her practice as a physician. Yet her private life was not as successful as her professional life. The family suffered a terrible blow when her divorced husband, Dr Jean Gold,* a

---

* Names have been changed.

prominent Johannesburg psychiatrist, committed suicide. Then Maria was diagnosed with cancer and had to have a double mastectomy. By 1998 she was suffering from financial problems and succumbed to a major depression. In her illness she could no longer cope with her own suffering, and nor could she contemplate the suffering of her four beloved sons. It was altogether too much for her to bear.

One night, in a delirious stupor, Maria gave her children sedatives and then set their luxury home in Morningside, Johannesburg, on fire. By the time the emergency services arrived, it was too late for two of her sons. She was sent for psychiatric observation and her children were placed in the care of their uncle. The court found that Maria could not be held accountable for her actions and she was acquitted. After years of therapy, she was reunited with her two sons in 2001 and she has reopened her practice. Her patients describe her as a good doctor and her sons have forgiven her.

Comment

Maria and her sons would like to try to carry on with their lives, away from media attention. The reason why her case is included here is to illustrate that South African law makes provision for crimes committed as a result of serious mental disturbance. It is also necessary to realise that people can recover, people can forgive and, despite terrible odds, they can build a new life and carry on courageously, if they make a conscious choice to do so. Never underestimate what the human spirit is able overcome. Dr Maria Fernandes and her sons are living examples of this.

5

Love Triangles

Kaplan and Sadock (1998) define an *obsession* as: 'pathological persistence of an irresistible thought or feeling that cannot be eliminated from consciousness by logical effort, which is associated with anxiety'. It is a fixed, largely irrational pattern of thinking, accompanied by unpleasant emotions that include fear, and a compulsion to carry out certain actions. Awareness of their inappropriateness is of no avail. An obsession is a thought, but a compulsion is an act. Both can be time-consuming and interfere significantly with a person's normal routine, occupational functioning, social activities and relationships.

Alfred Adler, a contemporary of Freud, defined the *inferiority complex*. A person is suffering from an inferiority complex when he or she has feelings of inferiority which are repressed. Several psychological defence mechanisms are employed to compensate for this complex, for example projecting it upon someone else, cultivating a macho image, bragging, over-control of another or the environment, cruelty and sadism. Both the psychological phenomena of obsession and inferiority complex come into play when one investigates the dynamics of love triangles which end in murder.

A person may believe that he or she cannot live without another particular person. On the face of it, this is already an irrational thought. One does not need another person in order to breathe. One might imagine one does, but in reality one does not. The belief that one cannot live without another is therefore fundamentally untrue, and marks the beginning of obsession. The one who believes he or she cannot live without the other begins to think about the other all the time. It becomes a time-consuming preoccupation which interferes with daily life, as will become evident in the case studies.

Since we have now defined *obsession*, it is easy to recognise that the people involved in the love triangles described in the case studies were obsessed. In love triangles, the obsession is usually shared by two people. Each feeds the other's obsession. They become 'soul mates', bent on forcing everything to conform to their set pattern of thinking. All their actions are justifiable when measured against the obsession. They do not pause to consider alternative options or the consequences of their actions, for their time is consumed by their obsession. The third party, who does not share the obsession, is usually the one who ends up dead. An obsession is irrational; therefore it is an illness.

Obsessed people believe themselves to be inferior and need someone else to validate their existence. This is where the inferiority complex comes into play. They believe they are not good enough to exist on their own. This is also irrational and also, therefore, an illness. The concepts of obsession and inferiority complex are always found within tragic love triangles. They are indicative of mental illness and neurosis.

An obsession born of an inferiority complex is not love. A person who enters a relationship based on an obsession is manifesting a narcissistic manipulative effort to have his or her needs gratified in an unhealthy manner. Narcissism is not love.

These relationships are typically characterised by lust, sex, adventure, deceit and, eventually, murderous thoughts. None of these are elements of love.

When one person says of another: 'If I cannot have you, no one else will', it is not love that is talking; when a person threatens to kill the supposed 'loved one' or the supposed loved one's family, it is not love, it is dangerous pathology; when one person tries to control another in any way, it is not love, it is an inferiority complex at work; and when a person tries to change a partner for the 'better', it is not love, it is manipulation. Abuse, tantrums, attempting suicide in order to manipulate, involving children in the relationship, storming off in anger, belittling the partner, infidelity – none of these represent love, they are all manifestations of infantile and narcissistic behaviour.

All the above are examples of manipulative behaviour by people who suffer from an inferiority complex and who will actually kill to meet their own needs. Clearly, it is not love. Nowhere in obsessive relationships does reciprocal give-and-take and granting the other the freedom and opportunity to individualise into his or her own potential as an adult human being enter into the equation.

Anyone finding him- or herself in a relationship with an obsessional partner should terminate the relationship immediately, no matter how many false promises may be made nor how attractive the sugar coating concealing the manipulation might seem initially. These relationships are dangerous and can lead to death.

Anyone recognising obsessional qualities in themselves should seek professional help without delay.

Characteristics of obsession and inferiority complex are also found within abusive relationships and in spree killings.

Another thought on the subject of love and fidelity. Many people, both men and women, when caught out having affairs or one night stands, tend to justify their behaviour by saying: 'It meant nothing.' They are admitting to having meaningless sex. They are also admitting that the person they had sex with was merely an object used to gratify sexual lust. The wronged partner should then ask him- or herself the question: Am I prepared to continue a relationship with someone who has the capacity to have meaningless sex, and who also has the capacity to view another person as an object used only to gratify lust? If such a wronged individual decides to remain in the relationship, they should realise that they have made their choice and must bear the consequences of their decision. If the wronged partner is not willing to share a future with an unrepentant, narcissistic person, he or she should terminate the relationship. 'It meant nothing' is not an excuse for infidelity, but people frequently get away with it.

What is notable in love triangles that lead to murder is that, almost without exception, once they are facing trial, or even before that, the couple who promised each other 'ever-lasting' love, turn on each other faster than you can say 'obsession'. Nothing brings one back to reality with more of a jolt than a murder charge and the possibility of life imprisonment. It is astonishing how quickly such a dose of reality cancels the earlier, all-consuming obsession. Suddenly the 'greatest love of my life whom I will die for' evaporates into thin air, and what remains are the consequences of immature adults who did not seek alternative solutions to their problems in the first place.

There is no guarantee that love will last for ever. It is a reality that people who once loved each other may cease to love, or may begin to love someone else. It happens. The rejected partner is resentful and hurt, for it is unfair. But no matter with what intensity the wronged party still loves the other, it will not bring back a love that is lost. No one can make someone else love them. People make the mistake of falling into a well of self-pity, or they resort to manipulation, or to the degradation of vengeful, petty and spiteful behaviour. The most mature path to follow in these circumstances is to let go. It happens also to be the most healing path. Mourn the loss, but get over it and get on with life.

Many people tend to confuse love with obsession. In a loving adult relationship there is no need for one to try to change the other. Nor is it a place where individuals with psychological or adjustment disorders can be allowed to act out their psychoses, either by taking it out on the partner or in conjunction with the partner. The place for acting out psychoses and neuroses is within a therapeutic environment, where they can be treated and healed.

Case study: Anna Rabie, 1842
Anna Knoetze was born on 13 November 1810

in Graaff-Reinet, in the Karoo in what is now the Eastern Cape province. At seventeen she had already acquired a reputation as a local beauty and it was clear from all the male visitors to her parents' humble home that Anna knew how to use her beauty to her best advantage. Men had to pay for her favours.

Twenty-three-year-old Jacob Rabie had heard of Anna's legendary beauty and he began calling on her when she was nineteen. Jacob had a quality which Anna found particularly attractive – he was the son of a wealthy local farmer. She soon became Mrs Rabie and the couple moved into a house in Cradock Street. Jacob was often away visiting the family farms and during his absence Anna would entertain friends at their home. These friends were all men, of course. Jan Bastiaan, Jacob's brother, warned him of his wife's inappropriate conduct while he was away, but Jacob was too much in love to believe him.

One of the most frequent callers was a widower named Johannes Liebenberg, father of three.

Jacob decided to take Anna with him on one of his trips, perhaps because he wanted her company, or perhaps to subdue the nasty rumours in town. At one of the farms the couple was entertained by the Koens, the managers of the farm. They were eager to impress the young owner and brought out a bottle of brandy. Sarah Koen noticed Anna adding something to the brandy and warned Jacob not to drink it. Jacob had the contents of the bottle secretly analysed. The results stunned him. There was enough arsenic in the brandy to kill an army. Anna denied having tampered with the brandy and since it was her word against Sarah Koen's, and Anna was of a much higher social standing than Sarah, Jacob decided not to pursue the matter. However, he was now alert.

One night he deliberately arrived home earlier than his wife expected him and found Anna in the arms of Johannes Liebenberg. Jacob packed a few belongings and moved in with his brother, Jan Bastiaan.

Anna realised she was about to lose the goose that had laid the golden egg and bought herself a house directly opposite the one occupied by the Rabie brothers, at number 145 Cradock Street. She took in a lodger, Thomas Bentley.

Despite the fact that her estranged husband was living across the street, Anna and Johannes continued their affair, much to the delight of the gossip mongers. Anna believed she had found true love with Johannes, but realised that if Jacob divorced her, she would be penniless. The best solution, the lovers decided, was for Anna and Jacob to reconcile and then to murder Jacob, so that Anna could inherit his estate. Then there would be nothing in the way of their happy future.

On 9 December 1841, Anna sent Thomas Bentley to invite her husband for tea. Jacob's first reaction was to refuse, but the next morning he decided to visit her in the company of friends. Anna called Jacob out of the room and soon they were spotted walking hand in hand in the garden. Jacob moved back that afternoon.

Shortly after the reconciliation, Anna tried to persuade a local good-for-nothing to murder Jacob, but he refused. Jacob enjoyed Christmas with his wife, not suspecting that she was plotting his murder.

On 4 January 1842, Anna poured some wine for herself and her husband after Thomas had gone to bed. At half past eleven that night a shot rang out in the house. The lodger Thomas Bentley did not investigate for he thought the shot had come from the street. Ten minutes later, Anna charged into his room, telling him that Jacob had shot himself. He found Jacob dead in his bed and called the neighbours.

At midnight, the local policeman, Hendrik Enslin, arrived on the scene. Jacob was lying on the right side of the bed with a gunshot wound above his right eye. Strangely, his hands were folded on his chest, his own firearm in one of them, pointing in the direction of the wound. Hendrik immediately noticed that the gun had not been fired recently. At that moment he knew that Jacob Rabie had been murdered and he also knew he would not have far to search for a motive. Residue on the pillow indicated that the shot had been fired from the right side. Hendrik noticed that there was a small window between the front bedroom and the kitchen which was behind it, and that the window was open. It was clear to him that someone had fired the shot from the kitchen, through the window. He noticed that there was blood splattered on the left side of the bed where Anna would have been sleeping when Jacob was shot, yet there was no blood on Anna, nor on her nightdress, an observation which Thomas Bentley had also made.

Hendrik left the room and began questioning Anna.

She told him the last thing she had done before going to bed was to close the windows and blow out the candles. One of the neighbours confirmed that no one had entered the bedroom after Thomas had found the body. When Hendrik asked Anna why the window into the kitchen was open, she said that she might have forgotten to close it.

Dr George Krebbs confirmed that Jacob had been killed by a lead bullet fired from a distance. He removed the bullet and handed it to Hendrik who noticed that it had strange markings on it. He found a circular mark on the kitchen floor close to the window. There was a large bowl in the kitchen and when he placed this over the circle, it matched. Someone had stood on the bowl, underneath the window.

As soon as it was light, Hendrik searched the garden and found interesting footprints. Clearly who-ever made the footprints was wearing only socks. Like a bloodhound, Hendrik followed the footprints. The trail led him through town, through the Sunday River and up the opposite bank, all along Planket Street to the front door of Johannes Liebenberg. Hendrik was not surprised, but footprints alone cannot convict a man of murder.

Johannes was not at home, but his daughter and the domestic worker were. The daughter confirmed that her father had been out the night before. The domestic worker told Hendrik that two labourers had helped Johannes cast lead bullets the previous afternoon. Each of them made three bullets, six in total.

He found his suspect visiting neighbours, discussing the terrible murder in their sleepy little town. 'I had nothing to do with it,' said Johannes when Hendrik came into the room. 'No one accused you,' replied Hendrik.

Hendrik took Johannes back to his own house. He made him take off his shoes and walk in his socks next to the footprints. It was a perfect match, but it was still not evidence. Johannes denied that he owned a firearm.

Hendrik visited the local general dealer, who told him that Johannes had bought a firearm on the afternoon of New Year's Eve. He had seen Johannes speaking to Anna Rabie in his shop that same afternoon. The day before the murder he had bought the lead.

Hendrik returned to arrest Johannes, and his daughter pointed out where her father had hidden the firearm. Johannes told Hendrik he had been target shooting with his other daughter near the river the previous day. He fired two shots. Hendrik found three bullets with the firearm, which left one missing bullet to be accounted for. In Johannes' jacket pocket he found unsigned love letters. The domestic worker told him that the day before Johannes had sent her to Anna's house with a bottle of wine and another of medicine.

Hendrik locked Johannes up and went to Anna's house where he confronted her with the love letters. She denied being the author, but he told her the handwriting matched her own, which he had checked at the local dealer. Anna then acknowledged that the letters were hers, but said that they were old. She and Jacob been reconciled after she ended the affair with Johannes.

A neighbour informed Hendrik that she had seen Anna burying something in the garden and when Hendrik investigated he found the bottle of medicine, prescribed for insomnia. Dr Krebbs confirmed it contained opium and remembered selling it to Johannes.

On 13 January 1842 Hendrik arrested Anna for the murder of Jacob. The trial commenced on 10 May 1842 with Mr Justice Kekewich presiding and a jury of peers was assembled. Three days later the jury found both the accused guilty of murder, although both denied it.

After several days in prison Johannes confessed

that he had killed Jacob. Anna had administered the sleeping potion to her husband before letting him into the house. He was too scared to kill Jacob in the bedroom so she took him to the kitchen. Anna stood on top of the bowl and held a candle for him, while he fired the shot. Then he slipped out of the house and went home.

On the morning of 8 July 1842 the townsfolk gathered at the prison. An ox-wagon containing two coffins was draped in black and purple silk. Anna Rabie was led from the cells and took her place on one of the coffins. Johannes Liebenberg took his place on the second coffin. Eight black oxen pulled the wagon, which was followed by a jeering crowd. Anna and Johannes rode in silence. Not once did they so much as glance at each other.

The gallows had been built on a hill outside the town. Many of the men who had previously visited the beautiful Anna were among the crowd. Just before she was led on to the platform Anna looked silently at Johannes. She was dressed in awful black sackcloth. Jan Bastiaan jumped on the platform, took a string from his pocket and tied the bottom of the dress around her legs. He did this for the sake of decency, in case her dress blew up when she swung from the gallows.

Anna Rabie did not acknowledge this gesture of kindness moments before she was hanged. A few minutes later, her lover's body dangled beside hers.

Magistrate van Ryneveld declared that they were not to be buried side by side. Johannes was buried at the north end of the town on Semelpoort heights and Anna Rabie was buried on the banks of the Sunday River at the southern end of the town.

Comment

The science of murder investigation has improved a hundred times or more since Jacob Rabie's death, but Hendrik Enslin possessed something that even the most sophisticated crime detection apparatus cannot match – instinct.

Case study: Mara Maria (Sonjia) Swanepoel, 1971

Sonjia Swanepoel and Fransiscus Wynand (Frans) Vontsteen, both in their thirties, met each other in 1967 when Frans joined the staff of the company where Sonjia was working. They were surprised to discover that Sonjia's husband and Frans' ex-wife were both inpatients at Weskoppies Psychiatric Hospital. Frans' ex-wife Hannetjie was a paranoid schizophrenic and Sonjia's husband Francois (Cois) was suffering from work-related stress. Cois, who was about ten years older than Sonjia, was a warrant officer in the police force.

Frans and Hannetjie were married for eleven years. Hannetjie was a dancer and the couple had three daughters but, tragically, the youngest one drowned in 1965 when she was two years old. Frans divorced Hannetjie in 1969 and moved into a flat in Sunnyside, Pretoria. Although he had custody of his two remaining daughters, they were both in boarding school. Frans had always been a dreamer, the kind of man who fell for get-rich-quick schemes. He never kept a job for very long.

Sonjia had been married before, but she fell in love with Cois and was already pregnant with his child when she divorced her first husband and married him two days after the divorce in 1960. It was also Cois' second marriage. They lived in a comfortable home in Eeufees Road, Pretoria North. By the time she met

159

Frans, Sonjia was also a mother of two.

Although Frans and Sonjia resisted a relationship at first, they had become intimate by February 1968. When Cois was fighting on the then Rhodesian border, Frans and Sonjia would treat themselves and their children to holidays. When Sonjia found herself pregnant for the third time, she told Frans he was the father. He visited his lover in the maternity ward in Pretoria.

The couple tried to end the relationship in early 1971, but they did not succeed. Whenever Frans brought up the subject of Sonjia's divorce, she told him that when she asked Cois for a divorce, he threatened to kill her and the children. She told Frans that Cois was a violent man who abused her. In 1971 Cois applied for a transfer. He never suspected that he was not the father of their youngest daughter. Frans and Sonjia felt trapped. Sonjia could not obtain a divorce, Hannetjie was causing trouble and threatening to expose their affair by sending Cois photographs of his wife and her ex-husband, and Cois' pending transfer was hanging over their heads. It would be only a matter of time before they were found out. Frans believed Sonjia and the children's lives were in danger and it was at this stage that they began contemplating getting rid of Cois.

Frans decided they should fake a burglary in which Cois would be shot. On the night of 3 July 1971, Sonjia, Cois and the children went to the drive-in cinema. She knew that during their absence Frans would break into their home, steal Cois' service revolver and wait for the couple to return home. Frans had told Sonjia to make sure they arrived home late, but she became nervous. She told Cois she was feeling ill and insisted they should go home. When the couple arrived home

Frans had already broken in and found the firearm, but had fled because they returned early.

Cois was convinced that it was a real burglary. A few days later Sonjia told Cois that a black man had arrived at their home and told her that he had stolen Cois' firearm and that he was going to kill him. Cois took his wife's statement. It is not unknown for criminals to threaten detectives, and Cois believed her. Unbeknown to him, the stage had been set for his murder.

Frans later admitted that he had made at least seven attempts to kill Cois. The plan was always that Sonjia would leave the lounge window open for him to enter the house, but the plan always failed because the window was never open.

On the night of 3 August 1971, Frans phoned Sonjia just before she and Cois went to bed. He asked whether the window was open and she confirmed that it was. As a matter of fact, Cois had opened it himself. At about two thirty on the morning of 4 August, Sonjia heard a noise as she lay next to her sleeping husband. She saw Frans creeping across the carpet towards the bed. He was wearing gloves. He silently leaned over her and fired two shots into the sleeping Cois' head and then disappeared. Sonjia waited ten minutes for Frans to escape, then got out of bed, shouted to her neighbours through the window and ran outside with her children.

Soon the scene was crowded with neighbours, family members and the police. Investigating officer Steve Oelofse arrived at half past four that morning. He was shocked that his close colleague and friend of five years had been shot in his bed right next to his wife. He remembered the burglary and the man who had threatened to shoot Cois, but his instinct as a detective warned him that something was not quite right. He began questioning Sonjia about the details of the murder. It bothered him that she had waited ten minutes before sounding the alarm. He took her to the police station for questioning. She insisted that her husband had been shot by a black man.

When Frans phoned Sonjia later that morning, she told him the police were harassing her. Frans phoned the police and complained about their treatment of Sonjia. The detectives smelled a rat. When Frans arrived at his Sunnyside flat at half past nine that night, the police were waiting for him. They took him to the police station where he made a statement. He admitted to being a friend of Sonjia's but told them that he was not involved in the murder. In his statement he mentioned a Mr Breedt, who had seen him and Sonjia together. Breedt was contacted and he told the police that Frans and Sonjia were lovers. Frans said he was visiting his family in Krugersdorp on the night of the murder and his sister and brother-in-law confirmed his alibi.

While Frans and Sonjia were in custody, the detectives continued their investigation. Mr Ehlers, a minister of religion, told them he had visited the Swanepoel couple on the night of the murder. Cois told him that someone was trying to break up his marriage. Mr Ehlers suspected it might have been Sonjia's first husband. The neighbours were unaware of the relationship between Frans and Sonjia. However, on 5 August a colleague of Frans, Adam du Plooy, informed the police that Frans had told him that he wanted to get rid of his lover's husband.

At about four o'clock on the afternoon of 5 August, Brigadier Stoffel Buys took over the interrogation of Frans Vontsteen. He played one of the oldest tricks in the book, telling Frans that Sonjia had confessed. Frans broke down and said he was prepared to take the blame for everything. 'It was I who shot him,' he confessed.

Both Sonjia and Frans were making confessions at the same time, independently of each other. Later Frans took the detectives to an empty plot in Sunnyside and pointed out where he had buried the firearm. It also transpired that he had taken his sister's vehicle that evening, leaving his own behind on the farm as an alibi. His brother-in-law acknowledged that he had only seen Frans on the farm the morning after the murder and that he had assumed he had spent the night there. Frans had made sure that his daughters spent the night with neighbours.

On 8 August, Frans and Sonjia somehow found themselves together in a cell and Frans asked Sonjia to change their story. He said she should tell the police that a black man had killed her husband, that she was frightened and phoned Frans. He came to her house and removed the firearm. Frans was actually planning to tell the police that Sonjia had shot her husband and that he had hidden the firearm to protect her. She refused to fall for this new story. She had her own ace up her sleeve.

As happens in most cases of this kind, once they find themselves fighting for their lives in court, lovers who previously swore undying love turn upon each other. Sonjia said she had never wanted to divorce Cois. Frans threatened to tell Cois that he was the father of their youngest daughter, and she feared Cois would then kill her and the children. She alleged that Cois had abused her on several occasions; she had reason to fear for her life. It was only because of this that she agreed to the plan to kill him.

Frans sent a message to Sonjia in the cells through an orderly. He said he loved her very much, but she should not be surprised if he told the court that she was a slut who had seduced him, because he was fighting for his life. The orderly did not relay the message to Sonjia, but told the prosecutor instead.

In the mean time, Sonjia's domestic worker informed the court that Sonjia had once told her that Frans was going to kill Cois. The domestic worker informed a friend who was a police constable, but he did nothing about it. Frans had confronted her one day, telling her that he would never kill Cois. Shortly after she returned from leave, she was fired.

Frans did not make a good impression on the court. He had a habit of using elaborate words in order to avoid giving straight answers. He testified that Sonjia had murdered Cois and that he had only removed the firearm.

On 25 October 1971, Mr Justice Victor Hiemstra sentenced Sonjia to fifteen years' imprisonment and Frans Vontsteen to death. On 4 October 1972 Frans was hanged.

Stories circulated that Sonjia had told fellow inmates in prison, and even while she was an awaiting trial prisoner, that she had pulled the trigger. But she later denied this.

Sonjia completed eight years of her sentence. She was released on parole in 1979. She went back to Pretoria and found work at a pharmacy. She was reunited with her two older children, but had no contact with the last daughter. On her release Sonjia told the world through several magazine articles that she was still in love with Cois. Two years later a picture of her sitting beside Cois' grave was featured in a magazine. She had never loved Frans, she said, and she would never love anyone other than Cois. She had been happily married to him.

At the age of forty-eight, Sonjia Swanepoel married again. She had met the man during her fourth year in prison, but he was married at the time. She waited four years for him in prison and another nine years after her release. After her marriage she once again said that Cois had abused her.

Comment

The case study of Sonjia Swanepoel illustrates the tragic consequences of a love triangle. Sonjia was extremely fickle in her relationships. She was already pregnant with Cois' child when she divorced her first husband. While she was having an affair with Frans and carrying his child, she still walked around the neighbourhood hand in hand with Cois. The neighbours never suspected this seemingly happy couple had marital problems. In fact, they said that although Sonjia complained of Cois' pathological jealousy, she was the one who always commented on the attention she received from other men.

Cois was described by his friends and colleagues as a peace-loving man who adored his family. He never lost his temper. While he was defending his country on the Angolan border, Sonjia was spending holidays with her lover and their children. She professed her love for Frans and was willing to assist in the murder of her husband to have him.

Frans' father, Henri Vontsteen, told newspapers that Sonjia had seduced Frans when he was vulnerable. He spent all his money on her. He had never believed that Frans was the father of her youngest daughter. He also disapproved of the 'seductive clothing' Sonjia wore when she posed for pictures after her release from prison. After her release, she told the world she had never loved Frans, but had always loved Cois. When she said this she was already secretly in love with husband number three, whom she married years later.

An interesting aspect of this case is that initially neither Frans nor Sonjia was connected with any evidence that linked them to the murder. Had Frans not confessed, he might have got away with it. It was only after the confession that he pointed out where he had hidden the firearm. Even if Sonjia had implicated him in her statement, there was no evidence that would tie him to the murder. She would have been charged with murder, for her confession indicated her guilt, but it would not have been used against Frans for there was no substantiating evidence against him. When Frans confessed he said he would 'take the blame upon himself' and reassured Sonjia she had nothing to fear. Was he protecting the woman he loved? If so, he paid the highest price for doing so.

Case study: Sandra Smith, 1986

Sandra and her husband Phillip, a fisherman, lived with her parents in Mitchell's Plain in Cape Town. They had two children and Sandra was described by all as a loving mother and a kind-hearted woman. Her life changed for the worse in October 1983 when she made the fatal mistake of sending a letter to local criminal and member of the Hard Livings gang, Yassiem Harris.

Everyone knew of Yassiem's reputation. At the age of thirteen he was a juvenile criminal. At fifteen, he robbed his employer of ten thousand rand in cash and twenty-six thousand rand in cheques. Since he was a juvenile, Yassiem was sentenced to corporal punishment, which was no deterrent to him. Shortly after his seventeenth birthday in October 1983, he was surprised to receive the letter from Sandra, inviting him to meet her in the park.

Perhaps Sandra was frustrated by the protected life she lived with her parents. At the age of twenty, with her husband away at sea and the burden of bringing up two young children, she wanted a little adventure and thought she would find it with the local bad boy. Just how bad he was, she did not realise at that time.

When she met Yassiem in the park she invited him to climb through her bedroom window that night. It was an invitation he could not resist. Sandra was one of the 'good girls' and he was flattered that she should be interested in him.

Sandra's parents knew nothing of the nightly visits their daughter was receiving from the criminal. As reward for his services, Sandra gave Yassiem the money her husband diligently sent home every month. After six months, Phillip returned from sea and could not understand why his beautiful wife was not over-enthusiastic about seeing him. The neighbours soon told him about Yassiem's visits to his wife. Phillip immediately rounded up his friends and they gave Yassiem a good hiding.

Scarcely had Phillip left for sea again, when Yassiem was once more climbing through Sandra's window. She welcomed him with open arms. After leaving just before sunrise, Yassiem would spend the rest of the morning hanging around the grounds of the high school.

One day he spotted a beautiful young scholar, Jermaine Abrahams, and he followed her home. He struck up a friendship with her and when Sandra's husband returned home, Yassiem spent most of his time with her. This arrangement continued for two and a half years.

In 1986 Sandra fell pregnant and told Phillip that the child was his. He went off to sea again, believing that the relationship between Sandra and Yassiem was over.

In March 1986 a terrible storm forced the fishing boats to anchor in Table Bay. Phillip caught the first train home, planning to surprise Sandra. To his dismay, he found her in bed with Yassiem, who promptly made a hasty exit through the window. Sandra decided the best course of action would be to follow Yassiem.

Phillip moved the children to his parents' care and left a message for Sandra that the marriage was over. She moved in with her lover who soon began involving her in his criminal activities.

On 31 August Yassiem saw Jermaine walking in the street. He went home and persuaded Sandra that they should break into Jermaine's home after her parents had left for work; he knew they kept cash in the house. At seven thirty on the morning of 1 September 1986, Yassiem knocked on Jermaine's front door. She was pleased to see him and invited him in, not expecting Sandra to slip in the door as well.

Sixteen-year-old Jermaine and twenty-something Sandra immediately realised they were adversaries. Sandra was not very happy when Yassiem and Jermaine disappeared into the bedroom and she was told to wait in the lounge. She followed them into the bedroom where she found Yassiem explaining to Jermaine that they were going to tie her up and then rob the house. Jermaine realised she did not have much option. While Yassiem was tying her up, there was a knock at the front door. Jermaine called out for help. Sandra ran to the kitchen, grabbed a dishcloth and began strangling Jermaine to keep her quiet. She had also brought a knife from the kitchen. 'Stab her,' she told Yassiem, and he did. The knocking at the door ceased.

Jermaine managed to free herself and stumbled out of the room. She fell down in the passage. Yassiem picked her up, carried her to the bed and asked the dying girl where her mother's jewellery was. Sandra began searching the cupboard that Jermaine pointed out. When she turned around, she noticed that Yassiem had covered Jermaine with a blanket. She lifted the blanket and saw that he had cut her throat.

Two weeks later the police arrested Sandra for the theft of a video machine. While in custody, she confessed to the murder of Jermaine Abrahams and implicated Yassiem Harris. Yassiem managed to evade the police for five days, but was eventually arrested.

Sandra was denied bail and both she and Yassiem were sent to Valkenburg Psychiatric Hospital for observation. Yassiem was diagnosed as a psychopath, but the psychiatrists could find no explanation for Sandra's behaviour and declared her mentally fit to stand trial.

On 22 December 1986, Mr Justice Munnik found them both guilty of murder. Yassiem was sentenced to ten years for robbery with aggravating circumstances and Sandra to seven years on the same charge. Both were sentenced to death for murder. Sandra Smith and Yassiem Harris were hanged at Pretoria Central Prison on 2 June 1989.

Comment
During the trial it became evident that Sandra was

jealous of Jermaine's relationship with Yassiem and this had led her to want Jermaine dead. The woman who was described as a kind and loving mother participated in the violent murder of a teenager because she believed herself in love with a ruthless psychopathic criminal.

Case study: Louisa Chatburn, 1992

Louisa Griffith was an only child who grew up in the Northern Cape town of Kimberley. When she was four months old, her mother deserted the family. Her father allegedly neglected her to such an extent that she was placed in the care of her grandparents. Shortly after completing school, she married Fanie du Toit and the couple had two daughters. The marriage lasted twelve years. On 30 July 1989 Fanie du Toit committed suicide with a firearm belonging to Louisa. Four months after his death, Louisa married Graham Chatburn, a man who had fathered five children in two previous marriages. Graham was seventeen and a half years older than Louisa.

On 18 February 1992, a council employee made the gruesome discovery of a body in the Black River in Cape Town. A crossbow bolt had penetrated the skull of the victim. Initially the body could not be identified because it had been in the river for a few days and was badly decomposed. Then forensic experts stripped the skin of the right hand, fitted it like a glove over the hand of an assistant and produced the fingerprints that identified the victim as forty-nine-year-old Victor Graham Chatburn of Hoff Street, Kraaifontein. The investigating officer, Warrant Officer Jeff Benzien ruled out robbery as a motive since the victim was wearing his gold wedding band and watch when he was found. He was clad only in his underpants and had been rolled up in a plastic sheet.

Warrant Officer Benzien called at the victim's home where his wife Louisa told him that her husband had gone for a walk at six o'clock on the morning of 16 February. When he had not returned later that day, she had reported him as a missing person. He was fully clothed, she said. Warrant Officer Benzien's instincts told him to make further enquiries.

The following week Louisa Chatburn was arrested for the murder of her husband and made a confession to a magistrate. She claimed that her husband had asked her to buy him the crossbow, which was stored in the attic. At five o'clock on the morning of his death, she found her husband in the kitchen, clutching the crossbow. There was a strange look in his eyes. She told him it was not a toy and tried to get it away from him. They struggled and she accidentally touched the trigger and the bolt penetrated Graham's skull. Panicking, she undressed him and rolled him in a blanket. She dragged the body to her car, heaved him inside and placed the crossbow on the back seat. She told her oldest daughter that she was going to look for her husband and drove to the Black River. She rolled her husband into the river and covered him with a plastic sheet. She dumped the crossbow in the veld in Kraaifontein. She tried to wash the blood from her husband's clothing and then placed it in a dustbin. She claimed that his death was a terrible accident.

Warrant Officer Benzien called in forensic experts to search for blood in the kitchen, but they found blood only in the couple's bed. Benzien also found a portfolio of Graham's insurance policies on the back seat of the car.

The trial commenced before Mr Justice Deputy President Hannes Fagan in October 1992. Louisa's advocate, Anton Veldhuizen, claimed that her confession had been made under duress and that Louisa had made another statement in which she claimed she had killed her husband because of his unacceptable sexual demands.

During the trial, where the crossbow and the penetrated skull of the victim were on continuous display, the state succeeded in proving that Louisa was unable to load the crossbow, did not have the strength to heave her husband's body into the car and could not point out the exact spot where the body had been found. It seemed obvious that she had had help.

State advocate Kevin Rossouw noted that the most obvious candidate was Gerhard Erasmus, an evangelist who supported her during the trial. Both Louisa and Gerhard – a married man – vehemently denied that they had even known each other before the murder, let alone had an affair. Gerhard also owned crossbows.

Elizabeth Cooper, a friend of Gerhard's, testified that she had overheard a conversation between Louisa and Gerhard during which Gerhard's role in the murder was discussed. She said Gerhard was supposed to have waited in the bathroom while Louisa killed her husband.

On 25 November 1992, Mr Justice Deputy President Fagan sentenced Louisa to twenty-five years' imprisonment for the murder of Victor Graham Chatburn. He found that Louisa had shot her husband in their bed and that she most probably had been assisted by Gerhard Erasmus in dumping the body in the river. The court established beyond reasonable doubt that the murder had been planned at least a few days in advance. The judge said there was a possible love motive for the killing and rejected

Louisa's claim that she was continually abused by her husband. There was not enough evidence to charge Gerhard Erasmus as an accomplice because his wife provided an alibi for his movements on the morning of the murder.

Two months after Louisa's conviction, Gerhard Erasmus agreed to meet a journalist for coffee. He was accompanied by a young girl. During this interview, Gerhard alleged that Victor Graham Chatburn had been a monster who had sexually molested a teenage girl and that this was the reason why Louisa had killed him. He alleged that Chatburn's own family was aware of these circumstances and that they had suspected the teenager of assisting Louisa in the murder. Gerhard vowed to do everything in his power to assist Louisa and ensure that the truth was told.

Comment

Had the judge found that Louisa had killed her husband because he abused her, this case study would have been discussed in the chapter on *Battered Women*; had it been found that a teenager had been involved in the murder, it would have been discussed in the chapter *Children who Kill*. But Mr Justice Fagan found that there was a possible love motive, and therefore this case finds its place in this chapter on *Love Triangles*. Only Louisa Chatburn herself would know where her case study should be placed. In her letters to Gerhard from prison she continually referred to her daughter's feelings and the fact that she never wanted to let her children down.

A particularly horrifying aspect of this murder is that it was established that Victor Graham Chatburn was still alive when he was dumped in the river.

Case study: Cecile Laetitia van Loggerenberg, 1994

At about twenty minutes past seven on the morning of 26 August 1994, traffic official J Muller noticed a burnt-out vehicle fifty kilometres north of Pretoria on the Moloto Road. On investigation he found a burnt body in the boot of the car. He called the Pretoria Murder and Robbery Unit and Warrant Officer Eddie Olivier took charge of the case. The body was transported to the morgue. Identifying the victim was Warrant Officer Olivier's first concern.

A few days later family members identified twenty-nine-year-old Andries van Loggerenberg as the victim. Andries' body was badly burnt and the family identified him by his ring and watch, which had stopped at 04:25. It was established that Andries' skull had been bashed with a blunt object and that he did not die in his car.

Warrant Officer Olivier visited Andries' home in Wonderboom South and called in the forensic unit to assist him with evidence he found there. At a quarter to one on 29 August 1994, he arrested twenty-seven-year-old Laetitia van Loggerenberg and her thirty-year-old lover Deon Pistorius on a charge of murder.

A friend of Deon's, Jan Bothma, told Warrant Officer Olivier that he had information for him and that he was prepared to testify, provided he could turn state witness. Olivier listened with interest. On the night of 25 August 1994, Jan and Deon went to the home of Laetitia and Andries. Jan was aware that Deon and Laetitia were having an affair, and he also knew she was eight months' pregnant with Deon's child. Deon had often talked about ways of getting rid of Andries, such as shooting him on the highway, but Jan never took him seriously.

174

But on this occasion Jan realised when they arrived that the couple was intent on killing Andries. Laetitia had earlier given her husband sleeping pills in a cup of tea, but he refused to drink it, saying that it tasted funny. She made him a second cup, which he drank and then passed out. Deon and Laetitia disappeared into one of the bedrooms to have sex. When they returned Deon carried the sleeping Andries outside. The plan was to place him in his car, connect a pipe to the exhaust and fake a suicide. Their plan went horribly wrong when Andries came to and put up a fight on the lawn. Deon seized a baseball bat and hit Andries on the head. With the third blow the bat broke, but Deon none the less continued to hit him. He told Jan to fetch a towel, which he wrapped around Andries' head, to prevent blood from spilling on the grass. Deon and Jan then heaved the body in Andries' Opel Astra. They stopped to buy petrol on the way to the Moloto road, where they set the car on fire. Deon promised Jan his bakkie as a reward for his assistance.

Mr Justice J Els presided over the trial in 1997. Although they initially pleaded not guilty, Laetitia and Deon changed their pleas to guilty after Jan had testified. Deon told the judge that he had met Laetitia when he was assisting her with her insurance policies. He became concerned about her safety when she told him that Andries abused her. Andries, a labour relations consultant at the City Council, allegedly drank a bottle of whisky a day, after which he would attack his wife. Laetitia was once admitted to hospital with a cracked breast bone. Deon was also concerned that Andries was neglecting his child, of whom Deon was very fond.

Laetitia testified that she had once given her

husband's firearm to Deon for safe keeping because she was afraid that Andries would kill her and the child. She said Andries had a terminal illness and had threatened to kill her and their child.

In April 1997 Mr Justice Els rejected Laetitia's claims of physical and emotional abuse. He also rejected Deon's claim that he had killed Andries because he was concerned about the lives of Laetitia, her child and his own unborn child. He found their motive was to get rid of Andries, who stood in the way of their relationship. Both of them knew they would benefit financially by his death and not by a divorce. He sentenced them each to twenty-five years' imprisonment.

Comment

While awaiting trial, Laetitia was released on her own recognisance and Deon was out on bail. He joined Laetitia in the house where the murder had taken place and she gave birth to their son. For a few months they could live the illusion of a happy couple – an illusion they had killed for.

Case study: Mariette Bosch, 1996

Mariette and Justin Bosch became friendly with Tienie and Ria Wolmarans in Botswana in 1990. They were all South Africans who had settled in the neighbouring country. Both couples had three children each.

In 1993 Tienie and Mariette began an affair. Ria had a domineering nature and would often berate her husband for his lack of financial insight. As financial manager of Kwena Rocla, she was in fact the breadwinner. Tienie, a construction worker, sought solace in the arms of the more docile and subservient

Mariette. Justin Bosch was a forceful, hard-working man who invested his time in earning a decent living for his family, rather than attending to his wife's more sensitive needs. It was easy to understand why Mariette submitted to Tienie's romantic seduction.

The wheels that eventually led to tragedy were set in motion when Justin died in a car accident in 1995. Mariette inherited his estate. Although she was now a relatively rich widow, she suddenly found herself in a position where she had to fend for herself. She had always been a dutiful housewife, but only that, and she was ill equipped to run her own financial affairs. The more capable and forceful Justin had always handled this aspect of their marriage. The Wolmarans couple took the lonely and almost helpless Mariette under their wing. Ria, unaware of the relationship that already existed between them, encouraged Tienie to assist Mariette in taking care of maintenance work that was required at her house. Ria and Mariette had become best friends over the years. They lived within walking distance of each other in a rather upmarket suburb of Gaborone.

In 1996 Ria had consulted a lawyer about her intention to divorce Tienie. She told her sisters that Tienie had once attempted to suffocate her, but her life was saved when her daughter walked in. On her frequent visits to Mariette she would complain about her husband. Outwardly Mariette sympathised with Ria, but inwardly she seethed because Ria was criticising the man she secretly adored.

On the evening of 24 June 1996, Hennie Coetzee, manager at Ria's employer Kwena Rocla, visited Mariette. He took some wine with him. The following day Mariette left for South Africa to visit Dennis Weber, a friend of her late husband Justin, in Pietersburg (now

Polokwane). She asked Dennis to give her Justin's firearm, which he had in safe keeping. She also visited Justin's brother Mike and his wife Christa and asked Mike to show her how to use the firearm. She returned to Botswana on 26 June, illegally smuggling the firearm over the border.

Tienie, who was working on a construction site in Maun, six hours' drive from Gaborone, alleged that on the morning of 26 June Ria phoned to tell him that she had uncovered evidence that Hennie Coetzee had misappropriated funds at Kwena Rocla. The auditors were to arrive at the company the next morning to investigate.

On the night of 26 June Mariette gave her oldest daughter and her boyfriend some money and asked them to take Ria's daughter out to a restaurant. This was unusual, for the two young women were not close friends. But Mariette's daughter complied with her mother's request. This meant Ria was alone at home, because Tienie was still in Maun. Mariette was at home with her mother and her youngest teenage daughter.

At about a quarter to nine that night Ria's neighbour, Janet Squire, heard two shots. She glanced out of the window, but could see nothing amiss at the Wolmarans home and so she ignored the incident.

When Ria's daughter returned home at about eleven o'clock that night, she found her mother's body in the kitchen. The contents of a tea tray lay scattered on the floor. She immediately phoned the neighbours, including Mariette, to come and assist her. The police arrived at the scene shortly afterwards.

Everyone was shocked and puzzled by the seemingly motiveless murder. Tienie alleged that he was driving from Maun to Gaborone that night, yet his daughter fetched him at the airport the following morning. His daughter moved in with Mariette, refusing to stay in the house where her mother had been murdered.

Ria's funeral was held in South Africa. Tienie and Mariette drove there together, and stayed with Ria's mother. The fact that Mariette accompanied Tienie to the funeral aroused no suspicion, for Mariette and Ria were best friends. Ria's mother had even prepared a bedroom for Mariette and her youngest daughter. The morning after their arrival, Ria's mother was shocked to find her son-in-law, the supposedly grieving widower, in bed with Mariette. They were consoling each other, he explained.

Upon their return to Botswana, Tienie made a statement to the police, framing Hennie Coetzee for the murder of his wife. Hennie happened to have the same calibre firearm that was used in the murder. Tienie alleged that Hennie had killed Ria to stop her from revealing incriminating documents to the auditors at Kwena Rocla on 27 June. The police were not interested in Hennie as a suspect. He had an alibi. He had attended a party on the night of the murder. Tienie then personally contacted members of the press and told them about his suspicions. Nosy people in the Gaborone community gossiped about Hennie, allegedly a man prone to violent outbursts. But suspicions died down when the auditors could not find any evidence that Hennie was guilty of fraud.

In the mean time the leases on both the Wolmarans and Bosch houses had expired and Tienie and Mariette decided to rent a house together. He was still living in Maun, and alleged that he slept in his daughter's room on weekends when he visited Gaborone. Mariette's teenage daughter was also living with them. Both Tienie and Mariette vehemently denied that a romantic relationship had existed between them before Ria's death. They said that it had only started months later, when Mariette and the children visited Tienie in Maun.

In September 1996, Tienie went with Mariette to visit Justin's brother Mike and his wife Christa in South Africa. She gave Justin's firearm to Mike and asked him not to tell anyone that she had had it. She also went shopping for her wedding dress. Mike and Christa realised that Justin's firearm was the same calibre as that used in the murder and they alerted the South African Police Service, who handed the weapon over to the Botswana Police.

Suddenly the investigation took a new turn. In October 1996, Mariette was arrested for illegally smuggling a firearm into Botswana. Tienie visited her in the cells and instructed her not to speak to anyone. He was promptly arrested for interfering with the course of justice, but was released the following day. Mariette kept her silence, claiming she was too confused to speak.

Tienie arranged for a hypnotist and a psychic from South Africa to visit her. Under hypnosis Mariette remembered that Hennie had drugged and hypnotised her two nights before the murder. It was under his 'magnetic influence' that she had gone to South Africa, fetched the firearm, returned to Botswana and left the firearm on Hennie's desk the morning before the murder because Hennie had said that he wanted to buy it. The police did not believe her. Why would Hennie want to buy an illegal firearm of the same calibre as one he already owned? He was a hunter and well aware of the stringent penalties for owning an illegal firearm.

Statements about Mariette and Tienie's affair had already been taken. Mariette's domestic worker,

Annaki Ntwayagae, said in her statement that Mariette had left home on the night of the murder. She said she was going to a parents' function at her daughter's school, but she returned home at about seven o'clock because she had got the date wrong. The police were convinced Mariette had the means, motive and opportunity to commit the murder. She was promptly charged and kept in custody.

This thwarted the marriage plans. Eventually, when Mariette was released on bail, she and Tienie were married in September 1997. Tienie married his mistress while she was awaiting trial for the murder of his wife. He thus became the stepfather of Mariette's children. Mariette made him the legal custodian of her teenage daughter, and the daughter took the surname Wolmarans.

Mariette received permission from the Botswana government to go to South Africa to attend the marriage of Tienie's eldest daughter. While in South Africa, lawyers advised her to break bail and remain in the country for South Africa would not extradite one of its citizens to a country where she could be facing the death penalty. But Tienie convinced Mariette that she should return to Botswana, assuring her that she would be found not guilty. Mariette was taken into custody again when she returned to Botswana.

By now, the Gaborone community was rife with rumours about an affair between Tienie and his teenage stepdaughter. Mariette, in prison, was not aware of these rumours.

Mr Justice Aboagye presided at the trial. Annaki Ntwayagae gave evidence that Tienie had threatened to kill her if she testified. She died mysteriously some time after the trial. Dr Louise Olivier, prominent South African forensic psychologist, testified that

Mariette had a low level of intelligence, was easily influenced and did not have the capacity to orchestrate or commit a murder. She said Mariette had suffered from dissociative fugue, a disorder brought on by severe stress. A person suffering from this disorder takes on a totally new identity for a period. They wander off from their current abode to live elsewhere. When they eventually recover, they cannot remember their actions during the fugue. Dr Olivier testified that Mariette had developed this disorder because she felt threatened by Hennie Coetzee. Mr Justice Aboagye rejected her testimony. When Mariette went to South Africa to fetch the firearm she did not take on another identity, she visited her in-laws and none of them noticed that there was anything wrong with her. She was therefore fully aware of her actions.

Ballistic evidence had established that the shots that killed Ria were fired from Justin's firearm.

To many who attended the trial it seemed clear that Mariette's first defence lawyer had taken instruction from Tienie and not from Mariette. She often gave answers that were clearly different from what he expected.

Mariette Bosch, a South African woman, was sentenced to death for the murder of Ria Wolmarans. The Botswana Centre for Human Rights immediately took up her case. Her first defence lawyer resigned from the case and the second defence lawyer, Mr Kgafela, was appointed to undertake her appeal for clemency. But before he could take any action, Mariette was executed on 31 March 2002.

The world was shocked by her execution because no one had been informed beforehand that it was to take place. Tienie and her children only received word of it the morning after. The Botswana government said that the court had found Mariette guilty based upon the evidence before it and they had the right to execute her.

Tienie flew into an indignant rage and during a press conference the morning after the execution, he vowed that he would prove Mariette's innocence. 'I know who really committed that murder and I will not rest until the world knows Mariette was innocently hanged,' he said.

Comment

The Botswana government was acting within its rights when it executed Mariette Bosch, but the question has to be asked: was *all* the evidence presented to the court?

Dr Louise Olivier was correct when she found that Mariette did not have the intelligence nor the capacity to orchestrate and execute a murder. Was Mariette acting under the influence of someone else?

No one contested or even checked on Tienie's alibi for the night of the murder, of which there are several versions. He alleged he was driving the six-hour route from Maun to Gaborone. He had left late because he had to pay his labourers. His foreman could testify to this. Yet this man was never asked to make a statement. Annaki Ntwayagae had testified that Tienie had threatened her; might he have threatened the foreman as well? If Tienie had driven through the night, how did it happen that his daughter fetched him from the airport on the morning after the murder? There were unconfirmed reports that Tienie had flown into Gaborone on the night of the murder on a flight of Kalahari Air. Later he said he was in Francis Town. No one knows if Tienie Wolmarans was in Gaborone on the night of the murder because no one checked.

Ria was shot while carrying a tea tray from the lounge to the kitchen. Two shots penetrated her body, fired from two different directions. Some of those who attended the crime scene alleged that there were three broken cups on the floor. Who would the third cup have been for?

Members of Mariette's family stated that while she was in custody she was made an offer to turn state witness. If she had, she would have received only a two hundred pula fine. When they asked her why she had not accepted the offer, she had answered: 'I can't, he's too good to me.'

After sentencing, Mariette's defence lawyer, Mr Kgafela, approached Tienie and asked him to make a statement to the effect that he had influenced Mariette to commit the murder. This would at least have saved her life. Tienie confirmed that this request was made to him.

Tienie married Mariette before the trial commenced, knowing that a wife cannot testify against her husband. So even if she had made a statement implicating Tienie in the murder, it would have been inadmissible.

Did Mariette Bosch have the motive to kill Ria? She knew Ria was planning to divorce Tienie. She could have waited for the divorce and then married her lover. No, she had no motive to murder. Tienie denied the divorce proceedings, but his daughter allegedly told her aunts, Ria's sisters, that he had instructed her to destroy the summons after the murder.

Who gained from Ria's death? She was effectively removed from Tienie's life and he inherited money from her estate. Were the rumours about an affair between Tienie and his minor stepdaughter true? After Mariette's execution Tienie took his stepdaughter on holiday in South Africa. They were spotted walking hand in hand on a beach. Mariette's execution also removed *her* from his life. Did he inherit what was left of Justin's estate from Mariette? Why did he persuade her to return to Botswana knowing that she could receive the death sentence? Why did he act against her lawyer's advice during the trial? Why did he not admit to influencing her, knowing that there was probably not enough evidence to connect him to the murder and that, as his wife, she could not testify against him? At the least, his statement could have saved her life. Does Tienie Wolmarans know who killed Ria?

Tienie Wolmarans is a free man. In 2002 he was living in remote Ghanzi, where his stepdaughter frequently visited him during school holidays. Mariette Bosch lies buried within the Gaborone prison yard. Tienie has not yet visited her grave.

6

Murder for Hire

It would be interesting to establish whether there is a correlation between women who hire hitmen to kill, and their chances of financial gain from the death of their victims. The hypothesis would be that women who hire hitmen are those who are motivated mainly by greed. Very rarely do they pay the hitmen before the job is done; in most cases they promise to pay them with the money they stand to inherit.

The supposition that some women would kill for money to gratify their basic need for security is discussed under the chapter *Female Serial Killers*.

Some of the case studies presented in this chapter depict women who were allegedly abused by their husbands. The reason why they are dealt with in this chapter and not in the chapter on *Battered Women*, is because during their trials the judges found their motives to have been greed, and not abuse. One may or may not agree, but that is what the law found.

An interesting phenomenon about women who kill their husbands for money is that they cannot resist a slight celebration shortly after the murder. An experienced detective or vigilant family member or friend might detect this. It is reason for suspicion. They may have their hair done, buy a new dress, go out for dinner. The celebration is small and mostly symbolic, but it signifies victory and new-found freedom. Search carefully among their faked, but often convincing manifestations of grief, and one will find the little telltale celebration. No truly bereaved widow would be interested in having her hair done or buying a new dress for a funeral. Her pain would be too great and overwhelming.

How can one understand the mentality of hired killers who are prepared to risk life imprisonment for the promise of payment for murder? What is the price of a life? The financial reward for murder often has little real monetary value. Although hitmen are mostly motivated by greed, in many cases they are also manipulated by the woman's sexual allure and 'helplessness'. Are they really so gullible? Surely this is taking chivalry too far?

These questions may seem harsh and extreme, but is it not time society reflected upon them? Lessons need to be learned about the relationship between greed and the value of a life. In my view, there is no relationship, for one cannot give life a price in monetary terms.

*

Case study: Dorothea Kraft, 1918

In September 1914 the farm Treurfontein in the Lichtenburg district in what is now the North West province, was a hive of activity. It was the place where several disgruntled burghers gathered to protest against General Louis Botha's decision to invade the German colony of South West Africa in an attempt to assist Great Britain in its First World War effort. General Koos de la Rey, on his way to address his troops at the farm, was accidentally shot and killed in a roadblock when the vehicle in which he was travelling was mistaken for one used by the notorious criminal Foster gang. This tragedy was a premonition of another to follow.

The farm belonged to the widow Dorothea Kraft who, with of her daughter Polly, struggled to eke out an existence on the barren land. Drought had taken its toll and labourers were reluctant to take orders from women.

It seemed as if providence had taken a hand when Louis Tumpowski, a Jewish immigrant from America who sought to make his fortune selling various wares to gold prospectors in South Africa, dismounted from his horse on Dorothea's farm. He was on one of his rounds to purchase provisions for his shops in town. Dorothea had little to sell. She bemoaned her fate to the attentive Louis and asked him to find her a manager to run the farm. Two months later he returned to the farm with an offer which she found most attractive. He would rent the farm for twenty-five pounds a year and she and Polly could remain on the land. Dorothea was delighted. She signed the contract without reading the fine print. Over the next year their situation improved considerably. Louis not only managed the farm, but he also kept Dorothea's bed warm at night.

Then Dorothea decided it would suit her better to sell the farm, for the price of land had increased dramatically with the increase in the local population. She would make a large enough profit to provide comfortably for herself and Polly. And it was by then clear to her that Louis had no plans to make an honest woman of her.

But Louis had no intention of letting the farm go, nor the widow's favours, and referred her to the contract, which stipulated that he was entitled to buy the farm for a meagre three pounds and five shillings per morgen, which was less than half the value of the farm. Dorothea was incensed at being cheated, but even more angry with herself for not having read the contract properly. She consulted a lawyer who confirmed that there was nothing she could do. She returned to the farm intending to use her feminine wiles to convince Louis to marry her, but he saw no reason to do so and refused.

Dorothea changed tactics and visited a witchdoctor (as they were then referred to) named Jim Bird on the neighbouring farm. Jim sold her a love potion, but Louis was immune to love potions. The only effect it had on him was to cause an upset stomach for a few days. He accused Dorothea of trying to poison him and from then on would not accept even so much as a cup of tea from her.

Dorothea paid Jim a second visit. He now required a lock of Louis' hair. The hair was mixed with magic potions and placed in a matchbox. Dorothea had to bury this under Louis' door and Jim assured her he would soon die of an illness. But once again, Jim's potions had no effect on the intended victim.

Early in 1918, Armanus Lambertus Swartz, an army deserter, arrived at Treurfontein. Maans Swartz, as he was known, was a man with no prospects and Dorothea recognised a good opportunity. He soon became Polly's suitor, but rumour had it that he also slept with Dorothea. Maans reasoned that if he married Polly and helped Dorothea get rid of Louis, he would eventually become the owner of Treurfontein. He suggested to Dorothea that it would be much more practical just to kill Louis rather than rely on magic potions. Jim Bird agreed to commit the murder for one hundred pounds. It is likely that his ego and reputation as a witchdoctor had been damaged by the useless potions he had provided for Dorothea and he needed to redeem himself.

On the night of 2 February 1918 a heavy thunderstorm broke over the farm. Dorothea, Maans, Jim and three labourers gathered in the old farmhouse. Polly had taken refuge in her bedroom.

As the thunder crashed around them, Maans opened Louis' bedroom door. Jim entered and attacked him with a knobkerrie. Maans, fearing that Louis might still be alive, strangled him and then cut his throat for good measure. Dorothea held Louis' hands while Maans murdered him. Jim fled the scene, but Dorothea and the three labourers carried the body outside and buried it beneath a rubbish dump, a fitting grave for the greedy Jew, she thought. While they were burying the corpse in the backyard, in the pelting rain, there was a knock on the front door. A couple with a sick child had turned on to the road to the farmhouse to seek help. No one answered the front door and the lights were suddenly turned off. They turned around and left, but not before they heard the sounds of digging coming from the back of the house.

By the time the storm had cleared the next morning, all traces of the murder were gone. Polly left for Johannesburg and Dorothea complained to the neighbours that Louis had abandoned her. She even went to stay with them because she said she was afraid of living alone on the farm. One of the neighbours, Michael Denysschen, and his cousin Johanna did not believe Dorothea, especially since mail was still arriving for Louis. Johanna took it upon herself to write to Louis' sister, Mrs Saltman in the then Rhodesia and to his agent in Johannesburg, telling them of his disappearance. Michael informed the local police of his suspicions regarding Dorothea and Maans.

In the mean time Mrs Saltman had received an offer from someone who was interested in buying the farm and attempted to contact her brother. When she received no response, and especially after Johanna's concerned letter, she sent her husband to look for him. Mr Saltman contacted the police, who visited Treurfontein.

Dorothea informed them that Louis had absconded without paying his yearly rent of twenty-five pounds and even had the nerve to ask the police to retrieve the money from Mrs Saltman.

Mrs Saltman retaliated by taking the contract Louis had entered into with Dorothea to the head of the Transvaal Detective Services. Her brother was a rich man and would not abscond without paying rent, she told him upon presenting the contract. If there had been only suspicion of foul play before, at least the contract now provided a motive for murder. The police had also received an anonymous tip-off about the mysterious digging on the night of 2 February 1918. Obviously the couple with the sick child had learned about the disappearance of a man from the farm they had visited that stormy night.

On 20 July 1920, Sergeant William Daniels and a group of convict labourers arrived at Treurfontein and started searching for clues. For six weeks they drained wells, pulled down walls, lifted flooring and dug up the garden, but to no avail. A reward of a hundred pounds for information as to the whereabouts of Louis was posted, but no one came forward.

Sergeant Daniels decided to ask the local witch-doctor for help. Jim Bird feared the law much more than he believed in his own powers and scarcely had the sergeant begun asking questions, than he had confessed to his involvement. He told Sergeant Daniels that he had fled before Louis was dead and had no idea what had happened to the body, if there was one. William took Jim to the farm and this time Jim's magic powers worked. He located the body beneath the rubbish dump. On 22 September 1920, Dorothea, who had in the interim married a man named Van der Merwe, Maans Swartz, and the three labourers were arrested for murder.

The fact that it was a white woman who was being charged with murder ensured that the courtroom was packed to capacity. Those present sat in shocked silence when Jim Bird, one of the accused, was led from the dock to the witness stand. He had turned Crown witness in order to save his own skin. He testified that Dorothea had rewarded him with sexual favours for his participation in the murder plot. She did not deny this. Dorothea and Maans were found guilty of murder and the three labourers were acquitted. Maans and Dorothea were both hanged at Pretoria Central Prison in 1921.

Comment

Had Dorothea Kraft not been so concerned about her financial plight that she blindly accepted the first solution that offered itself, she would probably have had the sense to read the contract properly. She was not the first woman to have expected a man to save

her from her financial predicament. In the end her
desire to lead a comfortable life was her downfall.
Was it necessary for her to kill Louis to secure a
better life? Surely not, for she later met and married
another man who provided for her.

Dorothea Kraft's case study illustrates how
irrationally women can behave when the fabric of
their security is threatened. She set the example for
many more to come.

Case Study: Maureen Katherine Smith, 1982

Maureen, daughter of wealthy insurance assessor
Harry Mullocks, married Roger Charles Smith, a
quantity surveyor, in Britain in 1974. Initially the
couple were happy together, and Maureen's nine-
year-old daughter from a previous marriage, Karen
Wood, called Roger 'dad'. The family moved to South
Africa in 1975 and settled in an expensive home in
La Lucia in Durban.

Maureen enjoyed a life of luxury. She was a popular hostess and weekly visits to beauty salons and
hairdressers were part of her routine. Karen was
placed in a private school, but she later joined her
grandparents in London where she studied dancing.
After a while the relationship between Roger and
Maureen deteriorated. Roger's business ventures
failed one after the other and his father-in-law Harry
had to pick up the tabs. Perhaps Roger resented the
fact that his wife's father had to bail him out of his
financial difficulties – Maureen had always been a
'daddy's girl' – and he took it out on her. Maureen
complained that Roger was abusive, particularly when
he drank too much.

In 1982, by which time Karen was seventeen,
Maureen and Roger had moved into another luxury

home at 10-368 Meadway, Kelvin, in Gauteng province. Unable to tolerate Roger's abuse and the humiliation he inflicted on her, Maureen had often left him, but he always persuaded her to return.

In December 1981 she asked him for a divorce, in terms of which he would receive a sizeable settlement of sixty thousand rand. Although he initially agreed, Roger later changed his mind. He blackmailed Maureen, telling her that if she tried to divorce him, he would expose her father for alleged tax fraud and illegal smuggling of money into the country. He allegedly even threatened to kill her parents. Roger exploited the fact that Maureen suffered from epilepsy and threatened to have her committed to a mental institution on the grounds of 'madness'. Maureen also later alleged that Roger had made sexual advances towards Karen.

Karen returned from London at the beginning of 1982 and moved in with her mother and stepfather. She had told her grandfather and her aunt, Daisy Sleet, a retired nurse, about Roger's abuse of her mother. Harry Mullocks was furious and allegedly threatened to send 'people' to South Africa to dispose of Roger.

Karen met twenty-three-year-old Lee Sparrowhawk in March 1982. He became her boyfriend. Maureen told Lee about her problems and soon a number of people had only one thing on their minds – the murder of Roger Smith.

Maureen even approached Lee's father to assist her. Her ex-husband, Raymond Wood, also allegedly offered to get rid of Roger. Maureen gave her domestic helper, Asnath Dekobe, four hundred rand to find a hitman. Asnath split the money with the Smiths' chauffeur Jack Ramogale, but neither of them made any attempt to find a killer. Maureen later gave Asnath a further four hundred rand, which she kept for herself.

Daisy Sleet arrived in South Africa on 16 July. She had allegedly been deputed by Harry to give Roger an injection of a substance that would induce a heart attack, but the plan was called off when Harry realised it would have been traced during a post-mortem. Maureen and Daisy decided to make Roger drunk one night and then smother him with a pillow. Lee played barman that night and saw to it that heavy drinks were poured for Roger. Roger eventually passed out, but the attempt to smother him with a pillow failed. Eventually Maureen asked Jack, the chauffeur, to find her a hitman. She promised to pay him and Asnath each five thousand rand if they were successful. Jack and Asnath drove Roger's car to Alexandra township and with the assistance of Jack's cousin, Sam Sekwela, they found a hitman, David Mnguni, who was prepared to do the job for ten thousand rand. By now all the domestic workers in the neighbourhood were aware that Maureen was plotting to murder Roger.

On 19 June 1982 Karen flew to Durban to withdraw ten thousand rand from her mother's private account which had been set up by Harry Mullocks.

On the evening of 20 July 1982, Maureen, Daisy, Karen and Lee were having supper. They all knew that Roger was supposed to meet his death in an 'accident' on his way home that night, so when he walked into the dining room at twenty past seven, everyone was stunned. Roger ate his dinner and then watched television in the den with Maureen.

Jack came into the adjoining living room and whispered to Karen, Lee and Daisy that the killer was outside in the garden, waiting for instructions. Lee's impromptu plan was that Jack should turn off the main electricity switch in the garden, which would lure Roger outside. This would give David his opportunity to kill Roger. Jack duly turned off the main switch and Roger went outside to investigate. He returned unharmed. About twenty minutes later the lights went out again. Jack ran to his room and hid under the blankets. Roger went outside with a torch and David attacked him. A struggle ensued and David stabbed Roger fourteen times with a knife. Roger died while he was crawling towards Jack's room, shouting for help. Lee watched the murder from the garden.

John Hinshaw, a neighbour, heard Roger's screams. He went out to see what was happening and saw a man bending over Roger and another running in the garden. He shouted at them and they fled. John ran home and told his mother to phone the police. He grabbed his firearm, but when he got back to Roger he found that he had been stabbed to death. John Hinshaw was astonished that none of the Smith family had ventured outside or called the emergency services. He asked his mother to phone for an ambulance. Karen then phoned the Flying Squad and the police arrived and began taking statements. Maureen was hysterical and had to be sedated.

The following day, Maureen wanted to pay David. Lee offered to take the money to him in Alexandra, but he was not at home and Lee returned with the cash.

A policeman standing guard at the murder scene noticed two men trying to jumpstart a car parked near the house. It transpired that on the night of the murder Sam was supposed to have driven the getaway car, but the car would not start and Sam and David left it behind, planning to come back for it later. They were taken in for questioning.

Sergeant Johannes Petrus Gouws of the Brixton

Murder and Robbery Unit met David Mnguni for the first time on 23 July. He retrieved the murder weapon from David, who made a full confession. Sergeant Gouws took David to Alexandra. At nine o'clock that morning Jack and Asnath arrived to meet David. They were promptly arrested and confessed to their part in the crime.

At midday on 24 July, Colonel Hermanus Arnoldus Barend van der Linde arrested Maureen at her home. She was alone at the time. She was taken to the police station where she made a statement in which she denied everything.

In the period after the murder but before her arrest, Maureen had made arrangements for Karen, Lee and herself to accompany Daisy back to London. Lee picked up the plane tickets on Saturday, 24 July. When he returned to the Smiths' house later that afternoon, Maureen was not there.

Family friend John Clayton arrived and invited the family to stay with him. That night he and Daisy went to the Brixton Murder and Robbery Unit to find out what had happened to Maureen.

Maureen, then thirty-nine years old, thirty-six-year-old David Mnguni and twenty-five-year-old Jack Ramogale, were charged with murder. Mr Justice H P van Dyk presided over the trial. Advocate Lionel Weinstock SC defended Maureen, advocate Andrew Booysen defended Jack and advocate Riaan Strydom defended David. Advocate A J de Klerk prosecuted. The trial caused quite a stir, to the extent that it had to be moved to a larger courtroom to accommodate the public.

Karen had turned state witness. She was promised indemnity if she told the whole truth and was held in a facility for juveniles throughout the trial. The same offer was made to Lee, who was also held in protective custody. Sam Sekwela and Asnath Dekobe also testified against the three accused.

On 19 November, Mr Justice van Dyk found all three accused guilty of murder. Maureen's mother Ros had flown to South Africa to support her daughter, but Harry stayed behind in London.

Now it was up to the defence lawyers to save their clients from the gallows. Advocate Weinstock argued as extenuating circumstances that Maureen had been both intimidated and blackmailed by Roger, that Roger was an excessive drinker and abused her, that Maureen's family, especially her father, had coerced her to have Roger killed and that she had been diagnosed as having an immature personality. Advocate Andrew Booysen argued that Jack had been a homeland herdboy who had only completed grade 3 at school. He had worked hard to make a success of his life, eventually becoming a chauffeur who earned a decent salary. He had participated in the conspiracy because he needed the money and he wanted to please his employer, Maureen. He had a subservient personality. There was not much that advocate Strydom could argue for David, save that David believed that Maureen's husband was having an affair. While advocate Booysen was pleading for Jack's life, Maureen had an epileptic fit and had to be rushed to hospital. They had to sit out the weekend, waiting for their sentences.

On 23 November 1982 crowds gathered both inside and outside the courtroom and the police had to use dogs to control them. There was a mixed reaction when Mr Justice van Dyk pronounced that he could not find any mitigating circumstances. 'No other sentence than the ultimate one would serve their dark and evil crimes,' the judge said, sentencing all three to death. He indemnified Karen from prosecution and said he had not yet made up his mind about Lee, since the latter had not been honest in his testimony. Maureen was granted permission to appeal against her conviction and sentence, and David and Jack were granted leave to appeal against their sentences.

Neither Maureen's mother Ros nor Karen attended the sentencing. Maureen's only support was her faithful friend, Monica Etheridge. Maureen was transported to death row at Pretoria Central Prison. The former socialite would be granted a few comforts – she was allowed make-up, hair conditioner, lipstick and deodorant.

Karen and Lee were released from custody. They were at the Rand Supreme Court to collect six rand witness fees when Maureen was sentenced, but they did not meet with her. Shortly after Maureen's sentencing, they were spotted having dinner in a restaurant. Maureen's mother invited Karen to join them in London. Harry went into hiding.

The sentence caused an outcry in England. Maureen's first husband, Raymond Wood, wrote an appeal to the Home Secretary, Mr William Whitelaw. But the British government refused to become involved since the legal processes in South Africa had not been completed.

After spending a year on death row, Maureen's appeal was successful and her sentence was commuted to twenty years. Jack's sentence was commuted to fifteen years. But David's appeal was unsuccessful. Shortly before he was to hang, David received clemency from the State President and his sentence was commuted to life imprisonment. Lee was finally indemnified.

In London Harry was happy to hear the news that

Maureen's death sentence had been commuted, but he vowed he would not stop until he could get his beloved daughter released from prison. He made a statement in which he admitted that he had pressurised her to have her husband killed and that he had supplied the ten thousand rand to dispose of Roger. Scotland Yard detectives began investigating the possibility of charging Harry with murder, conspiracy to commit murder, or perjury. According to British law, British citizens can be charged for crimes committed outside Britain. Eventually, however, it was decided not to prosecute Harry because of his failing health.

In May 1986 a two hundred and fifty page petition was sent to the South African Minister of Justice, Mr Kobie Coetsee, in which it was alleged that Harry Mullocks was responsible for the murder of Roger Smith. But in 1988, Harry changed his mind about testifying before a commission in London. He still feared prosecution. Maureen fell into a deep depression when she heard the news. In 1990 she appealed to be released on parole, but her request was denied.

On 8 July 1991, after serving nine years of her sentence, Maureen Smith was released as a result of a pardon granted by State President F W de Klerk to first-time offenders. She had forgiven her father, who was by then an old and ill man. She planned to visit her parents and her daughter Karen in London, and intended starting a business which would provide employment for ex-convicts.

Comment

This case study provides much food for thought. Roger Smith was no angel. He refused the divorce settlement offered by Maureen, because he wanted more money – in fact, he wanted it all.

He blackmailed his wife with her father's alleged crimes and threatened to commit her to a mental institution. He intimidated her and abused her. But did he deserve to die for this? Was there not another way out for Maureen Smith? If Harry Mullocks was innocent, why did he not call Roger's bluff? Why did he consider getting rid of Roger the easiest solution?

How could so many people all conspire to kill one man? How could all of them have come to the conclusion that the only way to solve the problem was murder? Did not one of them even consider another solution? Why did those not directly affected by Roger's behaviour agree so readily to have him murdered? Is life that cheap?

Asnath Dekobe and Jack Ramogale had been employed by the Smiths in February 1982. Four months later they were both willing to help hire a hitman to kill their employer. Jack admitted that Roger had never ill-treated him, yet he was the one who drove Roger home that fateful night knowing what awaited him. Jack's cousin, Sam Sekwela, introduced them to the killer and agreed to drive the getaway car. Asnath thought nothing of keeping the money Maureen had given her to find a killer, without producing results. Asnath and Jack told all their friends in the neighbourhood about the intended murder. None of these people informed the authorities what Maureen Smith was planning. Why?

David Mnguni, a backyard mechanic, was prepared to kill for ten thousand rand, and justified his actions by saying he did it because Maureen had told him her husband was having an affair.

The outsiders, Asnath, Jack, Sam and David had no motive to kill Roger Smith. He had never treated them badly. How could they have been so easily

201

persuaded?

Lee Sparrowhawk had known Roger Smith for three months only, yet he played a major part in planning his murder. Roger had not done anything to Lee but he justified his involvement by saying he felt sorry for Karen and Maureen. He was not even aware of the allegation that Roger had tried to sexually molest Karen, until it was brought up in court. When he was asked by Advocate Weinstock whether it bothered him that Maureen wanted her husband killed, he replied that it had nothing to do with him. After three months of integrating himself into a family, Lee Sparrowhawk thought nothing of murdering a man. He even offered to get his own father involved. What did Lee stand to gain by Roger's death?

Karen wanted to protect her mother and agreed to participate in the conspiracy, yet in the end she testified against her mother. Even her father, Maureen's ex-husband Raymond Wood, had allegedly offered to send in some 'heavies' to 'sort out' Roger. Daisy, who had no children of her own but regarded Maureen as a daughter, was willing to use her medical training to kill.

Harry Mullocks incited his daughter to commit murder in order to protect his business interests, then he failed her. Maureen had been indulged by her father all her life. She had always followed his commands. Once when she had wanted to go back to Raymond Wood, her father had forbidden it and she accepted his decision without question. When her husband failed to provide for her family, she ran to daddy. She did not support Roger when his business ventures failed and did not even attempt to see out the bad times with him. She enjoyed the life her father's money bought her far too much. Eventually she almost paid for it with her life.

What kind of people were these? Were they greedy, ruthless people, who found it easy to contemplate and plan a murder? In the end, they all turned on each other.

Case study: Lindi Nomsa Qunta, 1984

Lindi Qunta had everything a young girl could wish for. Her mother was a Dhlamini, a member of the Royal House of the Kingdom of Swaziland, and her father was an academic and a graduate of the University of Fort Hare. Lindi was beautiful, ambitious and intelligent. She grew up in Langa, near Cape Town. After completing grade 12, she moved to Port Elizabeth to train as a nurse. Her parents were very proud of her achievements, but did not approve of her boyfriend, Victor Mangaliso. Victor worked as a deliveryman at a liquor store. His mother was a domestic worker who could not keep down a job, and his father worked in the kitchen of the hospital where Lindi was employed.

To the Quntas, Victor was completely out of his league by setting his sights on the blue-blooded Lindi. But Lindi managed to convince her parents that Victor was the one she loved and the couple were married in 1972. The newlyweds and Victor's parents moved into a rented shack in Gugulethu on the border of Langa in Cape Town. Lindi qualified as a nurse and started work at Groote Schuur Hospital.

Lindi's ambition and intelligence soon changed her life. She bought a butchery in Langa with her savings .and within a year had bought a second butchery and secured the franchise of a Kentucky Fried Chicken fast food outlet in Gugulethu. Soon she was making enough money to give up nursing and establish herself as a successful business woman. Victor gave up his job as a representative at Nestlé and joined Lindi's business ventures. Lindi built her parents-in-law a new house and built a luxury home in Malungapark, Gugulethu, for herself and her husband. Here she entertained friends such as Winnie Mandela, then wife of Nelson Mandela, who was still in prison at the time.

Cracks began to appear in the marriage. Victor regarded himself as the 'boss' of Lindi's businesses. He drank too much and fell into the habit of entertaining loose women. Behind closed doors he physically abused his wife. After one such violent incident, Lindi phoned her brother and begged him to fetch her. Victor's abuse of Lindi was now public knowledge, but as a result of family persuasion and meaningless promises on Victor's part, Lindi returned to her husband. Scarcely had she set foot in their house, when he assaulted her and then added insult to injury by leaving the home with another woman.

During the winter of 1984, Lindi decided there was only one way to solve her problem. Victor had to be removed permanently from her life. She turned to one of her employees, Washington Manyosi Nxawe and asked him to find hitmen to kill her husband. He introduced her to Sipho Peter and Solomon Mbuzeli Shelini. Several of their attempts to murder Victor failed because of bad planning and because Lindi forgave Victor again and again for his infidelities.

Then Victor made the fatal mistake of having a relationship with a schoolgirl. When Lindi confronted him about this, he begged her to give him another chance, but she had had enough. On the night of 16 December 1984 Victor was drunk. During the night he was called out twice to the butcheries. Both were false alarms, which irritated him. He phoned Lindi and warned her to get out of the house before he returned or he would assault her. Lindi phoned the hitmen, who arrived just in time. Sipho had brought his own knife, but Lindi gave a knife to Solomon. They agreed they would wait until Victor was asleep before attacking him.

When Victor arrived home he told Lindi she was lucky he did not feel like beating her. He got something to eat from the fridge and went to bed, with a petrified Lindi beside him. She knew the assassins were hiding in one of the other rooms. She had already paid them two thousand rand. When she heard them entering the bedroom, she fled to the bathroom. The men proceeded to stab Victor to death. They locked the bathroom door from the outside and left the scene. Lindi climbed through the bathroom window and went to her neighbours.

The police were baffled by the attack. It was initially thought that the motive might have been political, but the investigating officer, Major Leonard Knipe, found some inconsistencies in Lindi's statement. Yet he had nothing with which to substantiate his suspicions. Major Knipe activated his informers and news soon reached him that Washington Nxawe knew something about the murder. Washington was interrogated and when he was offered the chance to turn state witness and avoid prosecution, he confessed.

The trial commenced on 18 March 1986, with Mr Justice de Kock presiding. Lindi did not deny having hired the hitmen and told the court about the abuse she had suffered at the hands of her freeloading, womanising, abusive husband Victor. The two hitmen blamed each other in turn. Eventually, on 12 December 1986, both Sipho Peter and Solomon Shelini were sentenced to death. Her husband's abuse of her was taken into account, and Lindi was sentenced to twenty years' imprisonment. Later both men's sentences were commuted to twenty years.

Lindi appointed a curator to administer her fortune, reputed to be worth millions, for her children.

Comment

Although intelligent and possessed of a shrewd business sense, Lindi Qunta, a wealthy woman in her own right, never considered divorcing her worthless husband and kicking him out. Surely, since her family had been against the marriage from the start, they would not have opposed a divorce? It is sad that a woman with the entrepreneurial skill to build a successful career for herself did not make the more sensible choice of divorce rather than murder. Did Lindi fear losing half her empire to her husband, did she fear the stigma of being a divorced woman with a failed marriage, or did she fear that Victor would continue taunting and harassing her? She had the financial means to protect herself and her children from him. She also had the political influence to make sure that he would have been prosecuted, had he tried to pursue her. What made her decide to commit murder? At least she admitted her guilt and took responsibility for her actions. Lindi Qunta, a royal descendant, intelligent, ambitious and beautiful, who contributed to the country's economy by providing employment for many people, ended up in Pollsmoor Prison because she made the wrong choice.

Case study: Nicolette Laurent, 1991

John Royce Fernandez, a thirty-seven-year-old financial manager at Omnimed in Johannesburg, disappeared mysteriously on 2 January 1991, after going to a bank at ten o'clock that morning. Three days after his disappearance police discovered his body on a dump site in Nasrec, south of Johannesburg. He had suffered a head wound and the police initially suspected he was the victim of a robbery. But further investigation quickly pointed to fifty-year-old Nicolette Laurent, a bookkeeper at Omnimed, as a suspect.

John, a married father of two, had given his wife a cheque to safeguard. After his death, she contacted her brother-in-law, who contacted Adrien Pule, the managing director of Omnimed.

The police established that since 1981 Nicolette had been defrauding Omnimed to the tune of well over two million rand. Two weeks after the murder they arrested Nicolette. Some of John Fernandez' personal belongings were found in her handbag. An urgent application to sequestrate Nicolette was brought before the court. It was established that she and her husband, Jean Michael Rene, had assets that included properties in Spain, a yacht worth sixty-eight thousand rand and a motor boat worth a hundred thousand rand, a plot at the Vaal Dam, a BMW 735I, numerous gold shares, and they had moved into a property valued at one and a half million rand at Ruimsig, Roodepoort, just six months earlier. Nicolette had defrauded the company by making out revenue cheques to herself and her husband. Jean was also arrested, but released soon afterwards.

During her trial, Nicolette testified that John Fernandez had discovered her fraudulent activities in 1987. She paid him a certain amount of money each month to keep him quiet, and she alleged that they also had sex regularly in an empty office on Omnimed's premises. On 2 January 1991 she invited him to her home for a drink and he suggested they have sex. But their activities were disrupted by her cat, whereupon John decided to leave. She fetched her husband's firearm and held it to her head, threatening to kill herself if John exposed her fraudulent deeds. He laughed at her and bent down to pick something up. She got a fright, she claimed, and accidentally shot him in the head.

Nicolette said she panicked. She fetched a blue plastic bag to wrap around his head to contain the blood and then attempted to drag him to an outbuilding, but the plastic bag came off. She tied the bag around his head with rope, wrapped his body in a duvet and managed to drag it to the outbuilding. Then she left to meet her husband and daughters at a restaurant. Since one of her daughters was getting married in three days' time, she decided to do nothing about disposing of the body until after the wedding. However, later that night she changed her mind. She went back to the outbuilding and managed to heave the body on to the back of the bakkie. She left the body there for a full day before driving to the dump site the following evening and unloading it. She told the court she wanted John's body to be found, because she knew his wife and children would be worried by his disappearance.

Her husband Jean claimed that he had no knowledge of either the fraud or the murder.

Dr Irma Labuschagne, well-known South African criminologist, testified during the trial. She argued that Nicole Laurent's loveless childhood constituted mitigating circumstances. Nicole had been rejected by her mother and the only love she received was from her uncle, who shared her bedroom and bed when she was a child, but who apparently did not have sexual relations with her. She fell pregnant at thirteen, was sent to a home for unmarried mothers, but the baby died three days after birth. Nicolette was made fun of as the fat, ugly under-achiever in the family. Her mother frightened her with stories about the devil to such an extent that she paid one of her brothers to protect her on the nights her uncle had to work. Her life had been an ongoing struggle for love.

Mr Justice Louis Weyers said that many people suffered during their childhood years, but this did not turn them into murderers. He described Nicolette's version of the sexual relationship between herself and the victim as a shocking and unfair attack upon the integrity of a man who could not defend himself, and said that it was embarrassing for the widow and her two children. He said that John Fernandez had most probably only discovered Nicolette's fraud on the day of his death and that she had lured him to her home on false pretences. There she offered him sex in exchange for his silence and when he refused she shot him in cold blood in the back of his head. Forensic evidence proved that John had been shot from the back and that Nicolette's version would have necessitated him performing an impossible acrobatic manoeuvre to explain the line of trajectory. He said that by dumping the body Nicolette was attempting to conceal the crime and he did not believe that she had felt any concern for Mrs Fernandez.

Mr Justice Weyers sentenced Nicolette to sixteen years for the murder and a further eight years for fraud. He said her claim to have had a difficult childhood was like crying crocodile tears.

Mrs Fernandez said the allegation that her husband had sexual relations with a woman much older than himself was hogwash. He was a happily married family man. She felt Nicolette deserved the death sentence. Jean maintained his silence, but held his wife's hands after the sentencing.

Comment

Nicolette Laurent clearly substituted money to gratify the basic security needs of which she was deprived during her childhood. Although she might not have intended to commit a murder when she first started to defraud her company, she became so attached to her financial security blanket that she was prepared to murder to protect it. Her case demonstrates that a woman who has been deprived of basic security needs will never have enough money, no matter how many material possessions she has.

Case study: Mignon Lombard, 1993

For two years Mignon Lombard got away with murder.

In 1993, thirty-one-year-old Mignon found herself trapped in a marriage which bored her to tears. Her husband Dave was a technician at Sasol in Secunda in Mpumalanga province. She was the daughter of a German baron who lived in Stellenbosch in the Western Cape. There are striking differences between picturesque, historic Stellenbosch and industrialised Secunda. Stellenbosch is a quaint little town, nestling among vineyards and framed by majestic mountains, with a lively student community. Secunda, on the other hand, is a dusty town built around the Sasol power plants. The earth is flat, brown and featureless and the town does not offer much entertainment, apart from the casino where one may be too easily recognised.

The noble-blooded Mignon sought relief from her boredom much closer to home. As a matter of fact, she found it right across the street in the form of twenty-eight-year-old Jasper Jacobus 'Cobus' Pieterse. Scarcely would her husband and children have left home in the morning than Cobus would arrive to find Mignon waiting for him in bed. When Dave worked night shifts, Cobus would keep his wife company, despite the presence of her sleeping children.

Their affair began in August 1993. Cobus later recounted that their sexual relationship went hand in hand with smoking dagga (cannabis). Mignon told Cobus that Dave abused her and that it was time to get rid of him. She had it all planned and just needed Cobus' help. She allegedly said that Dave had refused to grant her a divorce. Cobus testified that he had refused to help her on six separate occasions.

On the night of 15 October 1993, Mignon laced her husband's drink with sleeping pills. When Cobus arrived he was sleeping soundly. The time had come for getting rid of Dave, but not before the couple had first engaged in a sex and drugs orgy. Mignon and Cobus entered the main bedroom and Mignon sat on Dave's legs, while Cobus pushed a dishcloth down his throat and smothered him with a pillow. While she was sitting on her struggling husband, Mignon's nine-year-old son walked into the bedroom and asked what was going on. She told him that his father was having a heart attack and they were trying to assist him. She sent him back to bed. Dave regained consciousness, and promised Mignon he would divorce her if they spared his life. But the lovers continued relentlessly until there was no life left in his body. Then they removed his body from the bed, bathed him, for he had soiled himself, changed the bed sheets and replaced the body. They carefully placed the container of sleeping pills in his hand, trying to make it appear to have been suicide.

Mignon had carefully planned her alibi. Earlier that night, she had called her friend Annette Pieterse and told her that her husband was lying on the bed and she could not rouse him. At about half past eleven she called again, telling Annette that something was seriously wrong with Dave.

Cobus left after the murder and called the ambulance service. Dave was taken to hospital, with a hysterical Mignon in tow. At the hospital, one of the nurses heard Mignon's last words to her husband. She said: 'Fuck you.' The cause of death was given as heart failure; no one suspected murder.

During the funeral there were several incidents that raised suspicion among friends and family. The young son was stony-faced, showing no emotion. Cobus found it difficult to enter the church and would not approach the grave. Mignon refused to drop a red rose on her husband's coffin. A week after the funeral Mignon confessed to her friend Annette that she and Cobus had killed Dave. For reasons known only to herself, Annette kept quiet about it.

Soon after the murder, Mignon became bored with Cobus. She dumped him and began relationships with several other men. Cobus was distraught and bewailed his fate to Mignon's sister-in-law, Amanda Papenhagen. He told her that he had been good enough to assist Mignon in killing her husband, and now she was cheating on him. Strangely, Amanda did not inform the police either, despite the fact that her husband, Mignon's brother, was a sergeant in the police force. Later, during the trial, Sergeant Peter Papenhagen admitted that Mignon had told him about the murder.

Secunda was becoming too claustrophobic for Mignon Lombard and she moved to Stellenbosch, where she began another relationship. After a year, she had the man prosecuted and convicted for abusing her. But Mignon had made two mistakes. First, in a moment of passion, she had confessed to this man that she had participated in Dave's murder and, secondly, she did not bargain on his taking revenge. It was two years after the murder that the man, on his release from prison, told the police what he knew about Dave's murder.

Mignon and Cobus were arrested. Cobus claimed he could not remember anything and Mignon refused to speak. But while she was in prison, she wrote a letter to a man she had met in prison, confessing to the murder, but apportioning most of the blame to Cobus. She even admitted that she had told her family of the murder before she moved to Stellenbosch. She said that she had never been strong enough to embark on divorce proceedings.

Mr Justice L F Weyers presided over the trial. A former friend of Mignon's, Elize Kruger, testified that Mignon had complained that Dave had abused her for almost eleven years. She often expressed the wish that he would die. After his death, she laughed hysterically about it.

In April 1997, Mr Justice Weyers rejected Mignon's claims of abuse. Cobus had two previous convictions for burglary and attempted theft. Both were sentenced to twenty-five years' imprisonment.

Comment

What is interesting in this case is that Mignon Lombard admitted that she did not have the strength to file for divorce. Her allegation that Dave had refused to grant her a divorce was therefore untrue. Perhaps he would have divorced her and it was not necessary to kill him in order to be free. Was Mignon prepared to endure eleven years of abuse, instead of asking for a divorce? Surely her policeman brother and influential father would have helped her if she had really wanted to leave Dave.

It is appalling that Mignon's son had to testify that he saw his mother killing his father. He was only nine years old when it happened. Now he has no father and his mother is in prison.

A year after the murder Cobus had married and become a father. This child will also grow up not knowing his father. Through their selfish lust both Mignon and Cobus denied their children proper parents.

What kind of man allows himself to be persuaded to commit murder in return for sex and drugs? His indignation at being dumped after doing Mignon the favour of killing her husband is preposterous. 'It is wrong of her to dump me for other boyfriends,' said Cobus, not for one moment admitting the wrongfulness of the murder he committed, nor admitting the wrongfulness of adultery and the use of illegal substances, especially in a home where there are children.

Mignon Lombard was obviously more interested in sex than in values, as proved by her successive lovers soon after Dave's death. How did she find the 'strength' to have her subsequent boyfriend locked up for abuse, yet not have the 'strength' to lay similar charges against Dave? She resorted to killing him rather than calling upon the law to protect her from him.

It is ironic is that the man she had locked up was the one who informed the police. He allegedly told Mignon she would feel what it was like to be locked up. Yet after she was sentenced he told journalists that Mignon was the kindest, most soft-hearted person he had ever met.

Finally, several friends and family members had first-hand knowledge of the murder because both Mignon and Cobus confessed it to them. Why did they not speak out sooner? What justification did any of these people have for their lack of action?

Case study: Ansie Wostmann, 1995

In 1987 Heinz Wostmann divorced Madeleine, his wife of twelve years, to marry his mistress Ansie. Madeleine was sad about the divorce, but she knew her marriage with Heinz had reached a point where divorce was inevitable. Heinz, the owner of a tool manufacturing business and a butchery, regularly paid maintenance for his three children. Initially all seemed to be going well in Heinz' new life, until his children began complaining to Madeleine that Ansie was insanely jealous about their father paying them attention when they visited him at weekends and they had to spend the entire Saturday afternoon in the bedroom.

By 1995 it was clear that Heinz and Ansie's relationship had deteriorated. She had befriended policemen and traffic officers whom she invited to their home on a regular basis. She had also developed a serious gambling habit and was spending her husband's hard-earned money at an escalating rate. Werner Peiger, Heinz' business partner, also noticed that all was not well in the marriage.

Heinz decided to put a stop to Ansie's spending

and the male friends who visited her so regularly. Ansie, one of seven children who had grown up poor, recognised that her husband was now standing in the way of her addiction to money. She bargained on inheriting about two million rand on his death. She called in the help of traffic officer Tom van Baalen, seduced him and persuaded him to murder Heinz by promising him half of the estate. Tom, in the middle of his own divorce proceedings, was an easy target.

On the evening of 13 November 1995 Ansie decided to take her two children from a previous marriage, her brother and a friend out for a treat. While they were away, Tom went to their home in Midrand in Gauteng province and shot Heinz.

The police were puzzled by the fact that nothing was stolen from the property. So was Madeleine. Since the police investigation had drawn a blank, she contacted a private investigator, Piet Fourie, to look into the case. She was concerned because Heinz' maintenance payments had ceased and the estate would not resume them until the case was solved. After speaking to the executors, Madeleine found out that Ansie stood to inherit the bulk of the estate.

Piet Fourie found it unusual that Heinz' guard dogs had not attacked the intruder and that there were no signs of forced entry to the tightly guarded property. He concluded that whoever shot Heinz was not a stranger. He traced all the phone calls made from the house that day and found that one had been made to Tom van Baalen. It seemed strange to Piet that Tom had left the country shortly after the murder and that he had sold his firearm, which was of the same calibre as that used in the murder, to his son.

Piet also found out that Ansie had gone on vacation with another man barely two weeks after the murder.

This was not the kind of behaviour one would expect from a grieving widow. He decided to pay her a visit, aware that although Ansie was not an attractive woman, men found her strangely alluring. Ansie welcomed Piet's visit and seemed happy that someone was interested in solving the murder since the delay in winding up the estate was frustrating her. Piet acknowledged later that although he suspected her of being involved in the murder of her husband, she did have an effect on him. 'She is ugly and evil, but sit next to her and you get aroused,' he admitted.

Ballistic tests proved the murder weapon belonged to Tom van Baalen and he was arrested. He turned state witness. He told the court how Ansie had used her sexual allure to seduce and manipulate him into committing the murder.

But Ansie's allure did not influence the judge who sentenced her to twenty-five years' imprisonment. He acknowledged that Tom had been manipulated when he was in a vulnerable state of mind, but he none the less sentenced him to twenty years.

Comment

Unattractive Ansie Wostmann is an example of a woman who learned early in life to use her sexual powers to seduce and manipulate men to be at her beck and call and provide her with the luxury lifestyle she had missed out on as a child. Tom van Baalen, employed in law enforcement, must have known the risk he was taking, yet he could not resist her. Even Piet Fourie admitted to Ansie's sexual attractiveness. Madeleine, being a woman, was immune to her powers and it was her instinct that finally led to Ansie being put behind bars. The judge in this case did not heed Victorian standards and passed fair sentences on the killers of a father of three.

Case study: Suzanne de Sousa, 1995

Mr Justice Johan Els sentenced twenty-five-year-old Suzanne de Sousa to forty years' imprisonment for robbery and the murder of Graham Warwick Fletcher. Her motive for killing him was plain and simple greed.

Suzanne and her accomplices Byulent Schabanali and Sandov Smil, both Bulgarian nationals, lured fifty-year-old Graham Fletcher to a flat in Hillbrow, Johannesburg, on 6 February 1995. He owed her fifteen thousand rand for arranging the sexual services of three school girls for him. He had eventually offered to pay by cheque. Suzanne drugged Graham's coffee with sleeping pills, and he was then deposited in the boot of his own Mercedes Benz. Suzanne, Byulent and Sandov drove for thirty kilometres before unloading Graham at De Deur. They assaulted him and stabbed him thirty-two times.

After the murder Suzanne and her accomplices tried to cash Graham's cheques, but they were apprehended when a bank clerk suspected something was wrong.

The two Bulgarians fled back to Bulgaria, which has no extradition treaty with South Africa. Suzanne, pregnant with Byulent's twins, was left to face the music alone.

She was sentenced to thirty years for taking the lead in the murder, ten years for stealing cheques and credit cards, and five years for kidnapping. During sentencing, Suzanne hid her face behind a religious book and her mother, Francis Clarke, wept and prayed.

Comment

What is particularly distressing about this case is that Suzanne, a pimp for teenage prostitutes, extortionist, kidnapper, robber and killer, is the mother of five children. She married the father of her two youngest boys two weeks before she was sentenced, leaving her other children, aged seven, eight and nine, in the care of her first husband. She miscarried Byulent's twins in prison. After years of incarceration, it has been noted that Suzanne seems to be responding to rehabilitation. She is studying and teaching fellow prisoners. She has accepted her sentence, taken responsibility for her actions, and is trying to make amends.

Case study: Hazel Kidson, 1996

Money meant more to fifty-two-year-old Hazel Kidson than her husband did. Barry Kidson, aged fifty-three when he died, was a well-loved headmaster at Constantia Kloof Primary School in Johannesburg. He was also an active sportsman.

On the night of 23 January 1996 Hazel and Barry had just arrived back at their home when he was allegedly attacked by three men and bludgeoned to death. Hazel denied any involvement in the killing, but she had made a grave mistake. For several months before the murder, she badgered her gambling partner, Ashraf Alli (Ash) Rabani, to help her get rid of her husband. Hazel told Ash that she had lost fifty thousand rand of Barry's money. His death would not only conceal the gambling debt, but his insurance policies would provide her with a comfortable income.

Hazel got away with murder for fourteen months, until Ash could no longer live with his conscience and contacted the police. He had an astonishing story to tell. He had witnessed Hazel killing her husband.

Hazel was arrested on 11 April 1997. She denied that she had been involved in her husband's murder and immediately applied for bail. Her lawyer argued that Hazel was eligible for bail since she had not interfered with witnesses for fifteen months. The bail application was postponed to the following day. That night Hazel made another mistake. She phoned Ash on her cellphone from her prison cell. The following day the magistrate denied her bail because she had interfered with a witness.

Mr Justice Edwin Cameron presided over the trial. According to Hazel's version of events, she and Barry had just arrived home when three men attacked him as he was walking to the front door. He was hit on the head with a blunt object and stabbed. He shouted at her to run, which she did. She drove to her neighbours and told them on the intercom at their gate that Barry had been attacked and they should call the police. She rushed back home to find Barry unconscious. A member of the flying squad testified that when he arrived he found a hysterical Hazel cradling her husband's body.

Tony Bezuidenhout, the groundsman at the school where Barry had been headmaster, testified that he had helped Hazel to frame some pictures. After the murder he discovered that a rubber mallet that they had used for the framing was missing. The Kidsons' domestic worker, Dorcas Pula, identified the knife with which Barry had been stabbed and testified that it had gone missing after the murder.

Melvin Botes, a gambling partner, testified that Hazel had asked him to dispose of Barry in 1995. Another, Glenn Dulamo, testified that Hazel had told him she would pay a hitman ten thousand rand to kill her husband. And yet another gambler, Mabitsela Sape, testified that Hazel had told him she wanted Barry dead so she could inherit his insurance policies.

Silence fell upon the court when Ash took the stand. He testified that Hazel had phoned him on the night of the murder and asked him to come to her home. When he arrived he found her hitting Barry on the head with a rubber mallet. She went into the garage and fetched a knife with which she proceeded to stab Barry. Then she handed Ash a plastic raincoat, rubber gloves, the mallet, the knife and a can of insecticide and asked him to dispose of them. He took the evidence and left. He also told the court that Hazel had offered him money to kill Barry or to find a hitman for her.

The police used Ash to tape a conversation with Hazel in which she incriminated herself. She also spoke about her current boyfriend. The tape was eventually allowed as evidence.

Ash made another remarkable statement. He said that after an alleged attack on Barry in 1994, he did not think Hazel would try to kill her husband again. In 1994 Barry Kidson had been attacked in his home. Hazel alleged that at the time she and Barry were sleeping in different bedrooms because she had flu. She was woken at three o'clock in the morning by a loud thud. She went to Barry's bedroom and saw a man standing over him. She slammed the door and called the flying squad. Paramedics were able to save Barry's life, but his skull was fractured and he had to undergo several operations. He also suffered from memory impairment. The severity of his injuries resulted in his early retirement from work. He needed intensive nursing and virtually became an invalid. The attack on Barry remained unsolved. Bernice Otto, a friend of the family, testified that most of Hazel's friends deserted her after this incident; Hazel used to leave her frail husband in her care while she went gambling.

Hazel described herself as a caring wife who nursed her husband after he was attacked in 1994. However Hazel's telephone records indicated that Barry would phone her as many as twenty times in seven hours but she was out gambling and ignored his calls. The records also showed numerous calls to Ash.

Under cross-examination, Hazel's veneer of non-chalance cracked. She turned her aggression on the state prosecutor and tried to implicate Ash as the murderer, especially since he had been in possession of the murder weapons.

After a five-week trial, Mr Justice Cameron pronounced Hazel guilty of murder. No one was surprised at the verdict. The judge found the fact that Hazel ignored her ill husband's telephone calls despicable. He said a 'high degree of suspicion' surrounded the 1994 attack. There was a suggestion that Hazel had arranged for the attackers to enter the home, but they botched the attack and she had to complete the deed the following year.

Hazel's previous convictions were read out before sentence was passed. She had been convicted on seventeen counts of fraud in 1988, and on thirty-four counts of fraud in 1994.

In mitigation, Hazel said that she had suffered post-traumatic stress when her two young children and both her parents died in quick succession.

'Society deserves to be protected from middle-class murderers like yourself no less than from other murderers,' the judge said when he sentenced Hazel to twenty-five years' imprisonment. Her surviving son did not attend the trial.

Comment

Clearly Hazel Kidson had a bad record with money. She committed fraud, she gambled, and in the end was prepared to commit murder for money.

Hazel Kidson's life was certainly marked by tragedy. According to her, her second child drowned accidentally as a baby when her eldest son was bathing him. The third child died of a cot death. At one time, when Hazel and Barry were separated, she lived with her parents. During this visit, both parents died within hours of each other.

Case study: Johanna 'Poppie' Smook, 1997

Forty-nine-year-old Poppie Smook claimed she had endured twenty-nine years of abuse during her marriage to Gerald James Smook and that his abuse of their children became intolerable. During her trial for James' murder she told the court how he had struck his daughter and then kicked her when she fell to the ground, for no reason other than that she had gone out with her boyfriend.

Poppie alleged that she had asked her husband for a divorce on numerous occasions, but he threatened to kill her and the children and to burn down their house if she ever attempted to leave him. She claimed that when her son Albert told her that James was planning to buy a firearm on the black market in order to kill the family, she reached a turning point.

She asked her daughter's boyfriend, Francois 'China' Bezuidenhout, to help her kill James. China contacted a friend, Petrus 'Wimpie' Bezuidenhout (no relation), to help them. Wimpie was a paramedic and the plan was for him to inject air into James' veins. When it came to committing the deed, however,

Wimpie found that he was not equal to the task. He later confessed that Poppie had given them each one thousand rand to buy illegal firearms and that they took the money to placate her; they never had any intention of carrying out the murder.

Eventually the three of them devised another plan. On the evening of 4 May 1997 James Smook was watching television while Poppie and one of her daughters were in the main bedroom. There was a sound at the window and her daughter told her it was Wimpie. She instructed her daughter to go to her bedroom and went to ask James to investigate the noise.

Wimpie and China, each armed with a knife, were waiting for their victim. But they did not expect James to storm out of the house wielding a baseball bat. Wimpie fled. Eventually he returned to find China was kneeling next to James' body. He had been stabbed twelve times.

Poppie pleaded guilty but her two accomplices pleaded not guilty, so they were tried separately. During the Bezuidenhouts' trial China pleaded self-defence, saying he was trapped when James came at him with the baseball bat. Wimpie said he had run away. Poppie vehemently denied that she had offered to buy them both new motorcycles as payment for the murder. She claimed that they agreed to kill James because they were also angered by his abuse of her children. She said she had promised them they could move in after the murder, but that she expected them to pay rent.

Mr Justice S Mynhardt found that James had abused his wife and children earlier in the marriage, but that in later years he had no longer been abusive. He said the murder had been planned over a period of six weeks, during which time any one of the three accused could have backed down. He found that James had admitted to his children that there was no hope for the marriage and had asked one of his older daughters whether he could move in with her. This was not consistent with the allegation that he had planned to murder his family or had refused to divorce his wife.

Mr Justice Mynhardt rejected Poppie's claim that the motive for the murder was James' abusive behaviour and her fears for her life. He found that she harboured a grudge against James because he had told her that he was impotent, yet she suspected him of having affairs with other women. The main reason why Poppie decided to kill James was because he had told her she would not receive any financial assistance from him after the divorce. He sentenced Poppie to twenty-five years' imprisonment.

Comment

It was clear that at one time Gerald James Smook had been physically abusive towards his wife and children. It is amazing that a woman would endure this for twenty-nine years without making a serious attempt to leave. Why did she want to murder him when his abusive behaviour abated as he aged, and when he was finally ready to grant her the freedom she wanted? Did the fact that James threatened not to assist her financially after the divorce prove the final turning point? It seems that Poppie Smook was one of those women who are prepared to endure abuse, as long as the man was in a position to pay for her keep.

Case study: Rethea Bierman, 1997

Rethea married Andy Bierman, an electrician in Polokwane in the Northern province, in February 1990, but the couple were divorced at the end of 1992 for tax reasons. However they still lived together in the upper-class suburb of Bendorpark. They remarried in February 1997 and went to Mauritius on a second honeymoon. Little did Andy know, on this tropical holiday, that his wife was already plotting his death.

Andy had an employee by the name of Charles Nxumalo, who not only worked at his electrical company, but had also done odd jobs at the couple's home since 1995. During his trial Charles would testify that Rethea had first approached him to kill Andy Bierman in 1996; he was working in their garden at the time. She claimed that Andy was abusive when he was drunk, he had pressed a firearm against her head on several occasions and he was having affairs with other women. She offered Charles thirty thousand rand to kill Andy and asked him to obtain a firearm. When she returned from her second honeymoon she again pleaded with Charles to kill her husband, saying he could use her husband's firearm.

On the night of 28 July 1997, Rethea gave her domestic worker the weekend off. She locked the dog away, left the garden gate open, hid her husband's firearm in the fridge in the lapa and left a door open for Charles and his brother Sacharia, both Zimbabwean citizens, to enter the house.

During her trial Rethea testified that she was sleeping in her daughter's bedroom when she heard four shots. She ran to the main bedroom where she was assaulted by two armed men who tied her to the bedpost with a skipping rope. A car hooter sounded outside and the men became alarmed and fled. She shouted for help and her son heard her.

Charles, however, testified that Rethea was lying on a foam rubber mattress next to the bed on which her husband was sleeping. After he shot Andy, he assaulted Rethea and tied her to the bedpost in an attempt to fake a bungled robbery.

Initially Rethea was not under suspicion. She gave Charles work at her kiosk at the Pietersburg Hospital. When he began making demands for his money, she began a sexual relationship with him. She brought the same mattress on which she had been sleeping the night her husband died to the kiosk, where the couple made love after hours. Charles testified that he had fallen in love with her and thought she reciprocated his feelings, until one day when she told him to go away.

Someone tipped off the police, and fifteen months after the murder, they arrived at the kiosk to arrest Charles. Rethea at first said he was not there, but the police found him and arrested him. She later testified that Charles had arrived at the kiosk intending to rob her; he was armed and she had lied to the police about his presence because she was afraid of a shootout.

A short while later Rethea was arrested for the murder of her husband, when she and her daughter were leaving the movies one evening. Sacharia was not arrested as he was serving a sentence in a prison in Zimbabwe.

While in custody Rethea confessed to her minister, Gerhardus Bothma, that she had planned Andy's murder, and she admitted the same to her best friend, Hanlie Botha. Gerhardus Bothma struggled with his conscience; his legal advisers told him to speak to the police. Both Hanlie and Gerhardus testified against

Rethea.

Rethea was also charged with fraud relating to insurance payouts and Charles was charged with illegal possession of a firearm and ammunition. They were tried separately. Rethea remarried shortly before the trial commenced.

The case came before Mr Justice Ronnie Bosielo. The prosecution grilled Rethea because she claimed she did not recognise Charles on the night of the murder, even though he had been working for her husband for two years. She denied that she had asked Charles to kill her husband or that she had had a sexual relationship with him. She claimed she was happily married and had no reason to want her husband dead.

Mr Justice Bosielo sentenced both Rethea and Charles to life imprisonment. Rethea appealed to the Constitutional Court on the grounds that her rights had been infringed by the admissibility of the minister's testimony. She claimed there had been a breach of trust, since she was under the impression that her confession would remain confidential. If his testimony had been inadmissible, she would not have been found guilty. The Constitutional Court refused her appeal on the grounds that she had been found guilty not only on the basis of Gerhardus Bothma's testimony, but also on that of Hanlie Botha and Charles Nxumalo.

At thirty-five years of age, Rethea Wilson, a woman used to fur coats and gold jewellery was sent to Pretoria Central Prison as a category B prisoner. She would share her cell with ten to fifteen other women.

Comment
It is obvious that Rethea was motivated by pure

greed. Not once was there any indication that she had considered divorcing her husband because he was abusive. If indeed he had abused her, why did she remarry him? She was prepared to trade sex instead of paying Charles Nxumalo for committing the murder. Charles admitted in court that he was a 'fortune hunter' who agreed to commit the murder purely for the money. Rethea managed to dupe him for a while during their 'affair', but the moment she rejected him, he had no qualms about turning the tables on her. Gerhardus Bothma experienced a moral predicament about divulging Rethea's confession. He had received threatening phone calls before he went to the police, and one woman pleaded with him to think of the children who would have to grow up without a mother. What about the children who would have to grow up without a father?

Case study: Lynn Catherine Harvey, 1999

Forced threesomes, nipples and private parts being burnt with candles, sexual penetration with a banana, anal sex causing permanent damage, being flogged while forced to have sex with her daughter's boyfriend, and her husband kicking her private parts with his boots were some of the examples of the gruesome abuse forty-eight-year-old Lynn Harvey testified she had been subjected to during thirteen years of marriage to Steven Harvey.

The court listened in fascinated horror as Lynn Harvey, mother of seven children, testified that she had been sexually abused by her own father in Britain from the age of thirteen. By fifteen she was pregnant and did not know if the father of the child was her father or her boyfriend. She married Steven Harvey in 1986 and they moved to South Africa in an attempt to put Lynn's terrible past in Britain behind them. However, Lynn's nightmare continued for a further thirteen years as the victim of Steven's perverse sexual practices. Eventually, when Steven wanted to use dogs to assault her sexually, she could endure it no longer and asked her son from a previous marriage, John Hoare, to help her get rid of Steven. John hired a hitman, the illiterate Mpho Paulus Mokoena.

On the night of 18 September 1999, it was arranged that John would take the children away from the family's smallholding for the evening. Lynn alleged that one of her daughters had screamed, 'Kill him, Mummy, kill him,' as she waved them goodbye. Her daughter's cry erased all second thoughts about the impending murder, testified Lynn, convincing her that she should open the door of her home to the hired hitman that night. Mpho duly entered the house, while Lynn waited in the television room. He encountered the physically handicapped Steven Harvey in the bedroom. Although Steven tried to defend himself with his crutch, Mpho stabbed him to death with his pocket knife. Mpho returned to Lynn and said simply: 'It's done.' Lynn phoned a family friend, who arrived and allegedly removed the television and computer to fake robbery as a motive.

Lynn, John Hoare and Mpho Paulus Mokoena were all charged with murder. Initially, a wave of sympathy swept over the courtroom as the dreadful abuse Lynn had suffered was recounted, but the mood changed dramatically when Lynn's daughter Marie Ann turned state witness against her mother and stepbrother.

Marie Ann testified that Steven was not a violent man unless provoked. She said her mother had often bragged about her sexual exploits to her friends. She had killed her stepfather for money. After an insurance policy was paid out, Lynn had gone on a wild shopping spree.

This prompted state advocate Christo Roberts to cross-examine Lynn about the insurance policy she inherited from Steven. Lynn's reply was that she had not expected the policy to be paid out since it had lapsed, and she was going to have to sell their home in order to pay Mpho the sixty thousand rand she had promised him to commit the murder. 'It would have been evil,' she said, 'to use Steven's policy to pay for his own death.' She had never submitted a claim on the policy and did not know why it was paid out three months after her husband's death. She reaffirmed that the motive for the murder was the years of sexual abuse Steven had inflicted upon her. She added that she had persuaded Marie Ann to turn state witness so that she would not be charged as an accomplice. After Marie Ann's testimony, however, Lynn claimed that her daughter was lying and that she suffered from multiple personality disorder.

Mr Justice Ronnie Bosielo called for more information about the insurance policy. The trial took a last-minute about-turn when Jaqueline Jansen van Vuuren, an employee of the insurance company, arrived unexpectedly to testify.

In her testimony Jaqueline said that Lynn had visited her office soon after Steven's death and returned almost every second day, demanding that the policy be paid out. She was dishevelled and hysterical and claimed that her children had no food and that their water and electricity had been cut off because they had no money. Jaqueline explained to Lynn that the policy had lapsed. It had been brought up to date in March 1999, whereafter it had once again lapsed. Lynn returned with proof that the outstanding amount had been paid on 6 September 1999. Jaqueline said she felt sorry for Lynn and contacted her head office to enquire about the possibility of the policy being paid out. The head office replied that they needed to know the HIV status of the insured. When the post-mortem results showed that Steven was HIV negative the policy was paid out, barely three months after his death. Lynn received about half a million rand, half of which she spent on her children and a Christmas party.

The court was stunned into silence. The initial sympathy for the battered, sexually abused woman turned to disgust.

Before sentencing, Steven's mother, June Cox, spoke out. She objected to the fact that Lynn had depicted her son as a sex-crazed monster and provided information that painted a different picture of Lynn Harvey. Lynn had, indeed, been sexually abused by her father and her first husband. She had two children with that husband, but they were removed by the welfare department because they were neglected. She divorced him in 1974 and in 1976 she married Spencer Ian Hoare, the father of her fourth child, John. Lynn claimed that although she was fond of Spencer, she did not necessarily want an everlasting relationship with him. A year later she had an affair with a lodger, who fathered her daughter Marie Ann. Spencer left her, and the lodger abandoned her too. Her children were returned to her and lived with her for ten months before appealing to be returned to foster care. Lynn was denied access to them after this. She met Steven Harvey in 1981. At first she turned down his proposal, but finally married him in 1986. She stipulated three conditions before she agreed to marry him: she wanted a dishwasher and a swimming pool, and he had to promise her that he would not act out his sexual fantasies with a black woman. They had two children and moved to South Africa in 1990. Lynn had numerous 'swinging' affairs with men, including her husband's friends and her daughter's boyfriend. She had been plotting her husband's death for four years.

Before sentence was passed Lynn told the judge that she had loved her husband, but that he had turned into a monster. She said she did not have the physical strength to kill him and so she had to involve other people. She regretted involving her children and would miss her husband for the rest of her life.

Mr Justice Bosielo had no qualms about expressing his feelings during sentencing. He found it abhorrent that Lynn had played the racial card by using a black man to commit the murder. He said it would convey the message that 'another black barbarian had murdered an innocent person' which was not conducive to promoting peace in post-apartheid South Africa. He also found it abominable that Mpho Paulus Mokoena had attacked a helpless cripple and that he was motivated by greed to commit murder. He called Lynn an emotionless, lying manipulator and found the fact that she had involved her children in her evil plans constituted aggravating circumstances. Although he had some sympathy for John Hoare and Mpho Paulus Mokoena, he could not allow his emotions to influence his judgment.

Mr Justice Bosielo sentenced all three of the accused to life imprisonment. After sentence had been passed John Hoare described his stepfather as a loving man who did not deserve to die.

Mpho Paulus Mokoena said he did not want to kill Steven, but felt obliged to. 'I could not turn back on my word because they would think I am a bad person.'

'I loved him. When I looked at him I saw the man I loved, but it was only the shell remaining ... he had become a monster,' said Lynn. She added that the judge could take away her freedom, but that her love for her husband would always remain with her.

Comment

The question as to whether Lynn Harvey lied about Steven's alleged sexual abuse, or willingly participated in the exploits, remains hypothetical. Steven Harvey cannot defend himself. One wonders, however, if Lynn Harvey's life would have turned out differently if she had not been sexually abused by her father when she was a teenager. What link can there be between the rape of a teenager by her father, the subsequent death of a man, three people being sentenced to life imprisonment, and the lives of seven children being disrupted for ever? What about the family of Mpho Paulus Mokoena? Where did Mpho, a simple and uneducated man, acquire the distorted value system that it would be bad to break his word, but that it was not bad to rent himself out as a killer? The consequences of one man's lust erupted into a cycle of violence that spanned two continents. Lynn Harvey, John Hoare and Mpho Paulus Mokoena were all adults who could have stopped the cycle, but because of greed they chose not to, and they have to take responsibility for it.

Case study: Elizabeth 'Bettie' Cathrina de Vries, 1999

A local Pretoria newspaper, *Die Beeld*, carried a photograph of Bettie and her attorney husband Leon de Vries taken on 10 March 1999 at a Pretoria restaurant where they were allegedly celebrating their fifteenth wedding anniversary. The headline proclaimed that the photograph was taken only hours before Leon was killed in an attack at their smallholding at Bon Accord Dam. A second photograph showed a tearful Bettie describing what had transpired that fateful night.

When she and her husband returned to their property at ten o'clock, Leon got out and went to open the gate, his firearm in his hand, for they were always wary of hijackers. As he opened the gate he turned and smiled at her and then she heard a shot. Leon returned fire and shouted to her to drive to the house. She refused and he ran back to her. Another shot was fired, the bullet grazing Leon's head. After a third shot the wounded Leon pursued his fleeing attackers. Bettie drove home to call for help and when she returned to the gate, she found her severely wounded husband lying next to the fishpond. Abraham Cilliers, a neighbour, arrived on the scene and the bleeding Leon managed to tell him that his attackers were white men. Leon died in hospital with a weeping Bettie at his side.

Bettie was arrested eight months after the murder.

She had conspired with her brother-in-law, Nico Christiaan de Vries, to kill Leon. Bettie complained that Leon was abusive and she promised to set Nico up with a restaurant in the Cape once the estate paid out. She said she stood to inherit three million rand, of which she was prepared to give him one million. Nico succumbed to the suggestion.

On 10 March 1999, Nico met an unemployed friend, fifty-one-year-old Jacobus Petrus 'Jarrie' van Jaarsveld. He told Jarrie that he hated his brother and wanted to 'sort him out'. He asked Jarrie to accompany him to his brother's smallholding at Bon Accord. While waiting outside the locked gates, Nico asked Jarrie if he wanted to earn a quick buck. He would give him twenty thousand rand if he helped him to kill his brother. He assured Jarrie that Leon's wife Bettie was involved in the plan. They had to make it look like an attempted hijacking. Jarrie volunteered to do the shooting. When the couple returned home Leon got out to open the gate. Jarrie later testified that he had second thoughts about killing Leon and lowered the firearm and aimed at his stomach.

Bettie hired a private investigator, Wikus Willemse, to look into the murder. She was concerned because the estate could not be settled until the case was solved. Wikus later testified that his relationship with Bettie came very close to being an affair. She told him that she suspected Nico was responsible for her husband's death. Wikus suggested they go to the police, but Bettie refused, implying that Nico would have her killed if she did so. When she offered to pay him fifty thousand rand to steal the murder docket, Wikus became suspicious. And when she offered him two hundred thousand rand to get rid of Nico, his suspicions were confirmed.

Months after the murder, the police received information that a killer had been hired to murder Leon and they arrested Nico. Nico turned state witness and his statement led to the arrests of Jarrie and Bettie.

The trial came before Mr Justice Eben Jordaan. It took an unexpected turn when a mother of two, who claimed to be Bettie's lesbian lover, was called to testify. She said she had responded to an advertisement in a newspaper that sought ladies between twenty and forty years who dreamt of a discreet and exciting relationship with an attractive, married bisexual woman. Apparently the advertisement had been placed by Leon, who liked watching Bettie and her lesbian lover. The lesbian lover produced a letter written by Leon, in which he thanked her for making his wonderful wife happy.

The witness, whom the judge ordered should remain anonymous, testified that she regularly visited the couple, sometimes with her husband, although her husband was unaware of her sexual relationship with Bettie. Bettie told her that Leon was abusive and that she wanted to kill him. Two days before the murder she again told the witness that she planned to kill Leon. The witness became increasingly uncomfortable and tried to persuade Bettie to change her mind.

On the night of the murder Bettie phoned the witness from the restaurant to tell her that she and her husband had been reconciled. She called later to tell the witness that Leon was in hospital because he had been shot. She said he was a violent man who had died a violent death; if he survived he would think twice before lifting his hand to a woman again.

The witness found Bettie's behaviour after Leon's death very strange. She had asked the witness to help her to sort out the insurance policies, and made an appointment with a hairdresser and a manicurist. She went shopping and paid her accounts. On the advice of her therapist, the witness told her own husband everything.

Bank official Wilhelmina Strydom testified that Bettie had offered her a five thousand rand bribe to alter Leon's will so that she would inherit everything. The executor of the will, Jacobus Botha, testified that the estate amounted to only five hundred rand and that he could not locate Leon's last will.

Nico de Vries was indemnified. Jarrie and Bettie were both found guilty of murder and sentenced to life imprisonment. After sentencing, Jarrie apologised to the family and said he was prepared to go to jail for what he had done.

Bettie made the following statement: 'I had nothing to do with the murder. No matter what my husband did to me, I still loved him. My family, my advocate and my psychologist believe in my innocence. I will prove my innocence and I will be free. It's just a matter of time.'

Thirty-seven-year-old Bettie appealed against her sentence. She stated that she had two minor children (she had another son from a previous marriage), was a first offender and was the victim of domestic abuse and that these were mitigating circumstances that had not been taken into account. Judges T Spoelstra, D Basson and J van der Westhuizen disagreed. Mr Justice Spoelstra pointed out that family circumstances do not play a role in sentencing. Mr Justice van der Westhuizen added that Bettie herself had contributed to breaking up the family when she killed the children's father. Also, she had not provided concrete evidence about the alleged abuse. She was a voluntary participant in the lesbian sexual exploits and consented to her husband's extra-marital affairs. The judges found that she had committed the murder in order to inherit her husband's estate.

Comment

Bettie de Vries' case followed the rather typical pattern of a woman planning a contract murder on her husband. First, she offers the accomplice(s) a huge financial reward, payable of course only after the estate has paid out. The accomplices are usually blinded by the prospect of financial reward and are sometimes manipulated by the sexual prowess of the woman, and so they agree, never realising that no money will be forthcoming. An estate cannot be settled when foul play is suspected and it may take years before a murder is solved. They also do not realise that a woman who is prepared to kill for money, will be very unlikely to share it once she has obtained it. She will be more inclined to kill again to preserve it, as Bettie showed by wanting to hire Wikus to kill Nico, in order not to have to share the money with him. Who would she have hired to kill Wikus?

Secondly, the wife usually plays the role of the grieving widow, especially for the media, which Bettie accomplished by having the 'anniversary dinner' photograph published in the press. (It was in fact not their anniversary.) Thirdly, she cannot help celebrating her freedom, even if only by something small, such as having her hair done. She also gives herself away by her insistent enquiries about the insurance policies.

The murder is always thinly disguised as another crime – robbery, hijacking, etc. Criminals have a nasty habit of underestimating the investigative abilities of the police and private detectives. When such a murder is planned, the conspirators often do not pay enough attention to the staging of another crime. It is usually an afterthought. They are so concerned with the murder itself that they forget about the details. A crime may be committed within a short space of time, but the police have endless time to unravel every little detail and find an explanation for it. The time factor, combined with the state of the art forensic capacity in South Africa, and the experience and intelligence of police officers, are factors that criminals, especially murderers, do not reckon with.

Finally, as is often the case in contract murders, one party often spills the beans on the other as soon as the heat is on. It becomes a race as to who will reach the door of the state prosecutor first. However, not all state witnesses receive indemnity. This decision rests with the judge, who will evaluate the witness's truthfulness during testimony.

Case study: Elizabeth Johanna 'Bettie' Lotter, 1999

On 24 October 1999, Captain Ephraim Phiri investigated the case of a man who had been beaten to death near Siyabushwa on the Marble Hall Road in the North West province. The body was in the driver's seat of a car.

Captain Phiri ruled out robbery as a motive for the killing, as the victim was still wearing his expensive watch and had five thousand rand in cash in his pocket. Bloodstained newspapers and a plastic bag found in the boot of the car indicated that the body had been transported to the scene in the boot. Detective Sergeant Johannes Thessner, who also arrived on the scene, noted that the victim, a middle-aged man, had been assaulted in the face and had a wound on the back of his head. The victim was fifty-eight-year-old Martin Lotter, owner of several hair dressing salons in Pretoria.

While he was still at the scene, Detective Sergeant Thessner received a phone call from Mrs Bettie Lotter. She said she had received information that her husband had been murdered near a river. Ten minutes later, he received a call from a man claiming to be a friend of the family, who informed him that Bettie had earlier tried to kill her husband with *muti*.

The following day Bettie phoned Thessner again to enquire about the post-mortem, since she needed the death certificate in order to finalise insurance policy payouts.

Bettie Lotter was taken in for questioning. She said that she had married Martin in 1991. She claimed she was his sixth or seventh wife and he was her third husband. Their relationship was stormy and Bettie had left him on several occasions because he had allegedly assaulted and belittled her. She even divorced him in 1993, but moved back again. There was an ongoing pattern of moving in and moving out. Bettie said she preferred living at Martin's house, because he had a swimming pool. The last time she moved back, she decided she was going to stay.

Bettie discussed her husband's abuse with her domestic helper, Catherine Lala Mmoto, who suggested she consult a sangoma about the problem. She went to Mamelodi where she saw a man named Chauke, who promised that her husband would disappear before Christmas. He gave Bettie some *muti* to put in Martin's food, which she duly did. Martin lost weight and had bouts of nausea. Bettie panicked and told Chauke that if Martin died, forensic tests would prove that she had poisoned him, and also that she did not want him to suffer. Both Bettie and Catherine feared they would be caught if they continued the poisoning, so they stopped. Martin recovered and two weeks later he began abusing Bettie again.

Catherine then introduced Bettie to Fana Martin Makama, who in turn introduced her to Fransisco Mabanda, a sangoma from Mozambique. Fransisco promised Bettie that her husband would disappear within three days. All he needed was Martin's car keys.

Someone tipped Martin off and the day before he was murdered he phoned Bettie and confronted her with her visits to the sangoma. She told him that she had consulted the sangoma in an effort to improve their relationship.

The day after the murder Bettie told the police that the two men had arrived at her home. Fransisco threw the bones and smeared some *muti* on the kitchen door knob. Her husband did not return home that night and she received a call from the police the following night telling her that his body had been found in his car on the Marble Hall Road.

Bettie and her two accomplices were charged with murder and the trial came before acting Mrs Justice Lizette Meyer.

Nicky Snyman, a family member, testified that it was Fana and Fransisco who had phoned Martin and told him that his wife had offered them eighty thousand rand to kill him. He phoned his sister and told her about this. Nicky testified that about a month before his murder Martin had threatened to change his will to disinherit Bettie.

Matu Judas Maseko, also a sangoma, testified that Bettie had been trying to kill Martin with *muti* since 1998. She visited him on several occasions. He gave her *muti* to improve her relationship with Martin and to drive away evil spirits, but refused to give her *muti* to kill since this was against his ethics. When Bettie insisted that she wanted Martin dead, he told her to go away.

Louisa Kruger, Bettie's sister-in-law, testified that she had moved in with the Lotters for a while. She was supposed to cook for the family, but she became upset when Bettie repeatedly threw 'spices' into the food behind her back. Neither Bettie, her seven-year-old daughter, nor Catherine Mmoto ever ate the food. During August 1999 both Louise and Martin became seriously ill. They had severe stomach cramps and vomited. Once Louise made mashed potato and the little girl wanted some, but Bettie wouldn't allow her it. Martin, however, gave the child some, whereupon she became ill. Louisa testified that a sangoma once had supper with them and gave Bettie *muti* that would improve her finances.

Fana testified that he and Fransisco went to the Lotters' residence on 23 October 1999. Martin was playing golf. Bettie pointed out the main bedroom to him and he asked everyone to leave the house as he needed privacy to do his work. Martin arrived home unexpectedly and Bettie explained to him that the sangoma was trying to save their relationship. Martin attacked Fana, saying that he was going to kill him. Fana defended himself and a struggle ensued. Martin fell and bumped his head. Fana and Fransisco loaded the unconscious man in the boot of his car and left.

Bettie disputed Fana's evidence. She claimed that she had given him the car keys that night because they needed to fetch more *muti* in Mamelodi. She denied having seen Martin. She thought he was having a drink with friends and was not concerned when he did not return home that night, because he was with friends.

It was established that Fana told Bettie of Martin's death at a local shopping centre before the police notified her.

Both Fana and Fransisco claimed that Martin was alive when they left him in the car. They expected him to drive home once he regained consciousness. However, Fana was found in possession of Martin's car keys when he was arrested. He could not explain how he expected Martin to drive home without the keys. Forensic tests proved that Martin's injuries were not consistent with a bump on his head. It was more likely that he was killed with an object such as a golf club. He had also been wounded with a sharp object.

All the accused were found guilty. Fana was found guilty of being an accessory to murder.

Bettie broke down in tears and asked that her bail be extended for one night as her daughter was receiving a prize at school and expected her to be there. Mrs Justice Meyer refused the request.

The state also established that Bettie had never instituted criminal proceedings against Martin for the alleged abuse. She never received medical attention for injuries and she never asked for an interdict against her husband.

Comment

Bettie Lotter clearly enjoyed the luxuries of her husband's home. Whether or not he abused her cannot now be established. Her claims that she required *muti* to save their relationship are pathetic. Bettie Lotter risked the life of her child – the one she was so concerned about on the day she was sentenced – when she poisoned Martin's food. She showed no concern that her sister-in-law consumed the poisoned food. She callously risked the lives of innocent people to get her hands on her husband's money.

Because of her honest testimony Catherine Mmoto was not charged with being an accessory to conspiracy to murder.

The practice of sangomas is centuries old. They act as physicians and psychologists within their communities. There is no doubt that some of their remedies are effective. Mostly they use herbs, plants and animal products in their medicine. They also communicate with the spirits of the deceased ancestors. They have formed a national forum which registers legitimate sangomas to protect their profession. However, there are still some 'witchdoctors' who use poison and human body parts as *muti* and who no doubt commit evil deeds. Sangomas distance themselves very strongly from such practices.

7

Poisoners

Over the centuries female killers have always been attracted to poison as their weapon of choice. During the sixteenth and seventeenth centuries poisoning of adversaries was a common occurrence. Few people know that the practice of covering dishes with a silver hood originated as a way of preventing food from being poisoned as it was taken from the kitchens to the dining halls.

Douthwaite (1929) in *Mass Murder* says poisoning was so universal that ladies displayed poison bottles on their dressing tables as openly, and used them on others with as little compunction, as women of today display and use face cream and lipstick. Tophiania was a famous poisoner in medieval Rome who ran a lucrative business exporting her fatal potions all over Europe. She called her concoctions 'Manna of St Nicolas', referring to the miraculous oil of the tomb of St Nicolas, in order to confuse customs officials. The poison was better known among her customers as Aqua Tophiania.

Famous women in history who used poison included, of course, Lucretia Borgia who was said to have poisoned her husband and lovers; Catherine de Medici who poisoned her political adversaries in order to secure the throne of France for her children; Madame de Montespan who, with the help of La Voison, attempted to poison Louis XIV after he took a new lover; and Marie Madeline de Brinvilliers, a French noblewoman who poisoned her father and brothers in order to gain her inheritance.

Poison was a favourite murder weapon for centuries because it was mostly tasteless and left no traces. But in 1790 Johann Metzger developed the 'arsenic mirror' which could detect the presence of arsenic. When substances containing arsenic were heated and a cold plate held over the vapours, a layer of arsenic would form on the plate. This could not, however, prove that arsenic had been ingested. Dr Valentine Rose of Berlin improved on this technique in 1806. He boiled body parts of a victim suspected of being poisoned with arsenic. The resultant fluid was filtered through nitric acid to remove any remaining flesh and to convert arsenic into arsenic acid. Metzger's method could then be applied to prove that arsenic had been ingested by the victim.

In the late eighteenth to early nineteenth century, a Spaniard called Matthieu Joseph Bonaventure Orfila, a professor at the Paris School of Medicine, wrote *Traites des Poison* (1813) in which he developed several methods to identify poison. In 1836, James Marsh developed a more sensitive test to detect arsenic, which became known as the Marsh Test. Hugo Reinsch improved on the Marsh Test in 1842 and in 1850 Jean Stas of Belgium developed a test to identify nicotine. The Arsenic Act was passed in England in 1851, stipulating that arsenic had to be coloured with soot or indigo. The Pharmacy Act of 1852 made it compulsory for buyers to sign the poison register. Subsequent Acts in 1951, 1968 and 1971 made it virtually impossible for anyone but a doctor to buy poison in England (Marriner, 1991).

Brian Marriner in *Forensic Clues to Murder* (1991) classifies poison into four categories: poisons which affect the oxygen-carrying capacity of the blood, like cyanide; corrosive acids and alkalis, like chloroform; poisons that destroy body tissues, like arsenic and vegetable poisons; and poisons that leave no trace of entry, but can kill after being absorbed, like ricin.

During the twentieth century, techniques for the identification of poison developed to such an extent that vegetable poisons could be traced from crystals examined under a microscope. Column chromatography and spectroscopic methods were further refinements. In spectroscopy the spectrum of light is measured against a chart of known poisons. More than two thousand poisons can be identified in this way (Marriner, 1991). It has become so easy to identify poison that this method of killing has declined to a bare 6 per cent of all murders committed in the United States.

Although it might be relatively easy to establish death by poisoning, it is more difficult to establish who has administered it. Poisoning often takes place within family confines and the poisoner makes sure that the victim's death is confused with an illness. Poisoners are usually found guilty on circumstantial evidence, when it is proved they had both the motive (usually financial) and the opportunity to kill the victim.

Physicians have learned to identify the symptoms of poisoning, which in some cases are very similar to known illnesses, but warrant further investigation. Heavy metal poisoning, for instance, is consistent with the symptoms of Guillan-Barré Syndrome – an acute disorder of the peripheral nerves which causes weakness and paralysis of the limbs.

Arsenic was the favourite poison for centuries since it had no taste or smell, although a large amount is needed to cause death. It has lost popularity now, since it can be traced in every part of the body, even if the victim has been buried for years.

In South Africa tissue samples from victims suspected of being poisoned are sent to the toxicology laboratories of the Department of Health for analysis. The Forensic Laboratory of the South African Police Service in Pretoria is also equipped to conduct tests to detect and identify poisons, as are a few private laboratories.

South Africa has had its fair share of women who followed in the footsteps of their notorious sisters of old.

Case study: Maria Lee, 1947

Maria Lee was one of South Africa's most notorious sexual predators. Newspapers described her as highly sexed, much-married or possessed, extremely money conscious, cruel, callous, implacable and unmoved by the suffering of her victim. Maria was not an attractive woman. She could have been described as plump and matronly, but she exuded an irresistible sensuality that held men captive. And her looks disguised a sharp intelligence.

She was born Maria Helena Gertruida Christina van Niekerk and she was married in 1915 at the age of sixteen. She and her husband lived in the Lichtenburg district, in present day North West province, and had four sons. The marriage ended in divorce and Maria remarried shortly afterwards. The second marriage did not last long either. She had several affairs and then married twenty-four-year-old Jan de Klerk Lee, her third husband. He died of tuberculosis in 1941 and Maria inherited a comfortable estate.

During the Second World War, she corresponded with a soldier, whose identity has never been known.

In 1945, now aged forty-six, Maria met Alwyn Jacobus Nicolaas Smith, a man in his twenties, at a dance in Pretoria. Nico, as he was called, had just returned home after serving in the war. Maria, twenty years his senior, had already decided to move to Cape Town to take up a position at Lennon Limited, a pharmaceutical company. She and Nico met again on the train to Cape Town. Nico was not very intelligent, but his good looks and vigorous sexual appetite more than made up for that.

Maria rented a room from Mrs Sarah Jacobs, at 6 Prince Street, Gardens, in Cape Town. She and Nico lived as husband and wife and she called herself Mrs Smith. Maria found new employment at the American Swiss watch company and Nico worked as a taxi driver. One day they invited their friends to a smart hotel to celebrate their marriage. No such marriage had taken place, but their friends were not aware of this. Maria paid for the celebration.

After their 'wedding' Maria told Nico that she had to go to Pretoria to attend to her business affairs there. What she in fact did was meet the anonymous soldier, returning from the war, at the Johannesburg station. The next day she married him (this time, legally) in Pretoria and held a reception at a friend's home. Maria had rented a private mail box in Pretoria and she and Nico wrote passionate love letters to each other while she was away. Maria and her soldier husband moved to a town in the Free State. She arranged with a friend to forward her letters from Nico to this town and sent her replies to the friend, who forwarded them to the unsuspecting Nico in Cape Town.

Maria told her soldier husband that she was an advocate who had a practice in Cape Town, which provided her with an excuse to return to Nico. While she was there, she wrote love letters to her husband in the Free State, using the same private mail box and obliging friend to forward them. Sometimes her husband visited her in Cape Town, and she would book them both into a hotel, telling Nico she would be out of town for a while.

On one occasion when she was in Pretoria Nico met an old army friend who offered him a job in Durban. Maria, back in Cape Town, began stealing jewellery from American Swiss which she sent to Nico to sell in Durban. When he came home to Cape Town on leave, Maria begged him to hand in his resignation on his return to Durban. She gave him cash to buy a new car and also presented him with an expensive watch. He left for Durban on 23 October 1946, and became mysteriously ill on the train.

Nico was taken to hospital in Durban, where he recovered, but when he returned home to Cape Town, he once again suffered terrible stomach cramps. His physician, Dr Helman, was baffled. He was even more surprised when Nico told him, in Maria's presence, that he no longer required his professional services. For a while, Maria was the only person who attended to him.

The soldier husband was unhappy with his wife being out of town so often and threatened to divorce her if she did not return to the Free State. Fortunately for him, Maria agreed to the divorce. Nico was not so lucky.

On the morning of 2 May 1947, Maria phoned Dr

Helman and informed him that her husband was dying. Dr Helman wanted to call immediately, but Maria said she was not sure Nico would want to see him and that she would phone him later. But Dr Helman went to their apartment on his own initiative. He found a dying Nico and a very concerned Maria. Nico died while he was there. Much to Maria's consternation Dr Helman refused to issue a death certificate, but went instead to the Caledon Square police station and asked the police to remove the body to a mortuary for a post-mortem.

Two constables were sent to the apartment where they found a grieving Maria kissing the body of her dead 'husband'. State pathologist Dr Keen sent tissue samples to Johannesburg for analysis. Two months later he received the results: Nico had died of arsenic poisoning. Colonel Fred van Niekerk was appointed to investigate.

When Colonel van Niekerk arrived at Maria's apartment he found her in bed. She was wearing dark glasses and was still distraught about the death of her 'husband'. With her permission the police searched the apartment and confiscated Nico's pocket book. Colonel van Niekerk established that Nico had left a substantial estate, of which Maria was the sole beneficiary. The money consisted mainly of bonds. The car and the watch which she had given him were specifically mentioned in the will. He interviewed the landlady, Sarah Jacobs, who told him that Maria had come to her one day with Nico's will and had asked her and a friend to witness it. They signed the will, but not in Nico's presence. Sarah Jacobs also informed Colonel van Niekerk that Maria had begun seeing one of Nico's friends shortly after his death.

A clerk at a pharmacy where Maria had once worked

told Colonel van Niekerk that Maria had brought him the will, written out in her own handwriting, to type. When Colonel van Niekerk consulted the poison register at the pharmacy he found that Nico Smith had bought rat poison on 14 January 1947. It would appear that Maria had sent her lover to buy the poison she used to kill him.

Colonel van Niekerk also established that Maria had asked for the body to be cremated, but the request was refused. She then asked for it to be embalmed. She did not know that the state pathologist had already sent tissue samples to Johannesburg for analysis.

By October 1947, Colonel van Niekerk had enough evidence to charge Maria Lee with the murder of Nico Smith. Maria had fled to Pretoria, but he followed her there and arrested her in a hairdressing salon on 14 October 1947. By this time, Maria was already engaged to a man in Pretoria. While in custody in Pretoria Central Prison, she shared a cell with a Mrs M. Maria offered to pay Mrs M's bail, if she would undertake some errands for her in Cape Town. She also confessed to Mrs M that she had given Nico an overdose of arsenic. As soon as Mrs M was released on bail she went to the police. No mention had been made in the press that Nico had died from arsenic poisoning. Maria's confession to Mrs M thus established that she had first-hand knowledge of the crime.

The trial began on 6 April 1948 at the Cape Town Supreme Court before Mr Justice Gabriel Steyn. Women queued the night before in order to secure a seat in court. Maria, dressed to the nines with black ostrich feathers adorning her hair, acted the innocent, grieving widow. On 10 May 1948, Mr Justice Steyn read his judgment. A faint smile played over Maria's face behind the black net of her mantilla.

'I can but come to the conclusion,' read Mr Justice Steyn, 'that Mrs Lee never bore any love or affection for Alwyn (Nico) Smith. The attempts to convince those who came in contact with them in their private lives, of her deep devotion and attachment for him, were a feigned and hollow mockery. If true love was absent and there is this continuous pretence of doing whatever she could for Smith during his illness, then it must have been a deliberate attempt at camouflage. The question is then: why did she so conduct herself? The answer is that she was carrying out a foul design and engaged in a series of acts of poisoning which led to the death of Alwyn Smith. For these reasons I have no alternative but to find her guilty as charged.' By the time he had finished reading, Maria's smile had vanished and the haggard face of the forty-eight-year-old murderess was revealed.

On 17 September 1948, Maria Lee was led to the gallows at Pretoria Central Prison.

Comment

Maria Lee was the epitome of the classic psychopath. Women like her are not always beautiful – some of them are actually quite unattractive – yet they are so alluring and charming that one is almost tempted to use the words 'witch' or 'magic' when it comes to their ability to manipulate men. Every man who crossed Maria's path became devoted to her. Psychopaths are experts at pretending to love. They can express love eloquently, and show love arduously, but they are incapable of feeling it. They are motivated only to please and enrich themselves. Their emotional facades, as Maria demonstrated when the police arrived to remove Nico's body, are so convincing that most people cannot resist believing them. They feed on the sympathy of others in public, while behind the scene they find perverse pleasure in their uncanny ability to deceive.

Case study: Margaret Elizabeth Rheeder, 1957

Margaret Elizabeth Harker was born on 6 September 1922 at Platbos near Knysna in the Western Cape province. She was the eighth child born to a desperately poor family. When her father died, Margaret's mother had no choice but to remarry. She made a terrible choice, for her second husband, Cornelius Share, was a lazy man who claimed he was too ill to work. The family had to survive on a meagre welfare handout. Cornelius may have been too sick to work, but his illness did not prevent him from 'blessing' the family with another five children. He died in 1934 and the twelve-year-old Margaret and her two older sisters, Gwen and Olga, were sent to an orphanage. They probably fared much better there than at home, but when Margaret turned sixteen she decided it was time to seek her own fortune.

She found employment as a domestic worker in Cape Town for a few years, but returned to Knysna when she was about twenty and worked as a maid in the local hotel. Here she married virtually the first man she could find. She soon realised that he was a drunken layabout who was often involved in bar fights. Every time her husband was locked up for being drunk and disorderly, another man kept her company. Margaret became the mother of two daughters. Eventually she divorced her husband and left town with her little girls.

In 1951 she met Benjamin Rheeder in Groot Brak River. He was in the process of divorcing his wife and needed an able housekeeper to look after his children.

Margaret and her children followed him to Port Elizabeth in the Eastern Cape where she took up her new position. It did not come as a surprise to anyone when they married. Benjamin was a dockworker, but he managed to provide for his extended family. There was only one problem: his new wife detested his own children.

In 1955 the couple took in a young boarder. To the thirty-three-year-old Margaret, handsome twenty-two-year-old Johannes Strydom was the answer to her dreams and it did not take her long to find her way to his bedroom. As is so often the case when people are conducting clandestine affairs, Margaret began accusing her husband of infidelity. She confided to her young lover and her sister that she wished to be rid of him. She even told Johannes that she had once laced Benjamin's food with rat poison, but he smelled it and threw it away. Johannes asked why she did not divorce Benjamin. Her answer was the same as that of many women who contemplate murder: she would rather kill him so she could inherit what little money he had. The fact that her husband beat her now and again only sealed his fate.

On 27 April 1957 Margaret bought ant poison at a pharmacy. She signed the register herself. Two days later she diligently handed the two men their sandwiches to take to work. Benjamin returned home early that afternoon because he had been taken ill. The next morning he went to the doctor's rooms. Dr Edmund Bloch diagnosed fibrositis and prescribed medicine but Benjamin did not recover. By midnight he was in terrible pain and Dr Bloch was consulted once more. A few days later Margaret reported to him that Benjamin was better, but that she would keep him at home for a few more days. The good doctor visited his patient at home and felt satisfied that he was being properly cared for by his wife.

On 7 May Dr Bloch was called to the Rheeder home, where he found his patient very ill indeed. His tongue was swollen and he could not swallow, he had diarrhoea and had been vomiting. He complained of pain in his legs.

Margaret left her husband's bedside while the doctor was with him and chatted to her neighbour. She mentioned she would inherit some money if Benjamin did not make it. The neighbours also noted that Margaret turned up the volume on the radio to drown the sound of Benjamin moaning in the bedroom.

That evening, Margaret's brother came to visit the patient. At about ten o'clock Margaret gave her husband his medication with a spoon, in the presence of her brother. Benjamin Rheeder died before sunrise. Dr Bloch arrived, diagnosed gastro-enteritis and attributed the death to heart failure. He signed the death certificate there and then. He wanted to contact an undertaker to remove the body, but Margaret declined. She kept the body under her watchful eyes for the two days until the funeral.

After Benjamin's death Margaret began criticising Dr Bloch. She even told neighbours he had asked her what to write on the death certificate. These stories reached Constable Petrus Rheeder, who decided to investigate the death of his namesake. The first person he questioned was Johannes Strydom, who told him about the rat poison in the food.

Constable Rheeder visited Margaret. He was looking for poison, but found none in her house. Three days later he had established that Margaret had bought ant poison from a pharmacy and he went to see her again. She had thrown the poison away after they used it on the ants, she told the detective. She was worried that one of the children might find it.

Next, Constable Rheeder requested an exhumation. Analysis of the contents of Benjamin's stomach revealed enough arsenic to enable the pathologist to determine that it was administered at about ten o'clock the night before he died.

On 7 November 1957 Margaret Rheeder pleaded not guilty to the charge of murder. Nine days later, a jury found her guilty, but they suggested that there could be mitigating circumstances, because Margaret had suffered so much in her life. The judge did not agree, and sentenced her to death. On 6 May 1958, just before she was hanged, she admitted that she had killed Benjamin.

Comment

Margaret Rheeder's case is very similar to that of other women who poisoned their husbands. Many of them grew up in desperate poverty and were forced to marry young in order to survive. They did not have access to contraceptives and by the time they reached their mid-twenties, they had become middle-aged women. They longed to be free of both marriage and children and yearned for a life that had always been denied them. Usually they blamed their husbands – the ones who had rescued them from poverty – for their circumstances and justified their acts by reasoning that they deserved a decent life. Poison was once the easiest way to dispose of a husband but, decades later, it has been replaced by a tendency to hire hitmen and to stage a fake burglary or hijacking.

Case study: Maria Magdalena Groesbeek, 1969

Maria Magdalena Deyzel was born on 9 February

1936 in the Schweizer-Reneke district in the North West province. She was one of six children. Her family moved to Vryburg where Maria, or Miempie, as she was nicknamed, decided to leave school in grade 9 in order to earn a salary to help her parents. Her parents objected when she wanted to move to Harrismith in the Free State to work in a factory, but she persuaded them she was old enough to stand on her own two feet.

She met Christiaan (Chris) Stephanus Buys, an illiterate labourer twelve years older than her, in Harrismith. Six weeks after their first encounter, on 11 July 1953, the couple got married. Maria was eighteen. In the fifteen years of their marriage, Chris changed employment fourteen times. They moved from farm to farm, but eventually settled in Harrismith. By then they had four children. Chris worked for the railways, earning about a hundred rand a month. Every month he would diligently hand his salary over to Maria, who complained there was never enough money, yet who employed three domestic workers to help her in their small railway house. She also chain-smoked.

Gerhard Groesbeek had a below average intelligence. He left school in grade 8 and joined the railways where he met Chris Buys, who was about twenty-three years his senior. Both men were reserved and shy. One day, Chris invited young Gerhard home to look at his tame baboon and his fish. This was the first time Gerhard, who lived with his parents a few blocks away, met Maria. He thought she was fat, but friendly. He became a regular visitor and enjoyed playing with the children. In 1967, Maria and Chris moved into a slightly larger house in Vow Street and in September that year Gerhard moved in as one of two lodgers. By August 1968, Gerhard and Maria had become lovers.

She was twelve years older than him.

The affair soon became public knowledge. Maria and Gerhard openly held hands in the street, and nosy neighbours arrived to find them in bed together during the day when Chris was out. These neighbours tried to persuade Maria to mend her ways, but she refused. After the couple had admitted to the family that they were in love Gerhard's parents tried to intervene, Chris called upon Maria's parents, and Maria's brother-in-law even threw Gerhard out of the home on Christmas Eve in 1968. Gerhard moved back with his parents, Maria moved into a boarding house and they continued their affair. Later Maria moved back home and asked Chris for a divorce, but he refused. Gerhard was not yet twenty-one and his parents refused to give him permission to marry.

On 31 January 1969, Maria bought ant poison which she threatened to take in the presence of a neighbour and her children, but they persuaded her not to. When Chris asked her why she wanted to commit suicide, she said it was because he would not agree to a divorce, and that she would attempt it again. Chris steadfastly refused. She attempted suicide nine times and also told a colleague of Chris' that she would poison him if he did not divorce her.

On 27 February 1969, Maria bought the second bottle of poison. She administered a drop of poison in Chris' coffee that night and another drop the next morning. He became ill and Maria obtained medicine for him. But any misgivings she might have had about murdering her husband did not last long, for on 12 March 1969, she bought the third bottle. Again she administered the drops of poison in his coffee that day and the next. Chris became ill and was admitted to hospital. On 19 March she purchased the fourth bottle. When Chris returned home on 20 March, she repeated the process. On 24 March Chris was again admitted to hospital in agonising pain. He was transferred to the Kroonstad Hospital, where he died on 28 March 1969.

After the funeral Maria and her children moved to her parents' home in Wolmaransstad, where they stayed for a short while. She returned to Harrismith on 10 April 1969 and Gerhard asked her to marry him. He would turn twenty-one in two days' time. Maria agreed. On 12 June 1969, the couple were married in Ladybrand. With her children, they moved in with Gerhard's parents. Two weeks later, the police arrived on the Groesbeeks' doorstep to arrest Maria. Gerhard was already at the police station. A post-mortem analysis had revealed that Chris died of arsenic poisoning.

Maria confessed to killing her husband. She told the police that he had often assaulted her. She reckoned that if she tried to poison him and then nursed him back to health, he would either forgive her and work at their marriage, or divorce her. She said life with Chris was unbearable since he never bathed before he got into bed. She could not stand his abuse or his filthy habits. The children testified that they had never witnessed their father abusing their mother.

While Gerhard and Maria were awaiting trial prisoners her children were moved to a place of safety. Gerhard told fellow inmates that Maria was pregnant with his child and that was the reason she had poisoned Chris. He denied all knowledge of the murder. Maria pleaded with Gerhard to acknowledge that he was an accomplice, since she believed it would lighten her sentence. Gerhard refused.

Maria tried to implicate Gerhard in the murder.

She said he gave her the money for the poison. She also directed the police to love letters she had hidden in a mattress, which would implicate Gerhard.

On 10 December 1969, Maria Groesbeek was found guilty of murder and sentenced to death. She was executed on 13 November 1970.

Comment

Gerhard Groesbeek was acquitted. At the age of twenty-two he had to start a new life. He returned to his parents' house and sometimes visited Chris' grave. He admitted his affair with Maria was purely sexual. She had seduced him and it was his first sexual encounter. During the trial he found out that she had had several affairs with other young men. 'I don't know what I saw in that old woman,' he said finally.

Whether or not Gerhard Groesbeek knew about the poison, he was not involved in the murder. He was not intelligent enough to have organised it. Maria killed Chris because he stood in the way of her marriage to her young lover.

Case study: Theresa May Hall, 1986

Theresa May was the oldest of six children. Her father died when she was only five years old and her mother moved in with her grandparents. The children were placed in an orphanage. Theresa finished grade 11 and began working and taking care of her mother. She married Frank Ernest Hall, a man thirty-three years her senior. The couple lived in Rowellen Mansions in Noord Street, Johannesburg. Theresa's mother, Rhoda Dora Peyper lived in the same block of flats. For seventeen years, Theresa took care of her husband and mother, until one day she decided she had had enough.

Towards the end of 1985 Theresa asked the caretaker of the building, Mrs Heila Gericke, for rat poison. She wanted to poison the rats at the dustbins, she said, and there was also a rat in her flat. Mrs Gericke offered her a mousetrap, so Theresa said she would buy rat poison herself. She bought a bottle of arsenic at a pharmacy in Plein Street, Johannesburg, and from January 1986 she began systematically administering arsenic to her husband's brandy.

On 18 March 1986, Frank had a bad fall and broke his hip. He was admitted to the Johannesburg General Hospital. Frederick Johannes van Zyl, a patient who shared a ward with Frank, later testified that Frank, aged eighty-one, was a cantankerous patient. Theresa visited her husband three times during his hospitalisation, but the couple always argued. Theresa always brought her husband a flask containing amber liquid, which a nurse later testified was brandy.

On the evening of 25 March, Frederick heard Theresa say to her husband: 'I'll *sommer* give you arsenic to shut you up for ever.' A few hours later, Frank died. Scarcely had he breathed his last than Theresa was demanding a death certificate. She became quite agitated when it was not immediately forthcoming. She expressed no grief at the death of her husband and was stony-faced when she collected his belongings.

The post-mortem revealed that Frank had died of senility, pneumonia, a broken hip and arsenic poisoning.

Theresa told Mrs Gericke that Frank's death was a relief for both of them since he had been in a lot of pain. She was tired of old people, she said, and had no friends of her own age. She told the funeral parlour she was too busy too attend Frank's service and that they should scatter his ashes under a tree.

Rhoda Peyper, now in her late seventies, moved in with Theresa. She had undergone two eye operations and complained of pain and discomfort. Theresa decided to solve the problem by administering arsenic in her mother's tea. Fortunately, Rhoda survived.

Ten months after Frank's death, the police came knocking at Theresa's door. She made a mistake. She offered to bake Warrant Officer Jan Kock a cake without arsenic in it.

At work the following day, Theresa joked to her colleague Elizabeth Cloete that the police would not be able to prove anything since Frank's body had been cremated. She said they had asked for the flask she had used to take brandy to Frank in hospital and she had handed it over. She also told Elizabeth that she would be able to draw as much money from the bank as she wanted after Frank's estate was wound up.

No traces of arsenic were found in the flask. But the offer to bake him a cake led Warrant Officer Jan Kock back to Theresa's flat, where he seized everything in her kitchen. Arsenic was found in the baking powder.

Theresa was arrested on 3 February 1987 and charged with murder and attempted murder before Magistrate R E Laue. She pleaded guilty, but he changed her plea to not guilty and referred the case to the Johannesburg Supreme Court. She was sent to Tara Psychiatric Hospital for forensic observation and was found sane and fit to stand trial.

Mr Justice Irvin Steyn presided at her trial. Theresa claimed she had discovered the bottle of arsenic in January 1986 and confronted Frank with it. He told her that he was sick of life and wanted to die. She said he must have been taking the arsenic for quite a while, since there was not much left in the bottle. He asked her to administer the arsenic to him and she complied, although she had wanted to tell the police about it. She said she assisted her husband in a 'sort of mercy killing', but she never intended him to die. Of her mother, Theresa said that she had suffered a great deal since the eye operations and she administered the arsenic to relieve her pain.

Mr J A Greyvenstein, the forensic scientist who analysed samples from both Frank and Rhoda, found that Frank had two thousand times more arsenic in his blood than normal levels. Rhoda Peyper's health improved remarkably after she moved in with her younger daughter when Theresa was arrested.

Mr Justice Steyn found that the state could not prove beyond reasonable doubt that Frank had actually died of arsenic poisoning, since the post-mortem had also established that he had pneumonia. But since she had admitted to administering arsenic to Frank, he sentenced Theresa, aged forty-eight, to seven years and a consecutive seven years for the attempted murder of her mother. She would serve an effective fourteen years. Shortly after sentence was passed Theresa phoned her mother. She first enquired about her health and then told her about the sentence.

Rhoda Peyper said she bore no grudge against her daughter. She told the press that Theresa was fond of entertaining, but she could remember falling ill after she had eaten one of Theresa's cakes.

At that time, Theresa Hall was the only convicted woman in South Africa to have escaped the death sentence for poisoning, since it could not be proved beyond reasonable doubt.

The judge could find no motive for the crimes, apart from the fact that Theresa May Hall was 'sick and tired of old people'.

Comment

Unfortunately we do not know what Frank Hall's
estate was worth, but Theresa's comment that she
would be able to draw as much money as she wanted,
perhaps indicates her true motive. Theresa married
a man old enough to be her father; in fact, he was
almost ten years older than her mother. She needed
a father figure to take care of her and her mother,
something she had had to do for most of her life. For
seventeen years, Frank probably fulfilled this need,
but once he became old and ill, his usefulness was
over. When two months had passed, she probably
thought she had got away with it, and tackled her
second obstacle, her ailing and complaining mother,
in the same way. Theresa's flippancy betrayed her
when she offered to bake that cake for Warrant
Officer Jan Kock. Although he was fond of chocolate
cake, he declined the offer, saying that he was on a
diet. His instincts may have saved his life.

Case study: Unita Hendrietta Green, 2000

Unita Green had no one to discuss her problems
with. She lived with her long-time lover on the farm
Doornrivier in the Zeerust district of North West
province. No neighbour, friend or confidant would
listen to her complaints about her lover's alcohol and
drug abuse and his affairs. No one understood the
humiliation she had endured. She was fifty-one years
old and felt that she did not deserve such treatment.
The only solution she could think of was to get rid
of fifty-seven-year-old Gert van Rensburg. So she
laced his tomato and onion sandwich with Temic,
a rat poison. He died in bed right next to her that

Wednesday night in February 2000, but Unita just rolled over, snuggled down behind the dead man's back and slept on.

The next morning she was faced with the problem of getting rid of his body. She dragged it to the kitchen and heaved it, head first, into the freezer. While pondering what to do next, Unita stroked the head of her dead lover. She quickly closed the lid when the owner of the farm, Mr Wouter Kirstein, arrived. Two days later she asked Wouter to bring her some petrol from town.

On the Friday night Unita switched off the freezer and removed the body. She drenched the body, blankets and clothing with petrol and set them alight. While Gert burned on his pyre, she talked to him and told him she would scatter his ashes in the veld, so he could return peacefully to nature. When the fire turned to ashes, Unita noticed Gert's skull was still discernible. She cut it off with a knife and fried it over the coals. She kept her promise to Gert and scattered some of his remains in the veld. She shovelled the rest of the burnt body into a suitcase, and dropped it in a cattle dip.

Eventually, news of the missing man led to a police investigation and on 5 May 2001, Mr Justice N J Coetzee sentenced Unita Green to life imprisonment.

Comment

The horror of this case is beyond words, yet no one should ask the question: How could a woman do this? Obviously, a woman did. There was no mental illness at play here. Sane people are quite capable of committing horrendous acts. The judge found that nowhere in her confession did Unita attempt to justify her acts. She knew exactly what she was doing. She had solved the problem of an abusive man and afterwards she solved the problem of getting rid of the body. Her actions were cold and calculated. In court, Unita told the judge that she had not meant to kill her lover, she merely wanted to scare him so that he stopped drinking. At the age of fifty, Unita had not yet learned to take responsibility for her miserable life. She did not regard herself as being in control of her own life. She did not leave her abusive lover, nor did she attempt to find other employment or accommodation. Unita Green did not implement any alternative solutions to her problems. Murder was the only solution she could think of.

8

Spree Killers

Serial killers are often confused with mass murderers and spree killers. There are several important differences between these categories of homicide that should be addressed if confusion is to be avoided.

A *mass murderer* is defined as a person who kills several victims during one event at one location. There is no cooling-off period and the victims may be family members. Barend Strydom, who killed several people on one day at Strijdom Plein in Pretoria, is an example of a mass murderer. Mass murderers usually want to make some kind of statement, which may be political; or, as in the case of family murders, emotional.

A *serial killer* is a person who murders several victims, usually strangers, at different times and not necessarily at the same location, with a cooling-off period in between. The motive is intrinsic; an irresistible compulsion, fuelled by fantasy which may lead to torture and/or sexual abuse, mutilation and necrophilia (Pistorius, 1996). The motivation of the serial killer is the principal factor which differentiates him from all other murderers.

The *spree killer* is defined as one or more persons who kill their victims during one event, which could be of long or short duration, at two or more locations, with no cooling-off period. Spree killers literally get a 'kick' out of senseless violence. In many cases a male and female team perpetrate this type of crime. Spree killing became famous with the real-life American couple Bonnie and Clyde, and the fictional film 'Natural Born Killers'.

Case study: Charmaine Phillips, 1983
Charmaine Phillips met Peter Grundlingh on 24 December 1981. He was the worst Christmas gift she could ever have hoped for. Charmaine, who was living in Durban at the time, wanted to buy dagga (cannabis) for her father. An ex-boyfriend introduced her to his 'connection', Peter Grundlingh, who would be able to provide her with the dagga. From the very first moment they met, there was a fatal attraction between Charmaine, aged seventeen, and Peter, aged thirty-four. They were inseparable from that moment on. Peter took Charmaine to Johannesburg to meet his mother. She also met his son Martin. She recalled later that she witnessed Peter's temperamental outbursts in his dealings with his ex-wife, but she did not think he would ever vent his temper on her. They were too much in love.

Peter became obsessively jealous of Charmaine. He insisted that she have his name tattooed on her belly so no other man would touch her. During the fourth month of their relationship Charmaine fell pregnant. Peter's possessiveness increased. He burnt Charmaine's clothes and ordered her to wear only what he chose for her. When their son was born, Peter was initially furious that it was not a girl and continually assaulted Charmaine. One night she went to sit in the car with her baby, while Peter was enjoying an alcohol and drugs orgy with friends. He later joined her in the car, banged her head against the gear lever and bashed her face with his fist, while she was holding the baby.

The couple had left Johannesburg by then and Peter was doing odd construction jobs as they travelled south. By May 1983 Charmaine had become terrified of Peter and fled to her brother, Robert Dubery, in Vryheid. Peter arrived to fetch her, but Robert ordered him away. A few days later Peter was back. Now armed, he threatened to shoot Charmaine, their child and her family if she did not go with him. Charmaine capitulated. He took her back to Durban and they spent the night in his car, parked on the beach. They sold some of their clothing and the baby's pram and then went to a hotel in Point Road. There Peter met Gerald Douglas Meyer in the bar and invited him to go for a drive. Near Stanger, Peter pulled over into a sugar cane plantation. He and Gerald got out of the car to smoke dagga. Charmaine remained in the vehicle with the baby. The next moment a shot rang out and Charmaine saw the first of their four victims fall to the ground. Peter got back in the car and threatened to kill her if she ever told anyone.

They drove to Richards Bay where they spent another night in the car. The following day, Peter went into the local hotel and emerged with an old friend. He had been working in Richards Bay when he first met Charmaine. His friend offered them a place to stay and they spent three days with the man.

On one of these days, a Saturday, Peter arrived home with a stranger, Vernon Alexander Swart, and a case of beer. He told Charmaine that they would be giving Vernon a lift to Empangeni. At Melmoth, Peter pulled the car off the road and parked among some trees.

He ordered everyone out of the car. Charmaine knew what was going to happen. Peter told her to tie Vernon to a tree. While she was doing this she begged Peter not to shoot him, but the next moment the fatal shot rang out. Peter stole Vernon's wallet. They returned to Richards Bay and slept at their host's house. The following day they left for Durban and booked into a hotel. Peter paid with the money he had taken from their second victim. A day or so later, they were on their way north.

On Saturday 25 June, the by now familiar pattern repeated itself in Ermelo. Peter entered a bar and emerged with a stranger. He told Charmaine that the man, whom he called Boet, needed a lift to Kinross. The man was Barend Greyvenstein. When they reached Secunda, Peter remembered that he had old friends who lived there and he drove to their home. The friends, Tjaart and Maria van Heerden, were having a braai with their family. When Peter asked if he might invite his girlfriend and their friend inside, Tjaart laughed and said as long as they behaved themselves, they were welcome. They watched rugby on television, and Barend wanted to place a bet on the winning team. He boasted that he had four hundred rand in his bank account. After the game, Peter began to get agitated and the three of them and the baby left. Peter drove to the Kinross Dam where he forced Barend out of the car. He demanded the pin number of Barend's bankcard, but Barend refused to give it, whereupon Peter promptly shot him. Peter drove to the home of another friend, about half a kilometre away. Only the domestic worker was at home, but Peter intimidated her into allowing him, Charmaine and the baby to spend the night. The next day they continued to Bloemfontein, where the same pattern was repeated for the fourth time. This time the victim was Martin Mofosi.

By this time the police had found the trail of bodies. Photos and descriptions of Peter and Charmaine were featured on the programme Police File on national television.

On 15 July 1983 Peter and Charmaine were arrested in Vereeniging. They had left the baby with Peter's sister-in-law.

During the trial Charmaine and Peter made a pact. She would plead guilty to shooting the men, hoping that because she was only eighteen when the murders were committed and because she had a baby, the judge would be lenient towards her and Peter would escape the gallows. Charmaine behaved abominably in court, shouting obscenities and spitting at people.

Mr Justice President John Milne had no sympathy for Charmaine. He found her as guilty as Peter. Peter was sentenced to death and although Charmaine's age saved her from the gallows, she received four life sentences. Before they were parted, Peter made her a promise. If he did not receive clemency, he would write a letter explaining her innocence.

Charmaine was detained at Kroonstad Women's Prison where she displayed the same delinquent attitude she had shown in court. She soon formed a gang, whose members she tattooed, and although she was so young, she emerged as a leader. She transgressed every rule, had sex with fellow inmates and generally created havoc. She was often placed in solitary confinement. It took her six years to calm down. However, a prison official later remarked that while in retrospect Charmaine might have put on a show, but she never actually hurt anyone physically.

After fifteen years in prison, Charmaine had

completed grade 12 and qualified as a hairdresser. She was also a talented artist. She had repented, become a Christian and turned her life around. It was only then that police officer Brigadier Ivor Human (now retired) handed over the letter that Peter Grundlingh had written to her just before his execution on 27 July 1985. In the letter he declared that Charmaine was innocent of the murders.

With this new evidence, Charmaine petitioned three State Presidents in a row, the latest being President Thabo Mbeki, for her release. Prison authorities were of the opinion that her good behaviour was enough reason to have her paroled. She was informed that she could apply for parole when she had completed twenty years of her sentence. At the time of writing in August 2004, Charmaine was still in prison eagerly awaiting parole.

Comment

Why would a young girl of seventeen become a spree killer? Charmaine was born on 22 July 1963, the fourth of seven children. Her mother was an alcoholic and her father a schizophrenic. At the age of seven the welfare authorities removed Charmaine and her siblings from their parents. She was placed in a children's home, where she was spanked for bedwetting. When the family's circumstances improved the children were sent back home. Her mother kicked her father out of the house, believing he had sexually molested one of her children. The family moved to Pietermaritzburg, where Mrs Phillips turned to prostitution. The children were once again removed to children's homes and then to foster families. When Charmaine's mother was murdered in a drunken brawl, there was no chance of them ever being reunited.

Charmaine ran away from her foster family to join a gang of street children in Durban. At the age of fourteen, she was already a streetwise prostitute. She was arrested for drug possession and released into the custody of her father. At age fifteen she had a police record and she was pregnant. She was placed in a home for unmarried mothers in Port Elizabeth, where she had her baby, Ricky-Lee. She was forced to give the child up to foster care.

After the birth, she was sent to an industrial school in Cape Town, but she ran away to Port Elizabeth to be close to her son. She continued her life of drugs and prostitution and was once more arrested. She received a suspended sentence. In Port Elizabeth, she met a Greek sailor, Gavnil Skubandis and married him for the sole reason that she would stand a better chance of gaining custody of Ricky-Lee. (Ricky-Lee was eventually adopted at the age of eleven and moved to Ireland with his new parents.) Gavnil was at sea but would return for Christmas in 1981. He intended taking Charmaine and Ricky-Lee to Greece. On the day before his return, Charmaine was in Durban, where she met Peter Grundlingh.

With a background like this, it is hardly surprising that Charmaine Phillips became party – whether willing or not – to senseless spree killing. Hopefully she will make a worthwhile contribution to society by counselling delinquents, once she is released.

Case study: Ansune Putter, 2001
There are similarities in the cases of Ansune Putter and Charmaine Phillips, but fortunately the one victim that Ansune and her boyfriend Albertus Jacobus le Roux shot, did not die.

Ansune was a pleasant eighteen-year-old school girl in Carletonville in North West province when she met twenty-nine-year-old Bertie le Roux in 2001. He impressed her immediately with his fake French accent and his alleged accomplishments as a world-renowned chef. She ran away with him. In November 2001 they were working in a restaurant in the town of George in the Western Cape. The manager of the restaurant, Shawna Oberholzer, said they introduced themselves as Ricky and Candy. Ricky boasted about his cookery programme called 'The Wicked Chef' on DSTV. He said he and Candy were travelling the country, teaching housewives how to cook. Ricky also maintained that he had written several cookbooks and was worth millions. One day Candy showed Shawna a gold ring set with sapphires and diamonds that Ricky had given her.

But behind the scenes, things were not so rosy between Ansune and Bertie. He often assaulted her, raped her and cut her clothing with a knife. He threatened to kill her and her family if she ever left him.

Bertie and Ansune hitch-hiked to Cape Town, where he forced her to use drugs. On the night of 25 February 2001, the couple found themselves at the Engen garage in Beaufort West, hoping to hitch a ride.

Unfortunately for thirty-year-old Mr Johann Strydom, a restaurant manager from Mossel Bay, he was the one they approached. Johann did not suspect anything at first. Yet in retrospect he remembered that Ansune, who introduced herself as Verushka, asked for a lift south, to Cape Town. He told her he was on his way north. Then Bertie, who introduced himself as Vantsho, asked for a lift north, to Three Sisters. Johann told the couple to hop in. As they drove north Bertie, who was sitting in front, noticed some restaurant T-shirts in the back of Johann's car. Discovering that Johann was also in the restaurant business, Bertie began one of his boastful conversations. Ansune sat quietly in the back of the car, with her bag between her legs. Bertie often reached back to stroke Ansune's leg.

When they approached Three Sisters, Bertie pretended to make a phone call, telling Johann he had just remembered about a friend who would be in Colesberg, and if they could travel with him to Colesberg, the friend would take them further.

Somewhere between Three Sisters and Colesberg, Bertie reached into the back of the car. The next minute he was pressing a pistol to Johann's head. He ordered Johann to turn off on a dirt road. Johann stopped the vehicle and Bertie ordered him out and into the boot. The couple drove on for a while and then Bertie stopped the vehicle and ordered Johann to get out. He made him walk into the veld. When Bertie told Johann he did not want to shoot him, since he was a 'nice guy', Johann knew he was lying. Scarcely had Bertie said this than he pulled the trigger. Johann fell to his stomach, covering his head with his hands, and begged for his life. A shot hit him in the head. Then the couple drove off.

Fortunately Johann did not die. He walked four kilometres until he reached a house, where he found help and was taken to hospital. He related his experience to Captain Fanus Olivier, who obtained a video clip of the two suspects from the garage. Newspapers carried the picture and the story on their front pages.

On 2 March 2001, Bertie and Ansune calmly walked

into a police station in the Strand in the Western Cape and handed themselves over as 'Bonnie and Clyde'.

Mr Justice Percy Sonn presided over the trial in November 2002 in Victoria West. Ansune told him that they had 'picked up the firearm next to the road near Ermelo'. Bertie had thrown it away after the attack on Johann Strydom, and the police were never able to recover it. Both Ansune and Bertie were found guilty. In February 2003 Bertie was sentenced to thirty-six years for robbery, attempted murder and illegal possession of a firearm and ammunition. He would effectively have to serve twenty years. Ansune faced the same charges and was sentenced to twenty-six years, of which she would serve an effective fifteen years. Her youth was taken into consideration. Johann Strydom recovered completely.

Comment

The cases of both Charmaine Phillips and Ansune Putter illustrate the somewhat typical pattern of an impressionable young girl seduced by an older man who promises her the world. Such men will typically lie and boast to conceal their feelings of inferiority. As soon as the girl is in his power, the man will begin to abuse her and break her down. Typically, he will also threaten to kill her or her family should she leave him. On the one hand, the girl finds their adventure exciting, but on the other hand she is too scared to run away. She also realises that as an accomplice she is in too deep, and the man probably makes her well aware that if he goes down so will she.

The young woman in this instance has the same psychodynamics as an abused woman and she also suffers from the same illusion about true love as women who become involved in love triangles.

9

Stalkers

Stalking is psychological terrorism. Its components are the surveillance and harassment of the victim, and threatening physical injury to the victim or his property. Stalking can even escalate to the murder of the victim. Inflicting terror upon the victim can be intentional or unintentional, but the fact remains that the victim of the stalker is unsafe wherever he goes.

It is impossible for anyone to comprehend how a normal person's life can be turned into a living hell by a stalker, unless he has himself been the victim of a stalker. Without proper psychological management the victim will become the psychological captive of the stalker. Just as the stalker continuously thinks about the victim, the victim is continuously aware of the stalker, and has to deal with a burden of unnecessary emotions, ranging from irritation and anger to absolute fear. The victim is not free to think his own thoughts or to feel his own emotions. Awareness of the stalker is pervasive, always lurking in the back of his mind.

Apart from the psychological consequences of being stalked, the victim's physical environment becomes a prison. He is reluctant to leave the safety of his home, travelling only to work and back. Friends and neighbours have to do his shopping, he does not want to socialise outside the home or seek outside entertainment and becomes socially isolated. The victim may even lose his job if the stalker turns up at his place of work and causes a disturbance.

Communication and contact between the victim and the outside world becomes limited. He is too scared to answer the telephone. Telephone calls at work have to be screened and answering machines connected to home telephones. Friends start avoiding the victim for fear of becoming victims themselves.

Victims may be forced to spend money on extra security systems, employing bodyguards, or even relocate and, in extreme circumstances, change their identities. The families of victims live in fear of their own lives, as well as that of their harassed relative. Their lives become complicated patterns of coded telephone rings and door knocks.

It is almost impossible to imagine how a stalker can disrupt the different aspects of the life of an innocent person and his family.

The following types of stalkers have been internationally identified:

Celebrity stalker/erotomanic stalker

Most of the stalkers of this type are mentally ill. They suffer from a delusional disorder with the predominant belief that a particular person, usually of higher status (such as a celebrity or public figure) is in love with them. A small number are just disillusioned fans of celebrities. They are self-absorbed loners, characterised by feelings of inferiority.

The erotomanic stalker has the delusion that he

is loved by the victim and believes that he has an idealised romantic love relationship with the victim in which they share a spiritual union, rather than a purely sexual relationship. The stalker generally does not understand the harm he is inflicting and is convinced that the victim enjoys the attention.

Celebrities often send autographed photographs of themselves to fans. The stalker will interpret this fairly usual public relations initiative as a personal invitation. Research has indicated that a personal confrontation, whether friendly or not, between the stalker and the celebrity is ineffective in changing the stalker's behaviour; indeed, such a confrontation may only reinforce his behaviour since he has now gained the personal attention of the celebrity.

Successful counteraction would involve the celebrity enforcing complete separation between himself and the stalker. All personal contact should be severed and the matter referred to a professional who can manage the case.

This type of stalker tends to engage in the following activities: phoning, sending letters, pestering family or friends of the victim, spreading rumours, surveillance, sending gifts, breaking and entering, showing up at the workplace. Damage to property, causing the victim physical harm or killing the victim is unlikely, but it has happened in extreme cases.

Stalking of this nature tends to continue for years. It is seldom that an erotomanic stalker will follow through on a threat, although precautions should always be taken.

Love obsessional stalker

This group differs from the erotomanic stalker in the sense that the erotomanic delusion is only one of several delusions and other psychiatric symptoms. Psychiatric diagnoses which are applicable to this group are bipolar (depression and mania) affective disorder, schizoaffective disorder or schizophrenia, and borderline personality disorder might also apply. The group might include stalkers who are obsessional in their 'love' for their victims, but do not believe that the victims reciprocate the love. The obsessional 'love' is therefore not necessarily a delusional disorder, but an extreme emotion directed towards the victim.

This type of stalker will perceive obstacles to their adoration of the victim as tests of love, which they have to overcome to win or be worthy of the victim's love. They are unlikely to engage in physically harmful acts, but this has been found in isolated cases. The duration of the obsession can last up to twelve years but the duration of actual contact with the victim, which might include anything from telephoning to letter writing, is brief.

Dependent, rejection-sensitive stalker/simple obsessional stalker

This type of stalker is usually the jilted lover of the victim. He will gather information about the victim and pester friends, family or neighbours to reveal the victim's whereabouts and facts about the victim's lifestyle. He will usually send love letters and gifts to the victim, having established the victim's preferences for certain items – for example, favourite flowers, perfume, etc. He will also often call or visit the victim and look for excuses to make contact.

This type of stalker has also been known to break into the victim's house just to read their mail, listen to their answering machines, or to watch them sleeping.

Such stalking is psychological torture, and it can also escalate to include damage to property, attacks on pets, threats to family members and friends and even murder of the victim. The stalker's usual perception is: 'If I can't have him/her, no one else will'.

Stalkers in this group will have experienced losses during their childhood years – for example, losing a parent through death or divorce, rejection by parents, abuse and neglect. They have suffered intolerable hurt as children and fear subsequent rejection by adult partners. They are unable to grieve naturally or accept the ending of a relationship. They are ultimately dependent on their partner, but at the same time hate the partner for their dependency. Some of them may suffer from mental illnesses and personality disorders. Many of the men in this category will hide their feelings of dependency behind a macho image and are generally abusive towards women.

Gavin de Becker in *The Gift of Fear* (1997) gives the following indicators of 'intimate enemies' where the ex-lover or ex-spouse is the stalker:

The person

- accelerates the pace of the relationship by premature commitment, living together or pressure to get married;
- mostly resolves conflict by intimidation and violence;
- is verbally abusive;
- uses threats and intimidation as instruments of control and abuse;
- breaks or strikes at things in anger – symbolic violence like tearing up photographs is relevant;
- has abused a partner in previous relationships;
- has an alcohol or drug abuse problem and cites these as excuses for behaviour;

- has a history of police encounters – even if they are not related to interpersonal violence;
- uses money to control the activities and purchases of the partner;
- is obsessively jealous and often projects this jealousy;
- refuses to accept rejection and is over-sensitive to criticism;
- expects the relationship to last for ever;
- minimises incidents of abuse;
- enlists friends, family and colleagues of the partner to keep in contact with the partner or as sources of information;
- has inappropriately followed or kept the partner under surveillance;
- resists change and is inflexible;
- identifies with other violent people;
- has moods swings;
- blames others;
- has an interest in or access to weapons and instruments of power, or weapons are a substantial part of his/her persona;
- has experienced or witnessed violence as a child;
- if male, uses male privilege and is generally derogatory towards women.

The victim fears that the stalker will harm or kill him/her.

Simple obsessional stalkers may include those who target persons with whom there was no romantic involvement, but some prior relationship such as a customer, neighbour, acquaintance or a professional relationship.

The duration of the stalking in these cases tends to last less than a year. This group is also more likely to make person-to-person contact with the victims and they issue more threats than other groups. They are also more likely to follow through on their threats.

Immature romantic stalker

This kind of stalker is a teenager who develops a crush on either a person known to him or a stranger. They seldom resort to making threats or injuring the victim and usually grow out of it.

The adolescent will write anonymous love letters, phone the victim and put the phone down, leave messages on an answering machine, watch the victim from a distance, leave notes or flowers on the victim's car, etc. Unfortunately this kind of behaviour can escalate into a more serious type of stalking.

The following mental illnesses have been associated with stalking.

Paranoid delusional disorder

A person with this disorder has non-bizarre delusions involving situations which might occur in real life, such as being followed, having a disease or being deceived, but in reality there is no substance to these delusions. Apart from the delusion, the person's behaviour is not otherwise odd or bizarre (Kaplan & Sadock, 1991).

A delusion is a false belief based upon incorrect inference about an external reality, not consistent with the person's intelligence and cultural background, that cannot be corrected by reasoning.

The following are specific types of paranoid delusions:

- erotomanic type: the person is convinced that another person, usually of a higher status is in love with him;

- grandiose type: the person has a self-perception of inflated self-worth, special powers or knowledge; or identifies or has a special relationship with a deity or famous person;
- jealous type: the person believes his sexual partner to be unfaithful without any substantiation;
- persecutory type: the person believes he, or someone close to him, is being malevolently treated. He repeatedly takes his complaints to legal or law enforcement authorities.

The development of a paranoid delusional disorder starts during the childhood years when the child grows up in the following environment:

- a high value is placed on achievements and pride, but an unhealthy pride;
- discipline is aimed at humiliating the child rather than rectifying behaviour;
- good behaviour is not praised but rather devalued;
- parents project their own shortcomings on to others;
- the child has no privacy from prying parents;
- there is a lack of basic trust between parent and child;
- there is no intimate relationship between parent and child, resulting in 'remote controlled' children.

Schizophrenia: paranoid type

A person suffering from paranoid schizophrenia will have one or more systemised delusions with frequent auditory hallucinations related to a single theme. There is no incoherence, loosening of associations, flat or grossly inappropriate affect, grossly dis-organised behaviour or catatonic behaviour (Kaplan

& Sadock, 1991). (A hallucination is a sensation or perception which occurs in the absence of any external stimulus. The person sees, hears, smells or feels something which is not there.)

Such persons have no sense of interpersonal boundaries and tend to 'fuse' with the victim, taking on the victim's personality. They may also be convinced that the victim has a bad double who should be exterminated.

Paranoid personality disorder

Individuals with this disorder have a long-standing suspicion and mistrust of people in general, refuse to take responsibility for their own emotions and are often hostile, irritable and angry (Kaplan & Sadock, 1991).

They function adequately in their daily lives, but their interpersonal relationships are characterised by friction and conflict. Their suspicious attitude is not only directed towards their romantic partners, but also towards family, friends and colleagues.

Borderline personality disorder

A person afflicted with borderline personality disorder cannot tolerate the dichotomy of opposites in a relationship. They will either over-idealise or completely disparage others. At one moment they can absolutely adore a person, only to hate them the next.

Borderlines have difficulty in differentiating between reality and fantasy. They therefore often perceive a celebrity in the role that the celebrity takes on in his professional life, for example, a movie or on television, and cannot conceptualise that the celebrity has a private life and personality completely different from his professional role.

Stalkers suffering from borderline personality disorder are impulsive, emotionally unstable and experience mood shifts and depression. The mildest criticism or perceived insult evokes feelings of rejection, abandonment and shame. This results in them venting their anger on the victim by ruining the victim's career, reputation, family life, friendships or even by killing them. Stalking the victim becomes a full-time preoccupation.

This type of stalker often commits suicide.

Case study: Nina Olivier, 1994

The day Nina Olivier walked into George Kellerman's office, his life turned into a nightmare. He was a prominent lawyer in George, a quiet town in the Western Cape. Little did he know the sassy, sultry looks and vivacious personality of Brazilian-born thirty-something Nina, a mother of two, masked a very disturbed psyche.

Nina hired George to represent her in her divorce, but by the time the divorce was granted, she had become obsessed with him. Although forty-seven-year-old George was single, he was not interested in Nina. He found her attentions intrusive and although he had been friendly towards his client, he felt she had misinterpreted his feelings completely. For a period of eighteen months Nina stalked George, his continuing rejection of her notwithstanding.

In May 1992 George told a friend that Nina had threatened to kill him. In June he wrote her a letter asking her to stop spreading rumours about their non-existent love affair as it was damaging his career. George was also a local politician and a prominent figure in his community.

In September 1992 George laid a charge of indecent assault against Nina when she placed her hand in his trousers, while holding him at gunpoint for two hours. George won the case and Nina's licence to own a firearm was revoked. Furious, she turned to George in the courtroom and hissed: 'This is only the beginning.'

In February 1993 Nina was still stalking George. She would sit in her car outside his office and watch the building for hours. She wrote letters to him, she talked to others about their 'relationship' and she phoned him. George, who by now had armed himself and improved the security arrangements at his home, obtained an interdict against her. Nina retaliated by appealing against the firearm and indecent assault conviction. In May 1993 a Supreme Court judge overruled the previous convictions. He was not convinced that George was completely innocent, and reasoned that since Nina and her children lived on a smallholding outside the town, she was entitled to own a firearm for her protection. Nina retrieved her firearm, a .38 revolver, from the police.

George pleaded with the Commissioner of Police to revoke her licence once more, alleging that she was unstable. He also informed the chief magistrate that Nina had threatened to kill him. In the mean time Nina had of course broken the interdict and George took her to court again. She was fined two thousand rand.

Nina manifested typical stalking patterns. She ordered a video called 'Till murder us do part' in George's name. He had no doubt about who had ordered it. He laid another charge against Nina. Nina went to visit George's ex-wife in Hout Bay, where she was living with their children, and phoned him from there. George was terrified she would harm his children. She said that if he withdrew the latest charge, she would leave him alone. George was not the sort of man who gave in to threats and he refused to withdraw. He warned her to stay away from his children.

Eventually the police requested two psychiatric evaluations of Nina to determine whether George's application that her firearm licence be revoked was valid. One psychiatrist found her fit, the other did not. Nina remained in possession of her firearm. Whenever the police tried to contact her regarding the latest charge, Nina would disappear. The case was postponed time after time. George took in a female boarder hoping to deter Nina, but she intimidated the boarder into leaving with death threats.

Finally on Friday 25 February 1994, almost two years after they had met for the first time, the trial regarding Nina's transgression of the interdict began. She submitted a medical report which stated that she had had an abortion; she claimed it was George's baby. George objected. Nina threatened him during the lunch break. She blatantly told someone at the court that she intended shooting George and then herself.

The court adjourned and at four o'clock that afternoon George was talking to the proprietor of a shop in town. He turned around to see Nina standing in the entrance. She denied following him. George phoned the police. When he replaced the receiver, Nina fired five shots at George, killing him instantly.

The police arrived, but Nina held them off for several hours, threatening to commit suicide if anyone approached her. With one hand she stroked George's blood-soaked body. Eventually with the intervention of her priest, a psychologist and a journalist, Nina gave herself up and was charged with murder. She was sent to Lentegeur Psychiatric Clinic for observation.

Psychiatrist Dr Magner testified that Nina suffered from erotomania and a personality disorder. He recommended that she not be granted bail as he considered her a danger to society and to herself. Nina was kept in custody.

During the murder trial, several people testified that Nina had threatened to kill them and George a number of times. On one occasion she told a policeman and a magistrate: 'Tell George Kellerman I'll tie him to a bed and fuck him to death by candlelight, or I'll blow my brains out.' The most damning evidence was given by Guilliame Louw, a former colleague of her ex-husband. While still married to Nina, Christo Olivier offered Nina's services to look after Guilliame's children. Scarcely two weeks after this arrangement had been made, Nina declared her love to the stunned Guilliame. At the company's Christmas party he learned that Nina and Christo were getting divorced because of her relationship with him. He eventually managed to convince Christo there was never any relationship between himself and his wife. Nina threatened Guilliame and his son. Every time Guilliame received a passionate love letter from Nina, he handed it over to Christo.

On 22 January 1995, while still in custody and on trial for George's murder, Nina Olivier hanged herself in her Pollsmoor Prison cell. So ended the life of the stalker Nina Olivier. But it was too late for George Kellerman.

Comment

The case of Nina Olivier typifies many aspects of stalking, not only in respect of her behaviour, but also in the failure of the authorities to recognise it as a serious threat, and the shortcomings within the law. Few people could understand the trauma that George Kellerman was subjected to. He had no better legal option than to acquire interdict upon interdict against Nina, which she would typically ignore. Interdicts serve only to aggravate the behaviour of disturbed people and are not worth the paper they are written on. There was no other law to protect George Kellerman. Currently, the only mention of stalking is in the Domestic Violence Act (1999) which stipulates that there should be some form of intimate relationship between two people before stalking is acknowledged. The relationship between George and Nina was a professional one and it would therefore not have given him protection, even if it had been in existence at the time.

Several states in America have strict laws against stalking that carry heavy prison penalties and victims are advised if the stalker is ever released from custody. In South Africa victims can rely only on interdicts, the law against abusive telephone calls, trespassing, crimen injuria, etc. to protect themselves. None of these carry major long-term prison sentences. If a charge of intimidation can be proved, a longer prison sentence would be possible. None of these penalties constitutes a deterrent to the stalker.

Stalking is common in South Africa. Not only between ex-lovers, but also between employees and employers, strangers and celebrities, disgruntled customers and service providers. Senior politicians and ordinary citizens alike are the victims of stalking on a daily basis. In 2003 the South African Law Reform Committee began examining the possibility of promulgating legislation to address the issue, but at the time of writing (2004), but there is still no law to protect the innocent and deal adequately with the guilty.

References

Abrahamsen, D (1973). *The Murdering Mind*. New York: Harper & Row.

Adler, F (1975). *Sisters in Crime: The Rise of the New Female Criminal*. New York: McGraw-Hill.

Alarid, L, Marquart, J, Burton, V, Cullen, F & Cuvelier, S (1996). 'Women's roles in serious offences', *Justice Quarterly*, 13 (3): 432-54.

Bowker, L H (1979). *Women, Crime and the Criminal Justice System*. Lexington: Lexington Books.

Browne, A (1987). *When Battered Women Kill*. New York: The Free Press, a division of Macmillian Inc.

Cape Argus

Caputi, J (1989). 'The sexual politics of murder', *Gender and Society*, 3 (4): 437-456.

Chapman, J (1980). *Economic realities and the female offender*. Lexington: Lexington Books.

Dagbreek & Landstem

De Becker, G (1997). *The Gift of Fear*. London: Little, Brown and Company.

Deming, R (1977). *Women: the new criminals*. Nashville, TN: Thomas Nelson.

Die Beeld

Die Burger

Die Transvaler

Douthwaite, L C (1929). *Mass Murder*. New York: Henry Holt & Company.

Epstein, S (1995). 'The new mythic monster'. In J Ferrell and C Sanders (eds), *Cultural Criminology*. Boston MA:

Northeastern Press, pp 66-79.

Ewing, C P (1990). *When Children Kill*. Lexington: Lexington Books.

Femina

Freiberger, K (1997). 'Application of prominent typologies to the female serial murder phenomenon', Master's thesis, Virginia Commonwealth University, Richmond VA.

Gerberth, V J (1983). *Practical Homicide Investigation*. New York: Elsevier.

Heckert, D M & Ferraiolo, M (1986). 'The female serial murderer', *Journal of Police and Criminal Psychology*, 2(2): 72-81.

Heide, K (1995). *Why kids kill their parents: Child abuse and Adolescent homicide*. Thousand Oaks: Sage Publications.

Hickey, E W (2002). *Serial Murderers and their Victims* (3rd edition). USA: Wadsworth Group.

High Court of South Africa

Hoffer, P C & Hull, N E H (1981). *Murdering Mothers: Infanticide in England and New England 1558-1803*. New York: New York University Press.

Hoffman-Bustamante, D (1973). 'The nature of female criminality', *Issues in Criminology*, 8: 117-136.

Hoofstad

Horney, J (1978). 'Menstrual cycles and criminal responsibility', *Law and Human Nature*, 2: 25-36.

Huisgenoot

Independent Newspapers

Jones, A (1980). *Women who kill*. New York: Rinehart & Winston.

Kaplan, H I & Sadock, B J (1991). *Synopsis of Psychiatry*. Maryland: Williams and Wilkins.

Keeny, B & Heide, K (1994). 'Gender differences in serial murders: a preliminary analysis', *Journal of Interpersonal Violence*, 9 (3): 383-398

Kelleher, M & Kelleher, C (1998). *Murder most Rare: The female serial killer*. New York: Dell.

Keur

Kirby, P (1988). 'The feminization of serial killing: A gender identity study of male and female serialists in female dominated occupations', Doctoral dissertation, The American University, Washington DC.

Langlois, J L (1985). *Belle Guinness*. Bloomington, IN: Indiana University Press.

Linedecker, C (1993). *Killer kids*. New York: St Martin's Paperbacks.

Mail & Guardian

MacDonald, E (1991). *Shoot the women first*. London: Arrow.

Marriner, B (1991). *Forensic Clues to Murder*. London: Arrow.

Marwick, M (1970). *Witchcraft and Sorcery*. Baltimore MD: Penguin Books.

Maslow, A H (1970). *Motivation and Personality*. New York: Harper & Row.

McDonald, R R (1986). *Black Widow*. New York: St Martin's Press.

Nash, J R (1981) *Look for the Woman*. New York: M Evans and Company.

Oggendblad

Pearson, P (1997). *When she was bad: Violent Women and the Myth of Innocence*. Toronto: Random House.

Piers, M W (1978). *Infanticide*. New York: Norton.

Pistorius, M (1996). 'A psycho-analytical approach to serial killers', Doctoral thesis, University of Pretoria.

Pistorius, M (2000). *Catch me a Killer, serial murders: a profiler's story*. Johannesburg: Penguin.

Pistorius, M (2002). *Strangers in the Street: A history of South African serial killers*. Johannesburg: Penguin.

Pollak, O (1950). *The criminality of women*. Philadelphia: University of Pennsylvania Press.

Pretoria News

Rand Daily Mail

Rapport

Resnick, P (1969). 'Child murders by parents', *American*

Journal of Psychiatry, 126: 325- 334.

Resnick, P (1970). 'Murder of the newborn: A psychiatric view of neonaticide', *American Journal of Psychiatry,* 126: 58 -63.

Ressler, R K, Douglas, J E, Burgess, A & Burgess, A G (1992). *Crime Classification Manual.* London: Simon & Schuster.

Rooi Rose

Rosenblatt, E & Greenland, C (1974). 'Female Crimes of Violence', *Journal of Criminality and Corrections,* 16: 173-180.

South African Press Association

Sarie

Scope

Seagrave, K (1992). *Women serial and mass murderers.* Jefferson, NC: McFarland & Company, Inc, Publishers.

Servamus

Shur, E M (1984). *Labeling Women Deviant: Gender, Stigma and social control.* New York: Random House.

South African Police Services

Sowetan

Sparrrow, G (1970). *Women who murder.* New York: Abelard-Schuman.

Ster

Sunday Times

Sunday Express

The Citizen

The Mercury

The Star

Vaderland

Weisheit, R A (1984a). 'Female Homicide offenders: Trends over time in aninstitutional population', *Justice Quarterly,* 1(4): 471-489.

Weisheit, R A (1984b). 'Women and Crime: Issues and Perspectives', *Sex Roles,* 11: 7-8.

Weisheit, R A (1986). 'When mothers kill their children', *Social Science Journal,* 23 (4): 439-448.

Wolfgang, M E (1967). *Criminal Homicide and the*

subculture of Violence: Studies in Homicide. New York: Harper and Row.

Zedner, L (1991). *Women, Crime and Custody in Victorian England.* Oxford: Clarendon Press.